THEY WANTED WAR

THEY

WANTED

WAR

OTTO D. TOLISCHUS

REYNAL & HITCHCOCK
NEW YORK

PRINTED IN THE UNITED STATES OF AMERICA
BY THE CORNWALL PRESS, CORNWALL, N. Y.

ACKNOWLEDGMENTS

THE author and the publisher wish to acknowledge with gratitude the kind permission of *The New York Times* to draw for purposes of this book on the dispatches and articles by Mr. Tolischus which have appeared in the news columns or Sunday sections of that newspaper. They wish also to express their warm appreciation to Mr. Robert Van Gelder for his invaluable assistance in the preparation of this book.

CONTENTS

vii

THEY WANTED WAR

PART I

The Man and His Aims

I

UPON WHAT MEAT
DOES CAESAR FEED?

THE NEW CONQUEROR

THERE are two Hitlers in the same body—the private Hitler who, though he has come up in the world, is still essentially a self-made man from little provincial Braunau in Austria, and the official Hitler, the dictator and war lord who, unlike Mussolini, does not act but lives that role.

The private Hitler appears to be a smallish, quite unimpressive man, with commonplace features that can be found by the dozen along the German-Czech ethnographic frontier, raised out of the ordinary only by the now famous mustache and the small, greenish-brown and almost poetically introspective eyes—a man who seems to retain an uneasy shyness in company which gives his gestures the semblance of awkwardness and attaches to his personality the unmistakable air of "the little man."

For reasons of health, conviction and self-discipline

3

he eats no meat and neither drinks nor smokes. He is of the Alpine rather than the Germanic type and it is an obvious fact that he is not a descendant of a master class which he seeks to create anew. This fact has been one of the chief objections raised against him by the old German ruling class which he has ousted.

But the official Hitler, the Führer, mass orator, dictator, war lord is quite a different person and the transition from the one to the other often is sudden and startling. This Hitler is jovial, self-confident, domineering, scornful and omniscient. He does not talk—he orates; he does not discuss—he pronounces judgment; he does not walk—he strides. His very appearance becomes different. He seems to grow in stature so that those who have seen him only in public and then meet him face to face are astonished at his "littleness." His features become transformed into a hard, domineering mask unless they are distorted in passionate oratory. His eyes assume a fanatic stare and his voice ranges from the low familiar dark, deep tones to the high falsetto until it breaks.

This Hitler is no longer a man with human characteristics but the incarnation of an idea, terrifying to dissenters contemplating his power but exerting a strange magnetism on the susceptible which compels obedience and inspires a fanatical following from which his Elite Guards and "Suicide Squads" of German parachute troops are only two examples. It is this strange, almost mystic quality in Hitler that gives his oratory its hypnotic power, however much it may elude sober analysis, and which tempts sycophants to suggest his elevation to the level of a deity.

There is also a third and secret Hitler known only to his intimates. It is the Hitler in whom the conflict between his two personalities and the load he is carrying have taxed human nerves until they have snapped. But he soon gets control of himself again and proceeds as if nothing had happened.

It is not known whether Hitler ever loved any man or woman except his mother, or acknowledges any loyalties except to his self-appointed mission. In his book *Mein Kampf* he expresses love for his mother and his Austrian homeland; the rest is denunciation, revolt and a cool estimate of the value of human motives and emotions in relation to his mission.

There was first his revolt against an overstrict father, for whom he expresses only "respect," and against his father's effort to force the son into a narrow official career. There was his revolt against school discipline which prevented his acquisition of a formal education. There was the hatred born of a bitter nationality struggle between the Pan-German Austro-Germans and Czechs in the border region in which Hitler was born— a struggle which colored his entire boyhood, shaped his first political ideas and inflamed that nationalism which found expression in the nationalist part of National Socialism. In fact, it bred a National Socialistic movement long before Hitler which propounded many of the ideas and slogans later adopted by Hitler himself.

There was resentment and wounded pride when the

Vienna Academy of Art refused to acknowledge his artistic talents and so blasted his hopes of a painter's career.

Under these circumstances the outbreak of the World War came, as Hitler says in his book, "as a redemption from the disagreeable experiences of youth," for which, "overcome by fervid enthusiasm, I sank to my knees and thanked Heaven from an overflowing heart that it had given me the good fortune to live at such a time."

For four years he did duty under shot and shell. He saw human life sacrificed at command, saw the moralities of civil life turned topsy-turvy, saw the principle that the end justifies the means raised to the highest morality. He never got over that, and the morality of war became the guiding morality of his life, to find amplification in the Hitler movement and the present war.

There was earlier the revolt against the social, economic and political system which forced him to eke out a precarious existence as a casual building construction laborer and postcard artist and live in the Vienna or Munich slums, and there was his resentment against attempts by "Marxist" labor unions to force him into their frame and discipline which often cost him his job. It was in these bitter days of penury and hunger that the anger of the dispossessed took hold of him to find first expression in a hatred of everything that stood for the existing regime—the Habsburgs, Parliamentarianism, "Marxism," and Jews who, though non-Germans, seemed to flourish under a system which denied him everything. And out of this anger grew ultimately the revolution which manifested itself on a national scale in National Socialism and on a world scale in the present Armageddon between the "haves" and the "have-nots."

After four years of the last war Hitler saw a nation in defeat and ruins and himself thrown back into nothingness. Personal humiliations and national resentments combined to stir the smoldering embers of revolt into open flames. And, miraculously enough, another avenue of escape presented itself.

While reporting on political activities for the *Reichswehr* he stumbled upon one of many little groups of serious thinkers seeking ways and means of national regeneration and, becoming interested, addressed its meetings and discovered that he was an orator who could sway people.

"I spoke for thirty minutes," he says in describing the discovery in his book, "and what I formerly had sensed without quite knowing it was now proved by reality: I could speak. After thirty minutes people were electrified."

His career as a political leader and as "the greatest revolutionary of all times" was launched.

It took, of course, more than oratory to lead Hitler to the top. Germany at that time was full of political messiahs but he alone survived. The explanation is that if aversions were the powerful motives of his career, he also had as equally important pilots an inborn shrewdness coming down from many peasant generations—an uncanny, almost feminine intuition and quick perception of essentials, wholly unhampered by restraining influences of tradition, class or creed.

He learned where and from whom he could and used all manner of men for his purposes. And what he lacked in formal education he made up by means of prolific reading that included much which is unknown to the ordinary school curriculum. And with success came outspoken contempt for the masses as well as the classes which he bent so easily to his will and oratory.

But if there is any one motive or set of motives that dominates all others, it is the conglomeration of aversions, resentments and hatreds born of his environment, his early personal defeats, social maladjustment and the great national débâcle—aversions first hardened in the soul-searing fires of the last war and later sublimated into a fanatic revolutionary fervor.

Now that fervor has been fed on the imagery and emotionalism of Wagner's operas and converted by success into an unshakable faith in his personal destiny and his mission to transform the world.

Whether he is still personally ambitious it is difficult to say. For a man of his simple, abstemious tastes the headship of one of the world's big powers and the riches that fell into his lap after his accession to power might have been considered more than sufficient. That they were not is explicable on the one hand by the fact that Hitlerism is bigger than Hitler and that he is the prisoner of his own movement which, being a movement, must, like a bicycle, keep on moving or fall; while on the other hand, aided by success, flattery and the adulation of the masses, he has rationalized his necessities into an ambition that transcends personal ends.

In fact, Hitler has so completely merged himself and his self-appointed mission that even in the opinion of his intimates he has sincerely come to regard himself as an instrument of Providence who goes his way, in his own words, "with trance-like surety." And in that conviction he finds the strength to take the fateful decision and carry the responsibility which he does.

And if a personal ambition remains it is to do the work of transforming the world according to his own ideas during his own lifetime and live in the esteem of posterity as the greatest man in history. That and not fear of a premature end is the explanation of the rapidity of his movements and the oft-repeated complaint that he has "so little time left" for this gigantic task.

He is a new conqueror whose dreams out-distance the ambitions of Alexander, Caesar and Napoleon and envisage not only the conquest but also the revolutionary transformation of the world.

The success or failure of these dreams has now been submitted to the arbitrament of the sword, which will decide whether Adolf Hitler, that man who rose from the slums of Vienna to become master of more than 100,000,000 people and the most powerful war lord in the world, will go down in history as a genius or a madman.

But irrespective of the success or failure or any judgment of his methods it is impossible to ignore the grandiose sweep of the dreams themselves, which in their scope of totalitarian character surpass anything men have dared to dream before, and whose successful materialization up to now lifts them far above the fancies of a visionary and converts them into a concrete political program backed by the world's mightiest military machine.

Nor is it possible to blind oneself to the elemental force of the willpower, shrewdness and tenacity with which that program has been put into effect, or do anything but wonder at the mental and physical stamina with which one single bundle of bone, flesh and nerves has borne the almost superhuman load for years.

Hitler is no mere gangster leader, as mistaken propaganda pictures him. Gangsters do not carry great nations with them. There is a far better clue to the Hitlerian strength in Germany than the too simple explanation that Germany is ruled by a gang with guns.

HITLER AND WAGNER

The last war, at least in the somewhat warped Allied view of the German side of it, was dominated by Friedrich Wilhelm Nietzsche and his superman whose will for power was beyond good or evil.

The present war, almost unbeknown to both the Allies and the Germans themselves, is dominated by Richard Wagner—not the Richard Wagner of the incomparable, though still debated, melodies, but the Richard Wagner who brought back to life the dismal, pitiless and forgotten world of Germanic antiquity, the world of fighting gods and fighting heroes, of dragons and demons, of destiny and pagan epics, which presents itself to other peoples as mere Wagnerian opera, but which has become subconscious reality to the German masses, and has been elevated to the inspirational mythos of the National Socialist movement that rules the Third Reich.

"Whoever wants to understand National Socialist Germany must know Wagner," Adolf Hitler has often told his friends; and the whole National Socialist regime, which finds its foundation in the Germanic mythos and the cult of the heroic, is in fact unthinkable without Wagner and all he represents. In that sense the whole present war resolves itself into a super-Wagnerian opera turned into grim reality.

It must be kept in mind, however, that they little know of Wagner who only Wagner's music know. For Wagner was the first totalitarian artist who strove to combine art, science and life—music, poetry, grammar, philosophy, sociology and politics—into a unitary and all-embracing expression of a new Germanic *Weltanschauung* that was to save the German people from the danger of modern civilization, under the ægis of Baireuth as the German Olympus from which was also to come salvation for all Europe. In that respect he became a synthesis of the German intellectual turmoil that began to separate the German from the rest of the occident early in the nineteenth century—a turmoil that was first a protest against the French Revolution, then a patriotic uprising against Napoleon, then a revolt against the German pygmy States and their reactionary policies, in which Wagner personally took a hand, and then a revulsion against the whole nineteenth century with its great industrial revolution and the social evils that followed in its wake.

It was a turmoil symbolized by such names as Arndt, Fichte, Jahn, List, Feuerbach, Treitschke and Konstantin Frantz, whose "metapolitics" especially interested Wagner, and finally, as an extreme outsider, Nietzsche. Though these men differed in stature and ideas, the end result of this turmoil was a nostalgia for the "Holy Roman Empire of the German Nation" through which, in its heyday, Germans ruled the known earth. It marked a break with French enlightenment, universalist humanism, and Hellenic classicism, of which Goethe was the last representative, and led to a concentration on the Germanic mythos which found its climax in an exaltation of Germanism as the remedy for the world's ills.

"Am deutschen Wesen soll die Welt genesen" (through German virtue the world will recover) was the final wisdom distilled from this turmoil, to which Nietzsche contributed a scornful and aristocratic philosophy for the "lords of the earth," the antithesis of the "Judean-Christian slaves' religion of the masses," while Wagner himself, influenced by Count de Gobineau's *Inequality of the Human Races,* added a good shot of anti-Semitism. In Wagner's English son-in-law, Houston Stewart Chamberlain, these ideas found their final crystallization in an "Aryan Germanic *Weltanschauung*" that is the direct precursor of the National Socialist racial dogma and its thesis of German superiority.

It is against this rather profuse and, in its decisive aspect, unequivocal, background that Wagner's work must be viewed. For Wagner was part of this turmoil all his life; and, though his personal ideology wavered successively and ranged from Buddhistic negation to heroic self-assertion, from pagan fatalism to Christian redemption, in the end he implanted the Germanic mythos far more successfully in the subconscious German mind than all the German philosophers and historians. For he presented this mythos not as a cold intellectual abstraction—as such it found its own refutation—but in the far more pleasant and far more subtle form of "musical dramas," which conquered the world with their revolutionary harmonies, but at the same time evoked in the German people certain emotional reactions that found their fruition in National Socialism.

Hitler took his ideas where he found them and in utilizing them proved to be the great synthesizer of opposites. Nearly every element of National Socialist ideology can be traced to some antecedent which, far from weakening it, gives it strength by a multiform and susceptive familiarity that makes it all things to all Germans.

But more powerful even than any political or economic ideas of National Socialism are its deeper emotional and mythological elements, which raise it far above a purely political organization and make it a fanatic pseudo-religious movement that is inexplicable to all non-German "unbelievers." And these elements come from Wagner, from whom have also been adopted even such details as the "heil" of the Hitler salute, the National Socialist battle slogan, "Germany Awake!" and the runes affected by the SS. The fiery solstice celebration and other Germanic cult ceremonies designed to replace Christian ritual were natural developments of the return to the Germanic mythos.

Wagner was a romanticist who has now been taken over by political realists. And lest it be thought from American precedents that operas are after all only for the select few, it must be kept in mind that nearly every German city has its opera house and that Hitler himself explained, "I am convinced that art, and the uncorrupted and most immediate reproduction of a nation's spiritual life, have unconsciously the greatest direct influence on the mass in combination."

Hitler himself has been a personal devotee of Wagner all his life. Like Ludwig II of Bavaria, Wagner's illstarred royal patron, he became an enthusiastic Wagnerite after witnessing, as a youngster, a performance of "Lohengrin" in an Austrian provincial town.

"At once I was captivated," he writes in *Mein Kampf*. "My youthful enthusiasm for the Baireuth master knew no bounds. Again and again I was drawn to his works and today I feel it a special good fortune that the modesty of the provincial performance permitted later augmentation."

As a result of this enthusiasm, Hitler had attended hundreds of Wagner performances, traveling from the cheapest seats in the highest balconies in his days of penury to the royal box in his days of power. He has steeped himself in the provocative Wagner melodies. Although he cannot carry a tune, he reads Wagner's scores, and so detailed is his interest that every little change in every performance immediately brings inquiries from him.

Though captivated by Wagner's art as such, he is even more captivated by the fact that it is German art and the most intoxicating expression of a Germanic mythos which Hitler transferred from the stage to the political arena and made a world issue.

Besides that, early in his political career Hitler became personally attached to Baireuth and the "Baireuth Kultur circle," led by Houston Stewart Chamberlain when the latter, after listening to Hitler's speech in Baireuth in October, 1923—at a time when few people took Hitler seriously—received the comparatively unknown at Haus Wahnfried and immediately hailed him as the savior of Germany. In 1934 Hitler laid the cornerstone of a national monument to Wagner at the composer's birthplace in Leipzig.

It was therefore only natural that immediately on his accession to power Hitler, with all the resources of his totalitarian power, exalted Baireuth to the position that Wagner had dreamed of. Baireuth and its Wagner festivals were and are in charge of an English-born woman, Winifred Wagner (nee Williams), widow of Wagner's son Siegfried. And lo! with a Wagner tradition, she ascribes to the Baireuth festivals a "religious character."

As late as 1931 she also demanded that Baireuth must be "a festival of pure art, away from the impression of day-to-day affairs." But National Socialism has no use for "art for art's sake," and Baireuth immediately became the Olympus of German art and the Valhalla of the Germanic mythos, to which Hitler's presence at the festivals gave the final sanctification.

Wagner's "musical dramas" are really dramatized philosophic dissertations for which he wrote not only the music but also librettos of undoubted poetic and dramatic power, in which he took his stand on the problems of the age. But because he sought and compassed in them God, man and the world, he soon burst through the limitations of historic opera as known before his time, and delved into Nordic mythology, which, being a personification of abstract concepts, enabled him to give dramatic life and blood to his own abstract ideas. The originally incidental, but in the end the paramount, result of this was that he led the German mind away from the rational, individualistic, utilitarian world of the time which hoped for escape from its shortcomings in scientific progress, and conjured up in its stead the ancient, irrational, mystic and heroic world of the Germanic gods, ruled by the ancient pagan ethics of the tribal code, the blood feud and the law of destiny and personal atonement for guilt, in place of the Christian sin and redemption.

The ancient mystic world, utilized by Wagner to personify his own philosophic ideas regarding the problems of the modern world, is portrayed with compelling vivid-

ness in the "Nibelungen Ring," that amazing series of
four interdependent "musical dramas" on which he
worked for a quarter of a century and which are the
towering monuments to his genius. Whatever ideas
Wagner wanted to express in them originally—and he
changed these ideas repeatedly until the clarity of the
work suffered—his own political pamphleteering and
National Socialist ideology have given the "Nibelungen
Ring" an interpretation reflected directly in National
Socialist practice.

In the terms of Wagner's own librettos, the essential
elements of this interpretation may be briefly summarized as follows:

Wotan, chief of the ancient Germanic gods, subject
to destiny and his own law, and as such the symbol
for a mundane ruler, seeks to increase his might in order
to safeguard his realm. For that purpose he concludes a
treaty with the giants Fasolt and Fafnir, who may be
taken as symbols of the bourgeoisie; the giants undertake to build for Wotan "a fortress peerless and proud"
—Valhalla—in return for which they are to get the Goddess Freia, who holds the key to the gods' eternal youth.
But Wotan regards the treaty as a scrap of paper from
the start and depends on the tricky half-god or demi-god
Loge or Loki, his "Chancellor," to get him out of any
difficulties. When, therefore, the giants call for their reward—and Freia may be regarded here as the constitutional guarantees that limit the rulers' powers—Wotan
refuses to pay. Therein lies his original guilt for which
he must later atone.

When the giants rebel, Loki suggests that Wotan pay the giants in gold. In order to get the gold, the two capture Alberich, ruler of the gnomes or Nibelungs, and make him pay all he possesses as ransom. Alberich in National Socialist interpretation is "the type of the money-Jew" who by renouncing "love" has succeeded in stealing the gold from the Rhine daughters, who may be taken as symbols of either the nation or the German people.

From this gold he has forged a magic ring that gives its owner power over the world—a symbol of the power of gold—in addition to which he has also acquired a magic helmet that permits him to assume any shape he wishes or to make himself entirely invisible. Thus equipped, he swings the whip over the Nibelungs—the "proletariat"—(and also over his own brother, Mime) making them work to increase his treasure.

Having seized the treasure as ransom, Wotan puts the ring on his own finger and exults: "It is mine now, the spell of might, That makes me lord of the world."

This lust for gold as well as power adds, of course, to Wotan's guilt, but the exaltation is brief. For Alberich puts a curse on the ring that its future possessor shall die of it, and ring and treasure must soon be surrendered to the giants to keep Freia out of their clutches.

The curse fulfills itself immediately; Fafnir kills Fasolt to get the ring and treasure for himself alone and then retires with them to a cave which he guards thereafter in the shape of a dragon and under the motto, "I hold what I have, let me sleep"—a motto which the National Socialists apply to England.

From this mythological setting, Wagner developed a complicated succession of events supposed to symbolize man's struggle against the curse of the gods, or the "tragedy of modern capitalism."

Wotan, knowing that Alberich is trying to regain the ring in order to destroy him, seeks to regain it for himself. But having given the ring to Fafnir as ransom for Freia, he cannot recapture it himself. Wherefore he puts his hope on heroes. And the final perfection of these is Siegfried, grandson of Wotan himself, but also a "free and natural man."

Siegfried kills the dragon and captures the ring and treasure but gives the ring as a love token to Brünnhilde. As the result both of them also fall under its curse. Siegfried is trapped and stabbed in the back by Hagen, "lust-child" of Alberich and a Queen he had lured with gold, on whom Alberich pins his hopes for the ring.

Hagen seeks to gain the ring for himself, but Brünnhilde foils him and returns it to the Rhine daughters while immolating herself on Siegfried's funeral pyre. Hagen jumps after the ring but is dragged off to the deep. And Wotan, who has long since despaired of success for himself, now atones for his double guilt by setting Valhalla in flames, which ends the gods and their world. The action leads to pagan atonement through general and self-willed annihilation, that holds so strange a fascination to the German mind.

This final effect has been further intensified by the

fact that Wagner's "Nibelungen Ring" has been inextricably intertwined in the German mind with the *Nibelungenlied* from which Wagner took his inspiration without following it. For the *Nibelungenlied* translated the Nordic myth to which Wagner reverted into a heroic epic of medieval knighthood, and the most powerful part of it deals with the gruesome vengeance of Kriemhild, Siegfried's widow, against Hagen, who emerges as a new hero.

In the *Nibelungenlied*, Kriemhild is the sister of the King of the Burgundians, who also are called Nibelungen, and Hagen is the King's "Iron Chancellor," of such terrifying mien that daughters of his hosts hesitate to give him the customary welcome kiss. This Hagen also kills Siegfried by stabbing him in the back after tricking Kriemhild into betraying Siegfried's one vulnerable spot and after carefully removing Siegfried's swords. He also robs the widow of her husband's Nibelungen treasure because he thinks all this is necessary to protect the honor and interest of his King.

In fact, Hagen's "loyalty" goes so far that when he and his King are captured alive he tricks Kriemhild into killing her royal brother on the promise of revealing to her the whereabouts of the Nibelung treasure. Then when Kriemhild shows him the head of her brother Hagen laughs at her, whereupon she chops off Hagen's head as well and is herself killed by one of her own vassals.

It is this "grim" Hagen of the *Nibelungenlied* rather than Siegfried who, in the revaluation of all values, is now presented to German youth as the ideal hero for emulation. The spirit of Hagen is in that strong tribal design for living that lifted Hitler from the ruck of failure.

"MEIN KAMPF"—BLUEPRINT OF REVOLUTION

Hitler made himself what he is with a book—*Mein Kampf*, meaning, "My Struggle." This book recreated the Hitlerian movement after its collapse under the *Reichswehr* bullets before the Feldherrn Hall in Munich in 1923, re-established Hitler's authority over the many factions into which the movement threatened to split, and kept it alive when all its other expressions were suppressed. The proceeds from this book financed Hitler and his followers until they were big enough to command the support of those anxious to climb on the bandwagon. For years it was the source book for all National Socialist propaganda and speech-making, and the guide of German foreign and domestic policy.

More than 3,000,000 copies of *Mein Kampf*, have been sold, and it has been translated into many languages, including the Chinese. It is a tome of 782 closely printed pages. To emphasize its similitude to the Bible, the Reich League of German Government Officials once presented Hitler as a birthday gift a unique copy of his work; seven graphologists labored for eleven months to transcribe it by hand on 965 pages of "leather parchment" in the script of the medieval Bible, producing a volume that has been bound in iron and weighs no less than seventy pounds.

In content *Mein Kampf* is 10 per cent autobiography, 90 per cent dogma, and 100 per cent propaganda. Every word in it, every fact recorded or view expressed, has been included not for the sake of the record, or for the sake of abstract truth, but solely for the propagandist effect. Judged by its success, it is the propagandistic masterpiece of the age.

Like Machiavelli's *The Prince,* Hitler's work is amazing for the bold frankness with which it casts aside all moral considerations in the interest of political expediency, on the principle that the end justifies the means. "Success," he writes, "is the only earthly judge of right or wrong," a dictum reiterated by thousands of Nazi speakers, led by Dr. Paul Joseph Goebbels, the Minister of Popular Enlightenment and Propaganda. Force, terror, battle, conquest, "one-sided assertions," racial hatred and racial egoism are thus lumped together with mysticism, patriotism and social justice as equally acceptable means of rallying the masses to the Nazi standard.

The book accepts only the "manly virtues," and if it gives any recognition at all to ethical or moral values, such as humanitarianism, charity, justice and fair play, or to the social amenities, such as manners and moderation, it does so merely to evaluate them as available means in the political struggle, especially in relations with foreign nations. For the rest, it repudiates these virtues as attributes of weaklings, bourgeois Philistines and decadent aristocrats. "Get hard," is its motto, and "get hard" is the slogan that is being hammered daily into millions of German souls.

Yet all National Socialists would bitterly resent the description of Hitler's book as immoral. They claim for it a morality beyond good or evil—a morality based on the aim which it pursues. For that aim is a bigger and more powerful Germany, and though not all non-Germans might appreciate the desirability of this aim, nevertheless to all National Socialists it is the ultimate good, beyond which there is nothing in this world or the next.

Baldur von Schirach, the Reich Youth Leader, summarized the essence of Hitler's book most succinctly when he said: "Our religion is Germany." In that new dispensation lies forgiveness for all sins committed in the interest of the new religion, and the authorities of the Third Reich place themselves protectively before those who err in the direction of excessive zeal, provided their intentions are for the good of the National Socialist regime.

At the same time, Hitler's book receives credit for two achievements besides making its author what he is. It made the German people, "the most unpolitical people in the world," politically minded; it taught them to speak and understand the language of politics, but with a reverse technique. Usually, political language is discounted for its necessary propagandistic exaggerations; but Hitler's book has expressed his aims with such brutal frankness, and has so thoroughly filled the German people with his doctrine, that he has the advantage over all other politicians in the world—he can say less than he means and still be understood at home.

Furthermore, the book definitely roused the German people out of the fatalistic and slightly somnambulistic attitude, pregnant with disaster, that found its most famous expression in the title of Oswald Spengler's book, "The Decline of the West." There is nothing fatalistic in the tramp of Germany's marching millions, whether it be the army or merely the Hitler youth. Germany is, indeed, awake, and plans to do great things.

In his book, Hitler represents hardness and moral imperviousness as the only political method that can achieve success, and he bases this conclusion on his view of the world and human nature. It is the view of a man who never got over the war.

Born of the war, with its throw-back to the law of the jungle, this view sees the world as permanently a jungle in which herds of humanity, called nations or races, fight for feeding grounds in a catch-as-catch-can struggle in which the individual is nothing and the herd is everything, in which all rules and niceties are suspended, and in which might is right. To that view the book is rapidly persuading a nation of 67,000,000. But it is also the view of the professional war veteran who in some countries is satisfied with a bonus and in others demands nothing less than the whole country like Mussolini and Hitler.

The book itself consists of two volumes. The first was written in 1924 in the fortress of Landsberg am Lech, where Hitler was serving a term of "honorary confine-

ment" for his attempted *Putsch* of 1923. Here, in perfect liberty, he typed on his little typewriter, or dictated
to Rudolf Hess, his secretary and now deputy for party
affairs, "A Reckoning" in which he showed up the mistakes and failures of the Kaiser's government, flayed the
existing Republican regime which had quashed his movement, and finally defended and justified his own course
and sounded a trumpet call for further action.

The volume ends on a note of triumph when, describing the first successful mass meeting of his career, Hitler
writes: "A fire was lit out of whose heat must some day
come the sword that will regain for the German Siegfried freedom, and for the German nation life."

When Hitler came to power, one of the first things he
did was to abolish such "honorary confinement" for political opponents, so that never while he rules will such
a book come out of a German fortress.

The second volume was written in 1926, in Berchtesgaden, where, already at liberty, he repeated and intensified the doctrines of the first.

Mussolini has censored himself by banning all his
earlier writings, which are now available only in libraries
to history students of proved harmlessness. Hitler says
that he "makes his corrections in his foreign policy," not
in his book. He has, however, expurgated from the later
German editions some of the embarrassing passages,
such, for instance, as the reference to the German people
as a particularly gullible lot, although, in the main, he
stands by what he has written. The popular edition sold
in Germany remains, on the whole, intact, and anybody

who runs may read it, and quote from it—except the German press.

Besides all its other distinctions, the book has the merit that it made Hitler a rich man—a millionaire who is able to renounce his official salary. Of all the National Socialist authors, only Alfred Rosenberg with his *Mythos of the Twentieth Century* and Julius Streicher with his *Stürmer* have achieved any comparable financial success, and they are running far behind.

How much Hitler personally profited from his book is impossible to put in figures. On the basis of the usual royalties paid successful authors, say about 20 per cent on a book, the popular edition of which sells at about three dollars, this profit should amount to well over $1,000,000 in Germany alone, besides the royalties on the foreign translations.

But a large, perhaps the larger, part of this income Hitler put right back into the business, especially in the beginning, when the sales were smaller. (They reached 600,000 before Hitler came to power, jumped by a round million in the first year of Hitler's chancellorship, and are still increasing rapidly.) This income helped finance the movement during its lean years, and formed the financial backbone of the Franz Eher Publishing House, Hitler's own, which issues the costly *Völkischer Beobachter*, the official party organ, and other propaganda publications.

In any case, *Mein Kampf* has become part of Germany's destiny.

THE EAGLE'S NEST

Mein Kampf is an expression of the public Hitler. The private Hitler most often made his appearance in the place where he was happiest with his friends, and where the second part of *Mein Kampf* was written.

In the years before war broke out, Hitler in a sense gave Germany three capitals. The country was administered from Berlin, capital of the Reich. It was inspired and spurred onward from Munich, capital of the National Socialist movement. But it was ruled from a mountain top—the mountain on which Führer Adolf Hitler had built himself a lofty country residence, where he spent the larger part of his time and to which he always retired to ponder events and to make those fateful decisions that so often startled the world.

The Berghof, as this residence is called, is more than 3,000 feet above sea level and 1,400 feet above Berchtesgaden, in the southeasternmost tip of Bavaria and only two miles away from what once was Austria. There Hitler took refuge from the clamor of Berlin that irritated him and from the daily grist of routine paper work that stifled him. There, amid the most gorgeous mountain scenery to be found in Germany, not in set conferences but in informal walks and talks with his closest collaborators and with chosen representatives from all walks of German life, the private Hitler mulled over new ideas for the public Hitler to expound, and new courses of action for the German nation to follow.

And there, in the solemn solitude of a higher region, where frozen mountain peaks symbolized the eternal pattern of this world that yet changes in appearance with the constant change of atmospheric moods, and where the little things of everyday life below seemed to drop away to let the essentials come out in all the clearer relief, the man who had assumed sole responsibility for a vast and powerful nation found the strength to continue on his self-imposed mission.

In the beginning there was a rustic and unsophisticated simplicity about the place—it was this that had attracted the private Hitler. But this simplicity could not endure. A formidable and a martial air—more sensed than obvious—replaced it.

Berchtesgaden, which means mansion of the Goddess Berchta, was once a little-known spa of less than 4,000 inhabitants. Because of its beauty it was always patronized by the Bavarian royal family and Hitler likewise selected it as a place of recreation while still a struggling party leader. With a company of friends to which belonged his early mentor, the poet Dietrich Eckart; his erstwhile foreign press chief, Dr. Ernst Hanfstaengl; and Max Amann, his publisher, who became head of the Reich Press Chamber, Hitler used to spend many pleasant hours in Berchtesgaden, especially in the Platterhof Inn which has now been absorbed as part of the Berghof estate; and the time had by all was so pleasant that some of his more puritanical followers protested. But

Hitler worked there also. The second section of *Mein Kampf*, written at Berchtesgaden, is the more substantial part.

As Hitler progressed with his program, Berchtesgaden was rapidly turned into a miniature national capital. A speedy motor road was built to it from Munich and a private airport was constructed on the Rossfeld, near Hitler's residence. A special building was erected to house a branch of the Reich Chancellery, because, as State Secretary Dr. Hans Heinrich Lammers explained at its dedication early this year, "the Führer is always on duty, even when on vacation." New homes were built for the staff of officials and new barracks for the guarding garrison. This garrison, incidentally, consisted not of army troops but of Hitler's own bodyguard, recruited from the SS, from which was also recruited the Gestapo, or secret State police. Despite efforts of the army generals to abolish the bodyguard as a semi-independent military unit, Hitler insisted on keeping it.

In the same way the Berghof grew from a little mountain chalet into a stately manor house on a large estate. Originally it was little more than a mountain cottage, furnished in the rustic but colorful Bavarian style, and run by Frau Angela Raubal, Hitler's sister, who later married Dr. Martin Hammizsch, a Dresden professor. It was then known as Haus Wachenfeld, and it was so small that when guests stayed overnight, even such prominent guests as Rudolf Hess, Hitler's deputy party leader, they had to sleep in tents outside or over the garage.

26794

In 1936 Hitler rebuilt and renamed the place. It lost the aspects of a chalet and turned into a modernistic mansion of indefinable architecture, with spacious halls and many rooms sumptuously furnished, with Roman arches above and foundations of "medieval romanticism" below, and with extensive side wings in which rattled the typewriters and rang the telephone bells of the secretaries. Rebuilt, it was able to accommodate two-score and more guests for the night, if need be.

Beyond that, the Berghof also was turned into an impenetrable fort. Most things connected with Hitler's mountain home became a mystery as closely guarded as a military secret. Nobody was authorized to talk about it; no publication about it was permitted except for a few official photographs and some lyric but vague explanations of them; even the workers who constructed it had been pledged to silence.

Nevertheless, talk would get around, and if that talk was to be trusted, the Berghof had been equipped with bomb and gas-proof cellars, had been surrounded by little fortified posts commanding all approaches and had been girded by anti-aircraft guns embedded in the adjoining mountain sides and able to release a concentric fire that would bring down any hostile plane or fleet of planes long before they had any chance at doing damage.

In fact, so elaborate were said to have been the precautions as to convince the native populace that Berchtesgaden was destined to become the real national capital in the event of any but a one-sided war.

The Berghof itself is situated on the northern flank of the Obersalzberg, just below the brow of the hill, and from its central hall the eye may roam among magnificent mountain scenery from the snow-capped Watzmann, towering in the south, to the ancient town of Salzburg on the Austrian side toward the northeast, and then northward to the wide Bavarian plains below. To visitors Hitler once explained that he had chosen the northern mountain side for his home because the sun did not burn down there as steeply as on the southern slope and because, in this particular locality, it afforded a wider view into the land than any other.

The house is whitewashed and the woodwork stained a dark brown, with a gorgeous display of bright flowers in the window boxes. The entire basement is taken up by the garages, built into the mountain slope. Above the basement, but level with the ground at the back where the hill rises toward a peak, is the central hall and other rooms for social functions. On this floor is the big dining room which opens on a spacious balcony that takes up one corner of the house and affords a magnificent view of the scenery.

The second floor contains the bedrooms, and the center of the façade is crowned by a broad gable with three windows set in Roman arches. The guest rooms are furnished in simple hotel-like fashion and the service is entirely in the hands of white-clad stewards.

Hitler's own rooms are strictly separate because on occasion he has come to the Berghof, not to seek company but to isolate himself, and sometimes does so completely. Nevertheless, there remains a thrill for the guest in the automatic self-connecting house telephone which has one button labeled "Der Führer." The guest may luxuriate in the feeling that all one has to do in order to talk to his host is to press the button. But, of course, he doesn't.

A splendid road, which curves up the flank of the Obersalzberg, after branching off the main road from Berchtesgaden to Salzburg, leads up to the estate, and a special mountain-climbing automobile with a four-wheel drive assures safe and speedy transportation to it in all kinds of weather. But whereas Haus Wachenfeld lay directly on the public road on which its garages opened, the Berghof has become more inaccessible. The public road has been diverted some 200 yards and now skirts the estate in such a way that it dips behind the top of the hill, rendering the mansion itself invisible from all but a small section.

Furthermore the entire mountainside, covering several square miles, has been fenced in with wire seven or eight feet high. There are several other chalets, including that of General Hermann Goering, which is further up the hill from Hitler's home, but everything else, including a children's sanatorium and a score of peasant homes, has been removed.

All points of vantage have been adorned by little turrets which look quite romantic in the wooded landscape, but are actually defense posts for the bodyguards. And the biggest of these posts is a pleasant looking log cabin in the Alpine style, set right on the road, guarding the heavy gates to the estate. From its windows the sentries have a clear view of all the curves of the approaching road.

To make assurance doubly sure Berchtesgaden and its neighborhood have long been cleansed of all "unreliable" elements, and all visitors to the spa even in time of peace were forced to answer more questions on the police registration blank than in any other part of Germany. Wherever they went they felt many eyes following them, eyes of strange-looking peasants, baggage carriers, and merchants who do not talk the native dialect. And again in peace time, those who took the road to Hitler's estate required a special permit.

With safety and privacy thus assured Hitler is best able to relax at the Berghof.

Of course, no man in Hitler's position is able to dismiss the work and cares of office anywhere or at any time. But at the Berghof before war came, Hitler's cares seemingly were reduced to a minimum. In line with the artistic temperament which Hitler's admirers extol as his biggest asset in the art of politics, Hitler always has led a somewhat Bohemian life—so much so that methodical people, accustomed to a strict daily routine, have (until proved wrong) whispered doubts of his complete devotion to concentrated work. From the days of his youth, when he refused to follow his father in the methodical career of a minor Austrian official, Hitler has always held purely official drudgery in abhorrence; he regards it as death to really creative work. Though he recognized a bureaucracy as a necessary evil of administration, he still warned party leaders not to get lost in deadly paper work, but rather to keep in touch with the people and the facts of life.

At any rate, that is the rule Hitler adopted for himself. He has been a great improvisator, and that his improvisation is not without merit is proved by his spectacular career. But these improvisations of his early years in power were born not out of burning the midnight oil over long official reports but rather out of visits to all parts of the country and talks with many kinds of people and, above all, out of protracted discussions and exchanges of opinion in the intimate circle of his old cronies and collaborators, stretching at times into the small hours of the morning. For these discussions the Berghof was an ideal place.

The proverb, "It's the early bird that catches the worm," did not apply to Hitler in those creative years. He rarely rose before nine o'clock in the morning, and sometimes even later, except when he was on tour. During breakfast, which usually consisted of milk, bread, oatmeal, honey, and cheese, he read the newspapers, especially his own *Völkischer Beobachter*. Then he took a walk in the mountains accompanied by some guests. He sometimes visited Goering's chalet, or stopped at a mountain cafe, or he might simply stroll about, stopping at times to emphasize the ideas he was expounding to his guests by drawing pictures in the sand with his stick. About eleven o'clock, however, he was usually at his desk where his mail and the official business that had come up in the pouch from the Chancellery had already been laid out by his adjutants, Wilhelm Brueckner and Julius Schaub, and his press chief, Dr. Otto Dietrich. These men were his steady companions, although, in important affairs, State Secretary Otto Meissner, Chief of the Presidial Chancellery, and State Secretary Hans Heinrich Lammers, head of the Reich Chancellery, were also on hand.

As a rule official business was completed by lunch time. Hitler's vegetarian lunch and dinner consist of soup, eggs, vegetables, and mineral water, although he occasionally relishes a slice of ham and relieves the tediousness of his diet with such delicacies as caviar, luscious fruits and similar tidbits. He is outspoken about having a sweet tooth and loves confectionery, especially chocolates. However, regular meals were served for guests. National Socialist co-ordination ended at the door of the dining room.

In the years of peace, unless other things intervened, the afternoon was usually devoted by Hitler to his favorite hobby—architecture. In his study or special studio built at the Berghof, he could be found almost any afternoon bent over architectural sketches with a pencil in his hand, changing, adding, correcting; or inspecting models of new buildings and other constructions and expounding his views to his entourage and the original designers. Architecture was not his first love merely; architecture in the Third Reich meant monumental buildings, and monumental buildings were to Hitler lasting symbols of a great epoch.

His evenings at the Berghof were usually spent

around the fireplace in the big hall in the company of his guests. These might include artists from the opera, the stage, and the films, especially musicians who might give a sample of their talent for the edification of the company. Most of the time, however, the evenings were devoted to informal discussion of problems of the day. In these chatty talks Hitler learned many things that would never have found their way into official reports. Through them he extended the antennae of his intuition, gauged the atmosphere around him and measured the forces that he must take into account in making his decisions. These discussions were so much the rule at the Berghof that some believed that Hitler hated being alone. But there were other moods.

Even many of those who came to the Berghof with a certain reserve were captivated by the Führer's complete naturalness in these surroundings. Before the swallowing of Czecho-Slovakia, for example, a Czech delegate of the Front Fighters' Congress, who admitted his initial skepticism, described his impressions of his visit to Hitler in his native Czech paper as follows:

"In his salon Hitler gave us the impression of an unaffected private gentleman. Before other statesmen of great name, the average person has a peculiar feeling of distance. With Hitler it was otherwise. He sat among us. It seemed to me as if I had spent at least two years with him in the trenches. He repudiated the word 'dictator' for himself. The Germans, he said, had elected him with more than 90 per cent of the votes. He compared the life of nations with the life of a married couple. Agreement was necessary, he said, and difficulties had to be removed. War, he insisted, was the last thing he would take on his conscience; it is terrible for the vanquished and the victors.

"I repeat, this statesman and head of the German nation did not seem stiff; his social manner was informal and, so to say, comradely. Ladies accompanying blind veterans had been informed before hand that Hitler does not like paint and powder. In the salon was a piano and a bust of Wagner. Yes, Hitler loves music and plays the piano well. The artists are well taken care of by the Führer."

In some respects this friendly observer must be by now disillusioned, but there is no reason to doubt the honesty of his general impression. Similar descriptions have been given by other foreign visitors, and though it may be too much to say that they came to scoff and stayed to pray, the fact is that visitors to the Berghof put stress on Hitler's informality, while visitors to the Chancellery at Berlin were more likely to be impressed by his preoccupation and earnestness.

And, finally, associated with the Berghof is a curious anecdote. This is that while Hitler and Amann were climbing about in the Bavarian mountains early in their careers, before they always knew where their next meal was coming from, Amann jestingly remarked: "When we get rich, we'll build our homes here."

Hitler is said to have replied: "I shall never get rich,

but some day, perhaps, my people will build a house here for me."

That dream, like so many others that Hitler dreamed, has come true to a degree surpassing dreams.

II

WORLD REVOLUTION: A CHALLENGE TO AMERICA

THE theme song of the German legions is:

> *"Today we own Germany,*
> *Tomorrow the whole world."*

How do Hitler's victories concern the United States, which still has wide oceans to protect it and whose wealth of resources makes it "the greatest nation on earth"? Surely Hitler cannot be planning to conquer the United States and make it one of the subject States of his world scheme?

To have raised that question only a few months ago would have stamped one as an irresponsible alarmist. Yet it has been in the mind of all who have watched the rise of National Socialism and realized its implications, and today only the irresponsible will presume to give an apodictic answer to that question.

The answer of a responsible American Government is a multi-billion armament program.

The battle now being fought is a life-and-death struggle between two cultures, two ways of living and dying, two moral concepts and two systems of social, political and economic organization. The outcome must not only demolish the present balance of power in the world but determine the future shape of the world.

That this struggle has assumed such world-wide ramifications is boldly proclaimed by Adolf Hitler himself and reaffirmed by every word that has come from National Socialist Germany. This new Germany has broken beyond the German frontiers with the elemental force of an exploding volcano, the fires of which are testing the fitness of the existing world order to survive. That France, Austria, Norway, Czecho-Slovakia, Poland, Denmark, the Netherlands and Belgium were earliest engulfed was owing merely to the accident of geography which placed these countries as the first obstacles in the path of the National Socialist world revolution.

Each conquered country has been only a base of departure for new conquests; the final goal is announced to be the world rule of the German race.

A few months ago such ambitions appeared to be merely mad dreams or propagandistic slogans. Now they have assumed a new reality amid the bursting bombs of German air armadas, the roar of motorized divisions and the tramp of legions.

Yet the National Socialist aims that lie beyond the conquest of any individual country had been revealed to the world long since with a calculating frankness that won them the death-defying allegiance of German youth —a fact which precludes their abandonment—and seduced the rest of the world into not taking them seriously.

Starting with the conquest of Germany itself under the "temporary slogans" of breaking the Treaty of Versailles and fighting bolshevism, Hitler proceeded to the unification of the German race and has now proclaimed as his next goal the consolidation of the European Continent, with Germany as its protector. (Hitler's New Year proclamation and January 30th speech; Rosenberg's Danzig speech, April 16, 1940.)

But even that was recognized as a mere "temporary slogan" beyond which already was rising the next, whose import may be gleaned from the following statements of Hitler himself:

"A State which, in an age of racial pollution, devotes itself to cultivation of its best racial elements must some day become master of the earth," he wrote in *Mein Kampf*, which today is the bible of National Socialist Germany; and, barring half-hearted imitations elsewhere, Germany is so far the only country devoting itself to that task.

"We all sense," he also wrote, "that in a far future mankind may face problems which can be surmounted only by a supreme master race supported by the means and resources of the entire globe."

And how these problems are to be solved is indicated by his view of the rise of the Aryan, whose destiny Germany has taken into her keeping.

"As conqueror," he wrote in the same book, "the Aryan subjected to himself lower humans and regulated their practical activity under his command according to his will and for his aims. By leading them to useful if hard work he not only spared the life of the conquered but perhaps also gave them a lot that was better than their former so-called 'liberty.' "

If these quotations seem to refer to the distant past or the distant future, it must be kept in mind that in National Socialist reckoning past and future merge into the present and that under that reckoning time is regulated only by the dynamics of the National Socialist movement itself. That these quotations are as valid today as ever is illustrated by the fate of Germany's conquered subject peoples, now working under German command for German aims. At the same time, the objectives that will follow consolidation of Europe are already suggested by the constant emphasis in the German press that only such a consolidated Continent will be able to employ the full force of "its immeasurable economic and spiritual resources in the struggle between the great world-political rooms."

It is pertinent to subject the situation facing the United States in case of a German victory over Great Britain to cold-blooded analysis. Such analysis must proceed from three fundamental considerations.

First, which is self-evident, is that all National Socialist slogans invoked in the war against France and Britain apply with redoubled force against the United States. According to its own vociferous proclamations, National Socialist Germany is pitting "blood against gold" in a fight against "decadent democracy" and "rapacious plutocracy," depending on a free economy and world trade, in order to substitute for them a new world order based on national and international "socialistic" planning under authoritarian governments and a peace guaranteed by German arms.

A second consideration, long overlooked but now also evident, is that power dynamics of authoritarian States have their own law of action, which is determined by opportunity rather than by any individual will—even the will of Hitler, who is a prisoner of the forces he unleashed. In contrast to the Western post-war mentality, which envisaged a world stabilized by paper treaties, power politics abhors a power vacuum and enters it—in Europe as in the Far East. Under the hammer blows of the German armies in France the world again was shocked into a realization that the only dam against power is more power—even if that entails the risk of war.

The third and most important consideration is that National Socialist Germany wages "total war," in which military might, economic warfare and moral disintegration of the prospective enemy play equally important roles.

If the European Continent should be really consolidated under the ægis of Hitler, and if its "immeasurable economic and spiritual resources"—not to speak of its military might—should be thrown into the balance in the struggle between "world-political rooms," the United States would face what is known in diplomatic parlance as a new situation, unprecedented in its history. But it may be pertinent to try to envisage the consequences of a crushing defeat for Britain and the imposition on it of an "anti-Versailles," already propounded in the German press.

Such an "anti-Versailles" would first of all involve total disarmament of all the defeated countries. That would leave the German army supreme and beyond challenge by any power or combination of powers in the world. But it might and probably would also involve surrender of the Allied navies to victorious Germany, as Germany was compelled to surrender her navy to the victorious Allies in 1918.[1]

That would put Europe's strongest navies on one side of the United States and an allied Japanese navy on the other side. Added to them would be the strongest air fleet in the world. Both would far surpass any defenses that America or all the Americas could create in years. Moreover, an "anti-Versailles" must be expected to include complete redistribution of Europe's colonies and dominions—redistribution between Germany and, at least for the moment, her temporary allies. And it must likewise be expected to include confiscation of all foreign investments of France and Britain, as Germany's foreign holdings were confiscated in 1918. Moreover, National Socialist Germany has developed its own technique for acquiring ownership of industrial and other resources of conquered countries. The result would be a complete change in the political and economic control of

[1] Since this was written, Britain has captured or destroyed part of the French fleet to prevent its falling into German hands.

Europe and Africa, much of Asia and Oceania and presumably Australia.

The economic consequences to America of such an upheaval are equally obvious. It would put America's entire foreign trade, not only with Europe but also with the rest of the world, completely under the control of Germany and her allies. That trade, it may be argued, amounts to less than 10 per cent of America's total production; but under America's methods of production that 10 per cent often determines profit or loss. True, America produces many things which even a totalitarian world would still need. But the things that world would need would be American raw materials, such as oil and cotton. In markets for finished goods employing profitable labor America would find the competition of a consolidated Europe, behind whose salesmen stood the military might of Germany.

What that means already is amply illustrated in the case of Rumania and other Balkan States. Moreover, whatever foreign trade remains to the United States would have to be conducted on terms dictated by Germany, which repudiates free private multilateral world trade conducted on a gold standard and substitutes for it a government-controlled bilateral barter trade based on an equal exchange of goods between two countries and paid for in "labor currency."

In practice this means that Germany buys from each country only as much as she sells to it, and measures the value of goods so exchanged not in terms of gold but in terms of hours of labor. But the value of hours of labor in each country is determined through the mechanism of a managed fiat currency; the exchange value is adjusted arbitrarily by agreement between governments, whose relative position, in turn, is determined by their relative might. Germany as the mightiest country in the world could herself determine how much foreign goods her fiat marks would buy and how much German goods the currencies of other countries should buy in return. Germany could determine employment and living standards in countries that must trade with her.

For America the more or less world-wide adoption of this system would entail a further development of still immeasurable consequences—namely, demonetization of gold. With such a development the $19,000,000,000 gold hoard in Kentucky would be reduced to trinket value. In such a case it might be doubted whether America's foreign investments would be worth the paper they are written on. Difficulties of America's "financial imperialism" already are the subject of mocking comment in the German press.

Such, in any case, would be some of the inevitable consequences of "socialistic planning between nations" and a victory of "blood over gold" which the National Socialist regime has proclaimed on its banners. It proposes to lead the world into the "socialistic millennium" to be formed—in Hitler's words—"not by the senile forces of a decaying world but by the young and productive nations to whom belongs the future."

This would leave the United States alternative courses. This nation could adopt an autarchic planned economy of its own and live mainly on its own resources within the confines of its own borders and militarize itself to the limit to assure its safety. But there can be little doubt that planned economy goes hand in hand with authoritarian government, and so this course might mean an end of America's political democracy.

To adopt the alternative might be to court economic catastrophe of still inconceivable dimensions, with social and political upheavals, and possibly make America ripe for the invader. German proposals for new and more "organic" organization of the United States already are at hand. According to all National Socialist commentators, the American people are not a nation but a conglomeration of undigested racial units. According to Colin Ross, much-traveled German author, whose views are widely disseminated in Germany, the vertical division of the United States into Federal States is purely artificial and should be replaced with horizontal organization according to racial groups. Such horizontal organization already has been introduced by Germany in Czechia, Poland and Slovakia. It goes without saying that in these subject countries the German racial organization dominates.

According to Ross, a like organization in the United States would give the German element in America a new rôle to play, according to its numbers, influence and importance, enhanced by Hitler's victories. And as a "fifth column" such an organization might decide American victory or defeat in war.

PART II

How Hitler Prepared

III

HOW HITLER MADE READY

As THE Western world reels under the staggering blows of the German armies and desperately seeks ways and means to keep German might from spreading to the whole earth, there also has set in a frantic effort to discover the cause of Western weakness and the secret of German success.

For the most part search centers on discovery of the "secret weapon" the Germans are supposed to possess which is held responsible for everything that has happened. But that is an oversimplification which German propaganda encourages for the evil it works on the enemy's morale and the obstacles it puts up against discovery of the real truth and the organization of effective defense.

The Germans have sprung many "surprises" in this war, but none of these "surprises" so far has been of a character either new or secret or incapable of being anticipated. As a matter of fact, German success is not attributable to any "secret weapon" or any single weapon whatsoever but to a combination and perfect co-ordination of many weapons forged in seven years of moral, military and economic mobilization of the entire German nation, carried out in the glare of worldwide publicity which Germany has courted rather than shunned.

"We demand arms," is the cry that runs through Hitler's whole book, *Mein Kampf;* and that book leaves no doubt as to what he proposed to do with the arms once he got them. For the last seven years he has been getting arms with a speed, application of science and ruthlessness unparalleled in history, and he has often boasted of his success.

It must be kept in mind that this mobilization was a total mobilization for total war with total objectives. This means that all the moral, military and economic resources of 80,000,000 people were organized and mobilized for the sole purpose of waging war with all means, which in itself dictates such a war's goal. For that goal can be no limited objective which would not justify such a tremendous national effort and leave the way open for later retribution, such as Germany herself now is exacting, but only Punic annihilation such as Rome visited upon Carthage.

"The war of the future," wrote the authoritative *Deutsche Wehr* as early as 1935, "will be total war not only in the employment of all forces but also in the sweeping nature of its decision. In other words, total war means the complete and final disappearance of the vanquished from the stage of history."

That the world and especially responsible governments were taken by surprise is a phenomenon that will always interest historians.

Military and economic mobilization by means of which Germany created the mightiest military machine that ever challenged the world will be discussed later. But even a machine is worth only what the mind that rules it makes of it, and the secret, terrifying impetus of the German war machine is the mobilization of the minds and spirit of the German people, especially German youth, which was Hitler's first concern—a mobilization that has created a fanaticism which as long as it can feed on victories repudiates all other human values and attains the stage of self-annihilation.

For the last seven years the German people, especially German youth, have been brought up in the spirit of the dictum of General Ludendorff, inventor of total war, that "war is the highest expression of the racial life," which is amplified by the *Deutsche Wehr* as follows:

"War has become a form of existence with equal rights with peace. Every human and social activity is justified only if it helps prepare for war. The new human being is completely possessed by the thought of war. He must not, cannot think of anything else."

Results of this training are now finding expression in the death-defying courage with which German soldiers fling themselves into battle—courage which, military observers agree, exceeds all military discipline. It manifests itself in the grueling work, under conditions of malnutrition, performed by German men and women in armament factories whose efficiency cannot be explained by concentration camps or SS firing squads alone, however much these may have been used to crush opposition. And the same applies to the "extended strategy" that reaches out behind the enemy's lines with parachute "suicide squads" on the one hand and a "fifth column" of German and native Nazis on the other.

Parachuters and the fifth column are among the "new German weapons" that surprised the world, especially countries which so easily succumbed to German attack. Yet German parachuters are copied from the Russian parachuters paraded before Hitler's foreign military attachés for years, and though infiltration of German fifth columnists was perhaps less easy to detect, native Nazis have paraded sometimes in uniform in most of the big cities of the world, including cities in the United States.

In itself, therefore, there is nothing new in the weapon of the fifth column. Developed from the most ancient artifice of the military trade—namely, espionage—it showed up in embryonic form even in the last war: for instance, in espionage and sabotage organizations in the United States, for activities in which Franz von Papen and Captain Boy-Ed were expelled. The name fifth column derives from the Spanish civil war, during which it was first applied to General Franco's secret adherents in Loyalist Madrid.

New, however, is the vast development of this as well as many other weapons with which Hitler's revolutionary modern warfare is forcing all other nations to seek new defenses. And the development of this particular weapon can be understood only when viewed against the background of the whole National Socialist revolution, the full implication of which the world only now is beginning to grasp.

For the fifth column in its most modern form is essentially a revolutionary weapon, a fact which virtually precludes its employment by non-revolutionary powers. Under the name of cells it has been a well-known expedient of the bolshevist "world revolution" since its inception, but it took German thoroughness and efficiency to make it an effective weapon.

Whereas a bolshevist "cell" is organized for the propagation of class warfare and enlists only class-conscious proletarians and some ideological sympathizers, the National Socialist fifth column derives its strength from two revolutionary principles which enlist men of action and have the backing of the world's biggest military power.

First is the German racial dogma which proclaims the world supremacy of the German master race and claims the undivided allegiance of all Germans everywhere, irrespective of their "state-membership" or citizenship.

Under this principle, on which is based the concept of a total war enforced with all means at the disposal of an authoritarian government, Germans are no longer regarded as private individuals, but as agents of the German folk or race as organized in the German Reich, who must implicitly obey the orders of the Reich Government and serve it with the same fanaticism demanded of Germans at home. In National Socialist eyes Germany does not end at the Reich borders but exists wherever the German tongue is spoken, and German organizational talent has provided appropriate organizations for all, adapted to varying circumstances in individual countries.

German nationals abroad, so-called *Auslandsdeutsche,* are included in a foreign organization of the National Socialist party headed by *Gauleiter* Bohle, who rules Germany's "foreign province" and is also State Secretary in the Foreign Office. Germans of foreign citizenship in foreign lands, or *Volksdeutsche,* who subscribe to the Nazi doctrine, whether native-born or naturalized, are organized in numerous "folk organizations" which are as National Socialist as they dare to be and maintain contact with Bohle's organization through camouflaged cross-connections.

And woe betide a "renegade" who, whatever his citizenship, refuses to obey orders. The German press poured out the vials of its wrath and invective against Prince Bernhard, the consort of Princess Juliana of the Netherlands, because he refused to act as a fifth columnist in the Netherlands Government. That such a system casts suspicion on even the most loyal Germans is their tragedy, a fact which National Socialists coolly include in their calculations because it is most likely to drive the reluctant into National Socialist ranks.

The second principle is National Socialist world revolution aiming at the creation of a new social, economic and political structure of the world which, while designed to promote world rule of the German master race, nevertheless also enlists the allegiance and support of partisans of authoritarian government everywhere who hope to get power under the new regime and, as shown by recent events, are at times even willing to sell out their own country to the enemy.

The support of such organizations throughout the world is far costlier than that of a mere espionage organization and the second biggest drain on the German balance of payments—food imports are the biggest—has been expenditures abroad for just such purposes, hitherto lumped under the rubric of propaganda. But in part these organizations finance themselves and in return Germany possesses in every country in the world an organization which supplies her with more extensive and more accurate information of all kinds than the secret service of any country can hope to collect and on which she can rely in case of need to perform all kinds of desperate deeds—even to efforts to capture the governments of invaded countries, as in Norway and the Netherlands.

Functions of the fifth column may be divided into peacetime and wartime activities. In peacetime chief functions consist in creating propaganda, which is not always merely pro-German or pro-Nazi; in supplying detailed information on commercial, industrial and political activities and national morale which, when collated in Berlin, gives a complete picture of every country's life; in maintaining surveillance of important citizens of the "host land"; in outright espionage and, above all, in preparation for an "emergency," to the point of training shock troops for the first blow.

In this work the fifth column skillfully utilizes all the social, political and idealistic ambitions and aspirations of various elements of the "host land" to lull that land into a false sense of security, undermine its defense preparations and sow political, class and racial dissensions; and there is joy over every involuntary because guileless member whose aid the fifth column can enlist.

Its wartime activities were disclosed with startling results in the recent past in Poland, Norway, the Netherlands, and France. But for wartime activities the fifth column usually is reinforced with determined men from Germany herself, who come in many disguises, principally as tourists, sportsmen, commercial agents and cultural representatives, and often carry their uniforms in their suitcases. They take charge of previously organized resident armies, which often in disguise or in the uniforms of the enemy's own forces seize strategic points, reinforce parachute troops, organize espionage and sabotage behind the enemy's lines and throw confusion into enemy army and population through false orders and reports. Its work, especially its constant stream of information, has been largely responsible for the "trance-like surety" and deadly accuracy with which Hitler so far has been able to evaluate the situation in each country, and for the amazing advance of German armies in sometimes small and isolated columns in defiance of all laws of military tactics.

Activities of the fifth column are so many-sided and so widespread that only the briefest kind of summary can be given here of some of its outstanding accomplishments. The ideal fifth column was first formed in Austria, where its representative, Dr. Arthur Seyss-Inquart, could be put right in the government and was able to turn the country over to the invading German armies without a fight. In Czecho-Slovakia both the Sudeten Germans and a good part of the Slovaks constituted such powerful fifth columns that, with the help of its allies, the country disintegrated.

In Poland a fifth column formed by German minority organizations fought down Polish military organizations, occupied bridges and strategic points, seized industrial and power plants and in general prepared the way for guided German armies in their Blitzkrieg.

In Norway Germans had not only full knowledge of every inch of Norway's difficult terrain and the sad state of its defenses but also possessed hidden or disguised resident armies which seized Bergen before any German ships arrived and occupied Narvik with the apparent connivance of its commander, helped invading airplane troops to seize Oslo and, under leadership of the German air attaché, almost succeeded in seizing the Norwegian King and the Government. Furthermore, co-operating with native Nazis, however few, they were able to establish a puppet government under Major Vidkun Quisling and hold it long enough for him to disrupt Norwegian mobilization and throw confusion into Norwegian ranks by false orders of non-resistance.

In the Netherlands resident armies, troops smuggled in beforehand in ships and innocent-looking canal barges, and parachute troops, aided and guided by Dutch Nazis, combined to seize airports and bridges and even important parts of Rotterdam, The Hague and other places, and vainly sought to kidnap the Queen. In fact, the quick collapse of Dutch defenses is attributed in large measure to fifth-column work.

The Führer's headquarters itself boasts that parachuters, meaning the fifth column, were a decisive weapon in the record conquest of the Netherlands, which had to be accomplished before French and British troops could come to their aid in order to lay the basis for the vast flanking movements that led to the Allied catastrophe in Flanders.

Luxembourg was almost completely seized by German tourists with machine guns even before German regulars arrived.

Just what happened in Belgium still is not clear, but the German press frankly acknowledges the cordial welcome given to German troops by Belgian Flemings, and even King Leopold's capitulation is being connected with press dispatches from Berlin to the effect that by grace of Germany he may become King of "the Greater Netherlands" under German protection.

As a result of these experiences almost all countries in the world now have taken measures to cope with a fifth column within their gates as well as with parachuters who may come to the aid of that column. Almost everywhere resident Nazis have been rounded up or put under surveillance, "tourists" and ship crews and other foreign visitors either have been barred or put under sharper control, and laws and agencies dealing with espionage and sabotage have been reinforced. Every ship approaching from foreign shores is watched with suspicion and searched for hidden or disguised soldiers, guns and bombs. Moreover, both belligerent and neutral countries have felt compelled to organize a special home defense army to guard themselves against the new menace and instruct the whole population on how to deal with it.

Fifth-column and parachute troopers have been successful so far only in weak or ill-prepared countries where they could count on quick support from invading armies. They have not been able to capture a country by themselves nor so far have they been able to do any real damage in Britain, however numerous reports of "fifth-column" activities in that country may be. As said at the outset, they are important but only one of many important new weapons employed by Germany in her total war. And the only defense against total war is a total mobilization which undertakes to deal not only with one weapon but with all of them.

IV

THE REARMING OF THE REICH

TWENTY years ago Germany was completely disarmed by her conquerors in the World War. The mighty Imperial Army created in a century of progressive militarization and powerful enough to hold the world at bay for four years was smashed, together with all German fortifications, all German airplanes, tanks and heavy guns; and the German Navy disappeared below the waters of Scapa Flow. Only a nominal army of 100,000 men armed with rifles, light field artillery and paper tanks for practice was left to Germany for domestic police purposes.

Today a new German army of millions, better armed than the army of 1914, again is rolling over one country after another like a juggernaut, waging war without mercy for the proclaimed goal of world revolution that is to establish the supremacy of the German master race and annihilate all who will not bow to its will. Before its might the hitherto best army in the world wilts almost overnight and the strongest fortifications fall like the walls of Jericho.

Creation of this army within the space of seven years represents a national effort on so vast a scale that it is without precedent in history. This effort coincided with the fateful paralysis of its prospective victims. While the democracies were solving their political and economic problems at the expense of national defense and national efficiency, Germany embarked upon a moral, military and economic mobilization based on a revolutionary ideology which, whatever else is said about it, produced a new fighting generation and equipped it with the multitude of modern weapons with which Hitler is now revolutionizing warfare and dictating the law of action to the enemy.

According to Hitler's own figures, Germany spent in this mobilization 90,000,000,000 marks before the war started; on the basis of German expert estimates that war expenditures have exceeded 3,000,000,000 marks monthly, perhaps another 27,000,000,000 marks must be added to that sum up to May 1, 1940. That makes a total of about 117,000,000,000 marks, or nearly $47,-000,000,000 at the nominal rate of exchange. The defense expenditures of the far wealthier democracies don't begin to approach that figure. But as Rudolf Hess told prospective officers back in 1937:

"Saving in armament is saving in the wrong spot. Saving of a few hundred million marks may mean loss of a war and so the waste of billions of marks and millions of lives."

As a result of that policy Germany not only erected the Westwall, which balked the Allies while she finished off Poland, Denmark and Norway, but was also able to throw into the battle an army composed of close to 200 fighting divisions approximating 3,000,000 men, while another 2,500,000 are believed mobilized for home defense, for occupation armies in various conquered countries, especially Poland, and for various auxiliary organizations behind the front, particularly police and transport units and the labor organization, which relieve the army of all work behind the front and permit the army to concentrate all its energies on the sole business of fighting.

These figures are considerably smaller than the total manpower mobilized in Germany during the last war, when up to 10,000,000 men stood under arms at one time. But, according to German calculations, such vast armies are no longer possible or necessary. They are impossible because of the toll of the last war and the fact that every soldier in the field now requires two or three times as many workers behind the front to produce his equipment and ammunition as during the last war; and they are no longer necessary because modern arms have increased the firing and fighting power of the individual soldiers many times.

Firing and fighting power of the German soldier is made possible by the greatest accumulation and diversity of mechanical weapons ever assembled. Though unable to change the eternal laws of strategy, they nevertheless enabled the Germans to surprise the Allies with new tactics, which, in conjunction with the revolutionary ideology that created the fifth column, have been responsible for German successes.

And chief among mechanical weapons has been the motor—the motor in German tanks, airplanes, motorized divisions and supply trains which converted the struggle into a war of motors. But this was possible only because, in line with its surprise tactics, the German command developed its motorized units into its foremost, and independent, offensive weapons. It did not use tanks, as the French and British did, merely as a cover for the infantry and make them victims of their own slowness; and only in Poland was it able to use the airplane, in the classic Blitzkrieg method propounded by Douhet, to cripple the enemy before he could mobilize. It worked out a new system of hurling these units in close co-ordination and in mass formation against selected points, and this system was responsible for both the German break through the extension of the Maginot Line and the Allied disaster in Flanders with all its consequences.

Thus in a few short weeks the German army overthrew all the military maxims on which French strategy had been based for the last twenty years—namely, that with modern fortification works the defense becomes stronger than the offensive—and re-established the validity of its own maxim that on the land at least the offensive is the best defense. Whether that maxim is valid also against British sea-power must still be demonstrated.

According to the best estimates, Germany went into

the Western offensive with 12 armored divisions numbering 500 tanks each, which would make approximately
6,000 tanks in service, with perhaps 3,000 tanks in reserve. These tanks ranged from the small, seven-ton
tank armed with machine guns only, to motorized for-
tresses of 70 tons armed with machine guns, cannons
and flame-throwers and protected by armor against
which the ordinary Allied anti-tank gun proved ineffective. As many as 2,000 tanks were thrown into battle at
the same time at one point, and against their impact
even armored concrete forts and pillboxes were unable
to hold out.

The number of German planes is Germany's greatest
secret, but the German war goal was approximately 12,-
000 modern planes and there is no reason to assume
that there are many more. The 300 German air bases
possess an estimated capacity of no more than 12,000
planes, and though the total strength of the German air
force, including anti-aircraft defense, exceeds 200,000
men, the trained flying personnel is put at only 16,000
pilots, including some 7,000 officers. However, in her
diving bombers, which now are believed to have been
the most formidable of Germany's boasted "secret weapons," she possesses a deadlier instrument of destruction
than anything on the Allied side, and in the recent campaign she was able to use her planes much more freely
because her production, and so her replacement capacity, exceeded that of the Allies.

Used in mass formation to bomb forts, pillboxes, railways, troops, transports and especially troop concentra-

tions for counter-attacks, these planes have become Germany's flying artillery and, used as transports for troops and supplies on an unprecedented scale, they have added a new dimension to the strategy which permitted vertical encirclement from the air.

Finally, extensive motorization of the German army enabled motorized divisions of specially trained riflemen and artillery to pour through gaps blasted by tanks and airplanes and race forward at a speed up to 150 miles daily behind the enemy's fighting front, to spread confusion in hostile armies and panic among populations.

Yet the extent of motorization necessary to achieve these results need not be overestimated. The total of motorized German troops is put at no more than twenty divisions, or 10 per cent of the fighting force. But these were sufficient to hold the advantage until the regular infantry and artillery could come up.

But tanks, airplanes and motorized divisions, however important, don't win wars by themselves. Many other elements go into the victory, and so far as the German Army is concerned these elements may be summed up as follows:

First, an infantry trained, equipped and selected for both a quick war of movement and death-defying storm attacks. Trained from boyhood to endure long-distance marches with "pack," which have become the main "defense sport" in Germany, the German infantry covered on foot up to forty or fifty miles a day despite the fact that it is now equipped with twelve separate weapons instead of the two or three of the World War.

One secret of its mobility is the fact that most of the infantry's equipment and pack moves on wheels, making the infantryman's load much lighter than it was a quarter of a century ago. Further, contrary to the French system of mixing all age classes, the Germans have created units of the same age classes for the tasks best suited to them. The youngest are used for reckless storm attacks; older classes, especially veterans of the World War familiar with all the ways of taking cover, are used mainly for front-line defense.

Second, the great number of auxiliary troops and weapons, among which the elaborately equipped German combat pioneers, the parachute troops, anti-tank guns and flame-throwers are the most important. The job of the combat pioneers is not merely to clear the road for the infantry by removing mines and barricades and by building bridges under fire, but theirs also is the task of conquering fortifications with hand grenades, flame-throwers and high explosives.

The parachuters, desperate young volunteers all, are used mainly in collaboration with the fifth column to seize strategic points behind the enemy's lines; but, in collaboration with the combat pioneers, they are used also against fortifications. Following methods carefully worked out on exact models erected for that purpose in Poland, they landed directly on the armored cupolas of Fort Eben Emael barring the German road into Belgium and blasted the mechanism of its revolving turrets, which limited the sweep of their guns. This operation permitted the combat pioneers to come up under the protection of the "dead spaces" of the fort, where the guns could no longer fire, and the fort fell.

Third, a vast and elaborately organized transport system which mobilized the country's entire privately owned motor resources for military purposes. It has succeeded in supplying a modern army of millions with all it needs along steadily lengthening communication lines. Though how the armored divisions that swept behind the Allied front in Flanders were supplied with fuel and ammunition remains a mystery.

Over and above everything else, however, stands the centralized, daring, ingenious German army command under Adolf Hitler, whose totalitarian authority guarantees the perfect co-ordination of all arms, which is an essential element of German tactics. Hitler so firmly believes in his destiny that he takes risks which an ordinary general would shrink from. On the other hand, the difficulty of co-ordinating the armies of four nations, and an all-too-cautious military leadership, spelled disaster to the Allies in Flanders.

But when all is said that can be said about the German achievement, the fact which history will record as the main element in German success is the political passivity and rigidity of the democracies, which stuck their heads in the sand against the approaching storm and even after the outbreak of the war settled back comfortably behind the Maginot Line and the British Fleet to wait for Germany's collapse. It was this factor which permitted Hitler to seize and hold the initiative from the start, to split his opponents and pick them off one by one.

In particular it gave him two inestimable advantages of almost decisive importance in war. It enabled him to wage his campaigns according to his own time-table and when his own preparations had reached, absolutely and relatively, their maximum strength—an advantage which the democracies also conceded to Mussolini. And it gave the German armies the benefit of the surprise attack that picks its own time and place.

German rearmament began even while the Imperial Army was being disbanded after the last war. Under Colonel General Hans von Seeckt, whose motto was "Work, keep silent and obey," Germany began at once to construct a cadre army of 100,000 men composed of picked officers and material, which took over the traditions of the Imperial Army and formed the basis of the new army. Based on the 12-year enlistment period provided by the Treaty of Versailles, it trained military experts who became the officers and non-commissioned officers of the present army, reinforced by a specially trained and often barracked police.

Military training in many political party armies, veterans' leagues and "technical emergency organizations" was encouraged by the military—including Hitler's own Storm Troops.

Attempts to form an illegal "Black *Reichswehr*" were defeated by its own revolts, but arms and ammunition were manufactured in German plants and in other lands, especially Soviet Russia, where German officers and men also were trained with arms forbidden to Germany. And the basis of the new air fleet was created within the German Lufthansa, government-controlled and subsidized air transport company, one of whose directors was Erhard Milch, Marshal Hermann Goering's right-hand man.

Immediately after withdrawal of the Allied Control Commission in 1927 and especially after the Allied evacuation of the Rhineland was completed in 1930—five years ahead of treaty time—the German army proceeded to increase its armament and its effectives under guise of "reorganization" of its units and formation of new "technical, machine (meaning tank), instruction, service, repair, and other squadrons." Simultaneously it began to lay the basis of its motorization on the principle of standardization.

Up to the end of 1932 German rearmament was hampered by the necessity for camouflage. But when in December, 1932, the Geneva disarmament conference acknowledged Germany's right to armament equality the camouflage could be dropped and rearmament became the paramount national task.

Franz von Papen, President von Hindenburg's own choice, proved too much of a political lightweight for such a gigantic job. General Kurt von Schleicher, the army's man, proposed to rearm as a "social general" with the aid of the labor unions, but met the fate of all German political generals and paid with his life. It became evident that after Hitler's election victories, won with the promise that he would forge the German sword, rearmament could not be carried out against him and therefore had to be carried out with him. Hitler became Chancellor and the blood-red dawn of the iron age broke over Germany.

On the very day of his appointment rearmament began on a vast scale under conditions assuming more and more the form of martial law. Hermann Goering was appointed Air Commissar and Lufthansa planes grew in number by leaps and bounds, although the expanding corps of pilots continued to train in mufti. By April, 1933, the army also was ready for expansion; its ranks were being filled up with volunteers and battalions grew to regimental size. Compulsory labor service was introduced and numerous special "police units" were formed which later were incorporated into the army. When the alarmed Marshal Pilsudski of Poland tried to intervene as early as March, 1933, he was frowned down by France and Britain.

By 1934 Germany was feverish with rearmament activity. New barracks, new flying fields, new fortifications, new war schools, new military roads began to take shape. German industry, working on the principle of standardization and mass production even at the expense of quality, boomed with the manufacture of war materials—and unemployment began to disappear. A threat to the orderly progress of rearmament coming from Hitler's own ranks was drowned in blood, and on March 16, 1935, Germany threw off all pretenses by going back to national conscription.

By March, 1936, Hitler had taken the measure of

his democratic opposites; against the advice of his generals he moved into the demilitarized Rhineland. The German army marched with orders to retreat immediately if France and Britain moved.

By this successful stroke Hitler won out not only against his future enemies but also against his own generals. Despite their continued passive resistance, the army was being Nazified step by step and its leaders put under Gestapo surveillance. In the army shake-up of February 4, 1938, Hitler ousted the most formidable opponents of this process and assumed personal command of all the armed forces of the Third Reich. A few weeks later he marched into Austria. His career of conquest had been launched.

V

HITLER'S ECONOMICS

DESPITE many spectacular German victories, the last war was up to the very last a military stalemate broken by economic warfare dictated by American support of the Allies and the allied blockade against Germany.

The present war is dominated entirely by the almost incredible striking power of the German war machine which is forcing decisions before American help can become effective, and whose conquests are beginning to nullify the effects of any blockade. But this striking power of the German war machine is a product of total national mobilization whose terrifying meaning is only now becoming apparent and which is based on three main elements:

One, the psychological mobilization of the German people which shocked the world by its brutality against opposition but which also produced a hard, fanatical and unscrupulous fighting generation.

Two, the superior military enterprise and ingenuity of the German army command.

Three, the economic mobilization which produced,

first, the greatest amplitude and variety of mechanical weapons ever assembled in history and second, made the country as blockade-proof as possible.

The German fighting spirit, the German methods and German mechanical weapons were amply demonstrated in the campaigns of Poland, Norway and France. But in so far as this is a war of machines, German victory is also a victory of German organizational technique and industry which render the military positions of predominantly agrarian countries hopeless and teach their own lessons to those who would resist the "German master race."

When the victors in the World War disarmed Germany they not only left her industrial war potential intact, but under the leadership of the United States also did everything to increase it—by loans, investments to the tune of some 32,000,000,000 marks of which only one-third went for payment of reparations, by construction of improvement for German industrial plants, and by technical aid. Germany made the most of it and today it is not too much to say that in part the German war machine was financed and even constructed by those it would destroy.

This in no way diminishes but only amplifies the magnitude of Germany's economic mobilization, and this economic mobilization also is the key to the whole National Socialist economy.

In principle this economy is simple enough. It is the total conscription of the entire nation's man-power and resources—of capital and labor, of producer and consumer, of men, women and youth and their co-ordination in a system ruled not by economic calculations but by iron discipline which still provides certain paternalistic "socialism" for workers and leaves the limited profit motive to employers to spur their energies.

Under this system a nation of 80 million plus still uncounted millions of conquered subject peoples has been converted into a gigantic trust which has no other aims or dogmas except total economic and military war in service of the National Socialist world revolution that is to establish German world supremacy. Based on a philosophy that this is a dynamic world ruled by the law of the strongest for the survival of the fittest, it acknowledges no rules except those serving its purposes and defeats its opponents by their own rules. And so effective have been its methods that those who could oppose them were compelled to adopt them in realization that such a system can be met only with its own methods and that the answer to total war is total mobilization.

What such total mobilization can accomplish Germany has demonstrated. When she started on her career of rearmament and conquest she undertook a desperate enterprise in the face of sheer insurmountable obstacles. She was a country with poor natural resources, deficient in all but three of approximately twenty war-essential raw materials; she was without gold or liquid capital and heavily in debt abroad; she was moreover in the midst of an economic crisis which had reduced her industrial production by nearly 50 per cent, had disorganized all governmental budgets and sent unemployment figures soaring.

But she did have idle industrial production capacity and idle labor which made her potentially Europe's biggest industrial country, second in the world only to the United States. By bringing her idle production capacity and idle labor together through total conscription in the service of rearmament, she created both an economic boom which abolished unemployment and a war machine which made her incomparably the world's strongest military power.

In practice this process carried out by the militarization of the whole national economy under name of *Wehrwirtschaft,* which worked mainly for the state under the direction of an economic general staff headed by Goering whose executives were colonels and generals. But to create this *Wehrwirtschaft* required thousands of individual measures and commands all complicated and often paradoxical, but all enforced by heavy fines and imprisonment, by economic annihilation, concentration camps and SS firing squads. When war broke out the machinery of war economy was already functioning as it had been functioning for years.

The main principles and measures of this *Wehrwirtschaft* may be summarized as follows:

For capital, trade and industry:

One, fixed prices determined by price decree of October, 1936, but adjusted currently by the price commissar on a cost plus basis. This prevented the vast credit inflation with which the armament program was financed from taking effect in soaring prices that would have produced fatal money inflation and raised the cost of the armament program itself. As it is, the German wholesale price index has risen only from 90.7 in 1933 to 109.6 in April, 1940, and though the cost of living has risen far above the artificially adjusted cost of living index, it has not risen more than an average of 25 per cent.

Two, limited profits—limited by price control and compulsory investment all profits above 6 to 8 per cent in government loans, though this investment was subject later to distribution to stockholders. Gross dividend declarations in Germany are still up to 14 per cent.

Three, compulsory investment surpluses in nationally important enterprises such as plants for synthetic oil, artificial rubber exploitation, and otherwise unprofitable domestic ores.

Four, prohibition or control of new plants or shops or plant and shop expansion in nationally unessential enterprises.

Five, full control of industry by allotment of government orders for raw materials and control of foreign exchange.

Six, preemption of the entire capital market including national savings, resources, banks and insurance companies, corporation funds for government loans (except for a few private security issues for nationally important tasks) either through compulsory subscription to government securities or acceptance of government I.O.U.'s in their manifold forms.

Seven, limited "entrepreneurs' wages" for corporation heads and directors.

For labor:

One, fixed wage rates based mainly on the deflated wage levels of the crisis low of 1932, but subject to minor adjustments.

Two, job control which conscripts workers for nationally important tasks and prohibits others from changing jobs at higher pay.

Three, abolition of the right to strike and prohibition of independent labor unions except for the German labor front which is the agency of the National Socialist Party, and technically embraces employers and employes.

For consumers:

One, rationing of virtually all food and most other necessities under the slogan "cannon instead of butter" which lowered living standards to the point of malnutrition.

Two, directed consumption by controlled allotment of all necessities and national propaganda for the consumption of what is plentiful.

For farmers:

Fixed prices and market regulation compelling fixed deliveries of products to specified control agencies.

If this system sounds rigorous it is not without its benefits. For government guarantees, propagandistically through the slogan of "crisis-proof" economy and actually through plethoric government orders, full employment for industry and labor. Under it the industrial production index rose from 54 in 1932 to 137 in June, 1939. Agricultural production rose from 10 billion marks in 1932 to 14 billion in 1939. National income rose from 45 billion for the old Reich in 1932 to 100 billion for expanded greater Germany. Employment rose from 12,500,000 in 1932 to 22,000,000 just before the war and unemployment, which exceeded six million in January, 1933, had been replaced by a desperate labor scarcity that can only partly be met by the labor of the conquered subject peoples. And if wage rates had remained virtually stationary or been even reduced after the outbreak of war, earnings due to steady employment and longer hours increased by some 15 per cent over 1933.

In addition workers enjoy a "socialism" which improved working conditions through "beauty of work" organizations, established paid vacations for all, organized leisure and vacation recreation through "strength through joy" organizations, provided labor courts for appeals against dismissal and honor courts for appeals against insults to workers' honor. Where a shortage of raw materials or workers compels industrial curtailment, industrialists receive aid from the industrial self help fund and workers receive part time unemployment support.

Farmers, finally, got reduced interest rates, cheaper fertilizer and other supplies, and higher prices which are far above world market prices though not what they could get in view of the food shortage.

To many that may not seem sufficient for less freedom, but while this system lasts it compensates for the loss of liberty with economic security even if under reduced living standards. When Hitler came to power he faced not merely vast unemployment, but also predominantly a "Marxist and internationally-minded proletariat" which had to be won for his program. But this program solved unemployment automatically and confirmed another maxim of Hitler's book, *Mein Kampf*: "The question of 'nationalizing' a people," he wrote, "is primarily a question of creating healthy social conditions." For German standards he has succeeded and though observers report increasing nervousness and irritability among workers due to war strain, German victories go far to alleviate it for the moment. Industrial per capita production is still above pre-crisis levels and the German baby crop increased from 971,000 in 1933 to 1,420,000 last year to add to Germany's future superiority in man-power over all other European nations except Russia.

But in mobilizing all these factors Germany had overcome two tremendous handicaps: her raw material shortage and her lack of gold and fluid capital to finance her armament program. The manner in which she overcame these handicaps is a triumph of German ingenuity and craftiness.

The insufficiency of raw materials was solved by three methods:

The entire foreign trade and especially all imports were put in the service of rearmament under strict foreign trade control which required the approval of every individual foreign trade transaction and permitted the import of nonessentials only where absolutely necessary as quid pro quo for German exports. That was the meaning of the "new plan" introduced in July, 1934, which required bilaterally balanced exports and imports for each country and therewith compelled every country wishing to sell to Germany to take German goods, however unwanted, in return.

Two, strict rationing of war materials according to the national urgency of the products for which they were to be used.

Three, Germany's "new plan" vastly expanded the yield of her domestic raw material resources by creating synthetic raw materials such as oil from coal, rubber from coal and lime, textile fiber from wood, by exploiting her low-grade raw materials such as her low-grade iron ore irrespective of cost, by replacing imported raw materials with more plentiful domestic raw materials, and by saving every scrap of waste. That was the primary import of two so-called four-year plans which denoted a policy of the greatest possible self-sufficiency to make the country as blockade-proof as possible. How they have succeeded is illustrated by the fact that German production of "production goods," meaning mainly armament, was almost twice as high at the outbreak of this war as in 1913 on half the imports of 1913, and that Germany drove to victory primarily on artificial rubber tires and synthetic gasoline.

According to best estimates Germany is able to cover two-thirds of her raw material requirements from domestic sources though she completely lacks some important key metals which must be imported at all cost. And four-year plan plants, which up to the outbreak of the war consumed raw materials in their construction, now produce all the more.

As a subsidiary four-year plan may be listed the much advertised German agricultural production battle which, however, has been less successful. By raising production but primarily by reducing consumption to the point of malnutrition Germany increased her self-sufficiency in food from 75 per cent in 1932 to 82 per cent at the outbreak of the war, but her fat shortage is still more than 50 per cent. Additional amounts she must import or starve.

The problem of finance was also met if not solved by three methods:

One, Germany mobilized her foreign debts by declaring in June, 1933, a transfer moratorium on all foreign interest amortization charges amounting then to about 1,200,000,000 marks yearly. This kept German money at home, reserved money earned abroad by exports, shipping and other services for purchase of foreign raw materials, enabled Germany to repurchase greatly depreciated German bonds at a few cents on the dollar to subsidize exports, and, in as much as German debtors still paid debt charges in blocked marks, put large amounts of cash at immediate disposal of the government. Creditor countries helped by devaluing their currencies.

Two, Germany created her own capital by a simple expedient: The government as head of the German "trust" issued securities and I.O.U.'s to whatever amount necessary. This raised the combined public debt of Reich states and municipalities and their agencies, which camouflaged rearmament, from 24,300,000,000 marks in 1933 to well above 80 billion now (and some estimates put it above one hundred billion), compared with about 160 billion marks piled up by Imperial Germany in four years of war.

But in as much as currency circulation also tripled since 1933, there also were some 10 billion marks of additional "printed money" plus billions of special "credit bills," other I.O.U.'s with which German armies pay their way in conquered territories. Despite this fact that official gold coverage is now only a tiny fraction of 1 per cent and that the German mark is virtually worthless abroad, the mark remains "stable" at home because of fixed prices and it is even proposed by the German press as standard exchange value for the European continent.

Three, the economic boom created by the gigantic rearmament program brought part of the money poured out by the government back into its coffers under a drastic taxation system. Taxes have risen from 25 per cent of national income in 1932, to approximately 47 per cent of national income now, but total revenues of "public hand," meaning the government and its agencies, in taxes, levies and compulsory contributions however called, also have risen from 14,131,000,000 in 1932 to approximately 31 billion in the current year.

There is no doubt that the whole German machine,

industrial as well as military, has been subjected to terrific wear and tear. And it is a question how long it can continue without breaking down. But as against that and as a token of its replacement capacity, the German conquests accomplished under the slogan "blood against gold" have now put the resources of the whole European Continent at its disposal. And if the British threaten to blockade the whole Continent until starvation and revolution overthrow the National Socialist regime, the German press already replies that in such case it won't be Germany who will suffer.

The war has become a struggle of continental system against continental blockade and the results of that struggle are still beyond all calculations.

VI

THE JUGGERNAUT OF MARS

FOR seven years, beginning on the day he became Chancellor, Adolf Hitler and his National Socialist movement armed, organized and trained Germany for the totalitarian war which they hoped to avoid, but did not shrink from waging in order to smash the treaty of Versailles, unite the German tribes and assure to a new Great Germany that place in the sun, that *Lebensraum*, that share in the world's riches that they consider the due of one of the world's leading master races.

For that purpose they created not only one of the world's mightiest military machines but converted a whole nation into a living juggernaut of Mars, in which each individual had his designated place and functioned as just one cog in a complicated mechanism such as perhaps only Germans could devise and run.

In size, in methods, above all in its unitary control and its demonstrated efficiency, it was by all odds the most formidable, ruthless, determined and ambitious instrument of power the world had seen, and it achieved such spectacular political and military victories that its creators proudly extolled totalitarianism as the answer to the problems of the age as against "decadent, fair-weather democracy."

Against the possibility that it would be forced to fight a traditional British war of attrition Germany was prepared in a manner and to an extent difficult to realize. This aspect of totalitarian war was the basis which was adduced for the abrogation of personal liberty and for the whole totalitarian control of all phases of life, including speech, press, education and religion, introduced in an attempt to assure national unity and moral stamina; and it was in particular the basis of military economy with its emphasis on the armament industry and its complete regimentation of industry, commerce, trade and labor through control of raw materials and production, of jobs, wages and prices, and its effort at the greatest possible food and raw-material autarchy through the four-year plan.

Long before Premier Mussolini formulated it, Germany followed the totalitarian maxim that not peace but an armed state of war is the normal state between European nations and, therefore, the only possible economy is a war economy. When the war broke out all Germany had to do was to rename her military economy war economy, tighten a few screws in her war machine, and she was ready to go, while the others must build up a war economy from the start.

And it was a matter of both pride and satisfaction to the German leaders that in the storm the "fair-weather" democracies which still regarded peace as the normal and war as the abnormal state of international relations were forced to resort to some of the same methods that Germany adopted beforehand. In this they early foresaw the victory of totalitarianism, regardless of the outcome of the war itself.

That the German war machine functioned is self-evident.

And the same thing can be said for the domestic front. The strain of a general mobilization of huge material demands a modern military establishment. Finally, the effect of the Allied blockade, which cut Germany off from all overseas supplies and reached out for German exports, necessitated sweeping readjustments in production and a rigid rationing system, not only of raw materials but also of all, even the smallest, necessities of daily life, especially food and clothing, which foreshadowed fundamental changes in the whole distributing apparatus. But these readjustments, long planned and prepared, were carried through almost overnight without a major breakdown.

German economy continued to produce at capacity and during the long period of comparative military inactivity, to store up all things essential for the conduct of the war and at the same time provide the population with supplies which, though insufficient, maintained the living standard and averted genuine privation.

The armament industry, running at full capacity, seemed amply supplied with men and raw materials. In this connection, as an indication of the effectiveness of the four-year plan, stood the claim of Professor Walter

Messerschmitt, noted German airplane designer and manufacturer, that German planes consisted of 99 per cent domestic raw materials; and though this claim perhaps was not 99 per cent exact, its general implication presumably applied to many other arms as well.

At the outbreak of the war consumption-goods industries and commercial undertakings, including shipping, were throttled, working short hours or being completely shut down, and so the supply of consumption goods was seriously reduced. But the machine was kept going, for their losses were equalized by an industrial emergency fund fed by profits from the war industries; and, in addition, after the original concentration of war orders in the biggest and most efficient concerns, the government during the breathing spell felt able, in view of the slow pace of war-material consumption, to spread orders as widely as possible. By avoiding a war against major opponents on two fronts, Germany was able—at least in the beginning—to keep down her mobilized man power and her armed forces to 3,000,000 men, or 4 per cent of her then population, instead of an average of 10,000,000 men, or 15 per cent of the population, needed in the World War.

The size of this force explains why so many men of military age could be seen in civilian clothes in German cities during the war's early months. They provided the man power of the domestic front, operated the national economy—which was further reinforced by a working population of more than 25,000,000 Czech, Polish, and Jewish subject populations—with the result that the total German productive capacity was far above that of Britain and France combined.

At the same time, though unemployment increased because of the readjustments mentioned, it did not reach dangerous proportions; first, because the selective draft took principally those who could best be spared; second, because the labor draft permitted the shifting of workers from throttled consumption-goods industries to war industries.

Moreover, despite the shock of war, despite an estimated war cost of nearly 100,000,000 marks daily—during the "breathing spell"—the German financial and credit structure continued to operate as usual. There was no panic in the rigidly controlled security markets, and the government was able to finance the war with short-term treasury notes and taxes. In fact, it had created an almost automatic system which enabled it to collect a large part of the sums it paid out in war costs for new war financing.

This was done, first, by means of war taxes that skimmed off outright some 40 per cent of the national income; second, by compulsory reduction of consumption through the rationing system and by means of rigid price controls which not only prevented visible signs of inflation but also set free substantial purchasing power. This, for lack of other possible employment, found its way back to banks and savings institutions, where it was mobilized for new war credits.

Claims of German official statistics that Germany actually reduced her living costs by 1.3 per cent during the first month of the war in face of substantial increases everywhere else may be set aside as fiction because they took no account of the impaired quality of the goods. But that does not affect the financial automaticism which in effect put the whole German people to work in the interest of the war economy at fairly high paper wages, but gave them rather low purchasing power. This cut down the standard of living for all, especially the well-to-do.

And this leads to the consideration that every war machine, even the German, consists not only of military and economic apparatus but also of a human element which in the end decides for victory or defeat. In appraising this element the world was at first prone to delude itself with wishful thinking and an overestimate of more or less spectacular incidents by failing to view them against the background of the whole.

There is no doubt that for seven years the German war machine worked at a speed and under a pressure which were designed to get the most out of the German people in the shortest time. This machine, therefore, was geared to the limit of human capacity and endurance and it sapped the nation's psychological reserves. There is also no doubt that in its single-minded effort to make the nation ready for a supreme effort, the National Socialist regime rode roughshod over individual interests and lives and inflicted wounds on many families and whole classes of the population which raised many hatreds against it.

And to this then was added the shock of war with its

uncertainties and anxieties, the intensified hardships of
the war economy, the blackouts, and the increased control and rationing system which impinged upon every
phase of German life.

This unceasing strain began to tell in the winter of
1939, especially since fundamentally, despite the years
of the National Socialist regimentation and excepting
perhaps part of the younger generation, the German
people had remained more or less what they always
were, with the same individual, regional, political, religious, and class differentiations that were not always
in accord with National Socialist aims and ideology. And
this gave rise to a growing irritation on which fed a
growing opposition, which, in turn, stirred up activists
on the fanatic fringe who then committed deeds like the
Munich bomb plot.

That the National Socialist regime was perfectly well
aware of this and watched the domestic front with anxious care was indicated by the fact that whenever the
pressure became dangerous it was eased, at least for the
moment, as was done with the restoration of part of the
former overtime bonuses and the slight increase in food
rations. And it was also indicated by the whole direction
of the wartime propaganda which was designed to explain the necessity of control measures and to minimize
their hardships as well as by constant admonitions to
silence to foil enemy espionage and constant warning
against "sabotage."

But though this irritation was a symptom that the
war machine was using itself up at a much faster rate

than during the last war, when the rested nerves of the German people enabled them to stand the strain much more easily, it did not mean that the war machine was in danger of a breakdown. On the contrary, it continued to function with an almost inhuman efficiency, which crushed any individual who dared stand in its path, be he industrialist or general or obscure worker. Soldiers at the military front and soldiers at the domestic front were subject to the same laws of war which punish disobedience as mutiny. And the Gestapo was efficient enough to detect mutinies in the bud and crush them, if necessary, with firing squads.

For that reason the opposition was neither numerous nor organized and, taking the population as a whole, irritation vented itself in nothing more than constant and often not even ill-humored grumbling, comparable to the traditional grousing of an army that still springs to attention at the word of command.

Moreover, if the war in those early months brought added strain, it also brought new impulses to compensate for it.

Germany was at war and whatever the attitude of the individual German, he, like the Frenchman, the Englishman, and the American, marched when the bugle called. He did his duty. The war was still too young, too unreal, to permit popular feeling to crystallize, but as was to be expected with a patriotic people, the first shock of the outbreak of war was quickly cushioned by the German victory in Poland and new exploits of the German U-boats and fliers swelled German breasts with pride and gave a lift to German morale.

At the same time, the bulk of the German people, irrespective of class or occupation, feared that the loss of the war would throw the country into chaos comparable only with the Russian chaos of 1917, which would have been worse than anything they suffered in that first Winter. And they also were aware that changing horses in midstream by changing the regime was not conducive to winning the war.

Furthermore, most Germans were so busy in the war machine that they had little time for anything except the immediate problem at hand, and all Germans were so completely dependent on the machine for very existence that it was suicide to oppose it. The peasants, who incidentally, were the most satisfied class in Germany and the backbone of the regime, depended upon it for the market prices, industrialists for their orders and raw materials, storekeepers for their supplies and workers for their jobs and wages and also their food.

And Hitler's pact with Russia, whatever its cost, proved to be a trump card for the moment, not only in the international arena but also in the domestic field. For it took the wind out of the sails of the last undercover Communists, whose talk of revolution if war came quickly ceased; to the mass of German workers, who at heart were still Socialists, the pact held the promise of the rapid socialization of industry. In this hope the workers met with the rank and file of the National Socialist party careerists who expected the war to usher

in the long delayed "second revolution" that would reduce the salaries of the industrial bosses to their own
scale, and the regime responded to these hopes with
denunciations of "capitalistic pluto-democracies" and
charges that it was socialistic Germany that England
hated.

German industrialists naturally viewed such a prospect with less enthusiasm, especially since the war economy already was leading to a rapid extension of State
control and State capitalism, which for one thing nipped
war profits in the bud. However, many refused to take
the threat seriously and most of them were captivated
by the possibilities that real and permanent collaboration with Russia, together with German control of Central and Eastern Europe, opened up to German industry
and commerce.

They saw a vision of a continental economic bloc, a
new "continental system," which would provide ample
scope for German technique and organizing talent and
not only assure Germany's vital necessities to make her
blockade-proof but perhaps also bring back the Russian
market to world trade, through the German as the
middleman, as it was before the last war.

For Germany, it was emphasized, was anxious to
trade with the world as much as possible, though not
under conditions which permitted another power to cut
off that trade at will. And Russia, these quarters insisted, had given up chasing the phantom of world revolution and was anxious to develop her national resources

under a system of national bolshevism and State socialism with which Germany could co-operate.

Of course, the most important faction in a nation at war is the army, and there is no doubt that the German Army often had been at odds with the National Socialist zealots in the past or that it greatly extended its power and influence during the Polish war. For that reason all Germans pinned their hopes on it to preserve order whatever happened.

However, recruiting itself from the younger classes who had grown up under National Socialism the army was perhaps more National Socialist at the base if not at the top than the German nation as a whole. And if National Socialism had changed anything, it had made the army more democratic than it was before, so that during the war, at least, every soldier really carried a marshal's baton in his knapsack.

From this summary it will be seen how inevitable or how practical were the motives that lined up the bulk of the German population behind the regime and the war and how remote from German reality was Allied propaganda when the leaflets came floating down.

How was the nation so regimented? Some of Hitler's moves are surveyed in the following chapters.

VII

THE LAP-DOG PRESS

AMONG Hitler's early acts upon coming into power was the destruction of freedom of the press. A witticism circulating in 1935 had it that when Hitler arrived at the Pearly Gates, St. Peter asked: "What good did you do in the world?" "Why," Hitler replied, "I united the German people, abolished all unemployment and made everybody happy."

St. Peter, being a sceptic, sent an angel to investigate. The angel soon returned and reported that he had gone into the highways and byways of Germany and talked to all sorts of people, but that, sad to say, he was unable to corroborate Hitler's claims; rather the contrary.

Whereupon Hitler growled: "What did he want to go snooping around for! Why didn't he read the newspapers!"

Nobody in Germany, not even the National Socialists, denied the justice of this satire on the German press. The German newspapers, ever strong in argument and weak in information, had ceased to present a true or complete picture of their country and had, in con-

97

sequence, ceased to be the main source of news for the masses. Like the bolshevist and the fascist press, they had lost whatever independence they formerly possessed and had been reduced to publicity organs of the government, forced in news and comment to serve the propaganda of the powers that were—to sing their praises and cover up their mistakes.

In the words of Walther Funk, State Secretary in the Propaganda Ministry, the German press was no longer a "barrel-organ out of which everybody is permitted to squeeze whatever melodies he likes, but a highly sensitive and far-sounding instrument or orchestra on which and with which only those shall play who know how, and in whose hands the Führer himself has placed the conductor's baton."

To the Western world, where freedom of the press is a sacred heritage, this is a strange doctrine, sufficient in itself to pass final judgment on the German system. But this judgment is beside the point in a land that spurns it —a land which had rejected Western liberalistic civilization and which sought to build a new world on entirely different foundations.

Like everything else in Germany the German press must be viewed from the perspective of the totalitarian State and the mystic and semi-religious National Socialist *Weltanschauung*, which is designed to mobilize behind that State those positive spiritual forces which make up national morale, and among which the call of the blood is the most important.

The vision of an empire of power and glory, in which

the individual and his personal rights are lost in the mighty onward march of the race, and which creates its own morality according to its needs, was not without grandeur. Further, it possessed a magnetic attraction for most Germans—including journalists.

In church and university the theory that the people were the organs of the state rather than that the state was the organ of the people was not at once accepted. But within two years after Hitler rose to office the press was 95 per cent in his grasp. This was not achieved without arousing reading resistance among the German people. First effects of the National Socialist rule on the publishing business are illustrated by the following figures:

Between March 1933, and March, 1934, according to post office reports, the total number of newspapers and periodicals dropped from 11,328 to 9,426, a decrease of 16.8 per cent. The periodicals suffered most, but the total number of newspapers published more than three times a week also dropped from 3,827 to 3,245. A count made in the summer of 1935, which included all weekly newspapers but was not strictly comparable with the post office count (the latter listing all trade papers), registered 2,623 newspapers toward the end of 1934, with a total paid circulation of 15,019,400. This marks a circulation drop of 1,668,145 between the spring of 1934 and the summer of 1935.

One reason for the decline of the journals was the destruction of the "Marxist" press. As against this, the National Socialist press had at first a rapid rise and filled in part the circulation vacuum. So rapid was the rise that many Nazi papers, then still in the hands of prominent National Socialist leaders, were tempted to plunge into enormous plant expansion. Soon, however, they were caught, not only by the general circulation slump, but also by a perceptible drift of the reading public to the older "co-ordinated" papers—all the more painful because with it went the advertiser. As a result many Nazi papers got into difficulties and the party had to come to their rescue.

As an illustration, the *Angriff*, founded by Dr. Paul Joseph Goebbels, Reich Minister of Popular Enlightenment and Propaganda, dropped from 94,000 in December, 1933, to 53,400 in December, 1934. It then merged with the Nazi Labor paper *Der Deutsche*, which had a circulation of 150,000, but the combined paper was 101,-117 in March of 1935 and dropped to 96,839 in April. The *Essener National Zeitung*, formerly Marshal Hermann Goering's personal organ, dropped from 183,857 in January, 1934, to 135,859 in April, 1935.

Even the *Völkischer Beobachter*, principal and official party paper published by Max Amann, President of the Reich Press Chamber, had in 1935 a circulation of only 182,784 in Berlin, and a total circulation in the Reich of 362,784. In December it had slumped to 336,527, but later gained through a promotion drive, behind which was put the combined force of the government and party machine.

When the whirlwind of the National Socialist revolution ceased tossing the German press about, it had left only two kinds of papers—the National Socialist and the "co-ordinated" press. Both approached in ownership, management and personnel, the character of a State press. The first was published in the main by the National Socialist party, which was by law part of the State; the second, though for the most part still in private hands in 1935, was under such rigid State control that State ownership would have made little difference.

These two kinds of newspapers constituted the "orchestra" with which the totalitarian State played its music under the direction of Dr. Goebbels. He controlled the radio and the films as well, but the press was the most important. As a revolutionary fighting weapon, the spoken word proved superior to the written, but in the day-to-day business of government the press was indispensable.

Even in 1935 the music for the daily press concert was written on the theory that Germany was at war against a world full of enemies—open enemies abroad and sneaking enemies at home—who must be fought on the principle that attack is the best defense. With drums and trumpets, therefore, the German press marched into battle every day, in the approved style of war propaganda. News was carefully sifted to stiffen home morale and to avoid giving aid or comfort to the enemy. Criticism of any kind was outlawed, and he was the best man who flayed the foe most and cheered his own cause loudest. The newspapers existed not for their own sake or for the sake of the public, but only for the service they rendered the State.

In conducting this program the attitude of the National Socialists was disarmingly frank—not unmixed with cynicism. The name of "Propaganda Ministry" speaks volumes in itself; but beyond that Dr. Goebbels, in speeches, scorned to dissemble his thoughts. The duty of the newspaper, in his view, was "not to inform, but to shake up and spur onward," without indulgence in "that liberal objectivity which seeks to be equally just to friend or foe, to one's own and foreign nations." On the other hand, "the right to criticize belongs to the National Socialist party alone and I deny it to all others."

In this spirit the press was instructed and supplied with material. The material came in the main through the sole and semi-official news agency, born of the consolidation of the former *Telegraphen Union* and the old Wolff Agency and now known as the German News Agency. As editors and reporters shortly discovered, since almost all of its news must be subjected to careful scrutiny for reasons of state, it laid no claim to speed, but since it was alone in the field neither it nor its clients could be beaten on news even if it was a day late.

Instructions were issued at a daily press conference in the Propaganda Ministry, but were supplemented with running orders which might designate even the type, the headline, and the position of some individual item. Moreover, in times of stress, the orders might change constantly—to play up this, to play down that, to eliminate another thing—with the result that the German editor worked always with his heart in his mouth. For a slip might cost his livelihood.

In desperation, therefore, many editors simply learned the way of least resistance, printed the official or semi-official news according to instructions, and renounced all creative work of their own, except perhaps to be particularly devoted to the ruling powers. But this, again, produced a deadly uniformity which not only killed the newspaper but also defeated the purposes of official propaganda. Which, in turn, might bring down on the harassed editorial heads another official thunderbolt.

"It is asserted that the press is too uniform and dull," Dr. Goebbels once said. "That is not the reader's fault; the journalist should be a little brighter." In fact, he went so far as to denounce the "lap-dog press," calling on the newspaper men to show more courage and decreeing that the press should be "monoform in its will, but polyform in expressing that will."

However, any paper that stepped out of the ranks was suppressed, and Ehm Welk, editor of the Ullstein *Gruene Post,* who waxed mildly sarcastic over this exhortation, went to a concentration camp, while others who committed similar offenses fared only a little better.

Thus the newspapers continued "uniform and dull." Papers died, circulations dropped and the public found other means of satisfying the universal craving for news that makes the whole world kin. Those who could, read foreign newspapers, some of which atttained for a time remarkable circulations in Germany. At various intervals *The London Times* was credited with selling 30,000 copies in Germany daily, the Paris *Temps* and the *Man-*

chester Guardian 35,000 each, the *Baseler Nachrichten* 50,000 to 60,000. But as foreign papers were constantly banned, their annual circulation in Germany is problematical. In the early years a small class was reached by illegal publications, usually Communist pamphlets disguised as innocent advertising distributed surreptitiously, or sent by mail anonymously to members of the army, the police and Nazi organizations.

Most important, however, was the "spoken newspaper"—that word-of-mouth transmission of news that seems irrepressible, even though it makes up in abundance what it lacks in accuracy. "Rumor-mongering" became perhaps the most widespread crime in Germany, and no punishment could curb it. So prevalent was it that the official organ of the Reich Press Association published the following remarkable admission early in Hitler's reign:

"Alongside of the printed, written and read newspaper, there has reappeared again the old oral newspaper. Beyond the visible reader of the printed paper there has formed a class of invisible readers of the unprinted newspaper. That is not the fault of the reader; the newspaper is to blame. For the newspaper is no longer a mirror of the times. It meets its epoch only by commands, not questions.

"The man who lives in this epoch and feels the many complicated problems deeply, is left without response in his many cares and needs, his joys and questions. He would like to know more, learn the connection between events, read more of the things that affect his life. But to his questions the paper has no answer. It permits no distance, no individual judgment."

This should be read in the light that it was made public when the church struggle was the biggest domestic problem in Germany. This wrenched the consciences of millions, yet found no echo in the press, which was forbidden to mention it.

But the author of this courageous indictment suggested no solution, and it may be doubted whether he knew one. For the solution that seems obvious to an American newspaper mind, namely, to print more news, met not only official handicaps but the opposition of the German press itself. This solution was, in fact, suggested by Dr. Hjalmar Schacht, then the Reichsbank president, whose middle names were Horace Greeley.

"The influence of the newspaper," he said, "shrinks in the proportion in which it expresses opinions and judgments. It should, therefore, confine itself to the reporting of facts, and at most comment on the facts." For this statement he was attacked so hotly that he beat a quick retreat.

The German press has never been a news-press, but an opinion-press, which cultivated the long leading article and looked down upon the mere "reporter." It always was the instrument of some party, cause or *Weltanschauung,* and its makers were crusaders and politicians before they were newspaper men. The news-press was reproached for degrading to a business what should be a great calling for cultural and political leadership. The decisive importance of accurate information as the foundation of democratic government was never recognized. Truth is always subjective, in the German mind, and words were invented, not as means of communication, but to cause action—that is, command.

Freedom of the press means different things in different countries. In Germany it always has meant freedom of propaganda. By concentrating on propaganda, the German press not only destroyed its own basic foundation, but also the foundations of the democratic State. It propagandized the German people into so many factions that they fell, like ripe fruit, into the hands of the National Socialists.

This provided, at least in German eyes, a certain justification for the destruction of press freedom. "Absolute freedom of the press never existed," said Dr. Goebbels, pointing out that German newspapers always served some party or other special interest, and the working newspaper man had to conform to the policy of his paper. If the press was merely a propaganda organ, then, to the National Socialist mind, it was logical that the totalitarian State should monopolize it for its own purposes.

Today the German press is governed by two fundamental laws designed to make the National Socialist spirit supreme in the publishing world. The first, proclaimed on October 4, 1933, and pronounced by Dr. Goebbels as "the most modern press law in the world," applies to the working journalists as semi-State officials and semi-independent of their employers in respect to their writings, for which they are answerable to the

State. This, said Dr. Goebbels, is true freedom of the press, "for it is better to serve the State than an employer."

The law provides that only those shall contribute to German newspapers or political periodicals through news or pictures who are German citizens in good standing, above 21 years of age, possessing at least one year's training, and not Jewish or married to Jews as defined by the Civil Service Law. This excludes all Jews and all those with Jewish grandmothers, and under this provision hundreds of the best-known German newspaper men have been drummed out of the profession.

Those qualifying are licensed by registration in a list of the profession kept by the Reich Press Association, a State institution. Anybody who does journalistic work without being on this list is punishable by imprisonment or fine.

The second law consists of decrees issued April 24, 1935, by President Amann, of the Reich Press Chamber. These decrees proclaim the right of way for the National Socialist press, where necessary by suppression of any "co-ordinated" competition, and for the rest provide that even "co-ordinated" newspapers shall be published under strict regulations regarding ownership.

The law does not apply to the National Socialist party, which under Amann's supervision publishes most of the National Socialist newspapers, and which enjoys the further privileges of tax exemptions for its real estate, official patronage in advertising and active support and promotion of its publications by all governmental officials, including the mailmen, who otherwise are threatened with dismissal.

According to talk once common in Berlin, Amann first demanded 30,000,000 marks from Dr. Schacht to buy up dangerous competitors. When Dr. Schacht refused, Amann passed his decrees to eliminate "unhealthy" competition—in opposition, it was said, to both Dr. Schacht and Dr. Goebbels.

These decrees kept the most prominent German newspapers, like the *Berliner Tageblatt*, the *Frankfurter Zeitung*, the *Kölnische Zeitung*, the *Deutsche Allgemeine Zeitung* and the *Lokal Anzeiger* alive, for one reason because the Foreign Office needed them for their influence on foreign public opinion. The decrees were supposed to be directed mainly against the Catholic press and the provincial news press, the so-called *General-Anzeiger Presse*, which was the most prosperous and dangerous competitor of the Nazi press.

As self-made men, the National Socialists worship success and declare it to be the measure of all things and methods. But as newspaper publishers and controllers, their success is subject to grave qualifications.

VIII

ARTISTS IN UNIFORM

THE German faith in propaganda extended to a point where propaganda was *Ersatz* for art. Nothing incensed the National Socialist masters of Germany more than the charge that their rule was throwing the country back into tribal barbarism. In the years of preparation, this charge hurt not only their sensibilities but their political program: first, because to the "nation of poets and philosophers," Kultur remained sacred and above all political change: second, because Kultur had always been put on a par with power as a weapon of national consolidation; and, third, because the vision of a National Socialist epoch replacing the Christian epoch was predicated on the creation of a new mystical Reich that would conquer not only by its armed might but also by the glamour of its Kultur—a Reich that would combine the discipline of Sparta with the glory of Athens and so dominate the modern world as the divided Greeks never could the ancient.

If this vision strikes the outsider as a hallucination of the national ego run amuck, it was nevertheless seriously entertained in highest quarters in the Third Reich; and there was no doubt about its propagandistic usefulness at home and abroad. The traditions of the past and the demands of the future impelled the National Socialist regime, therefore, to do everything possible to combat this charge of "barbarism," and, since the best answer to it was actual cultural achievement, the National Socialist Government in fact attempted to outdo every other regime in the world, except possibly Soviet Russia, in setting itself monuments in stone and bronze, in verse and paint and melody.

It built more representative buildings, spent more money on art and artists, put up more prizes and created more titles to encourage talent, and exerted more organizational energy on cultural promotion than any previous regime in Germany. Hitler, Goering, and Goebbels vied in patronizing the arts, officially and privately.

The Reich Kultur Chamber, with its Reich Kultur Senate and its subordinate chambers for the static arts, for literature, for the theatre and for music, in which were organized all the active artists in Germany, was the most ambitious and certainly the most elaborate and costly cultural organization in the world, supervising both the productive and commercial ends of all the arts, seeking to discover and promote new talent, and providing for the relief of artists in distress or too old to work.

The classic drama had no better performance in the world than in the State theatres of Berlin, and there was no better opera in the world than in the State Opera in

Berlin. The Wagner festivals at Baireuth had been raised by Hitler to a sacrificial rite.

Furthermore, through nearly two hundred publicly-owned theatres, through numerous art exhibitions and reduced entrance fees to the museums, and, lastly, through the "Strength Through Joy" organization of the German Labor Front, which maintained "Theatres of the People," numerous "traveling stages," and a special symphony orchestra of its own, the regime tried to do more than any previous one to bring art home to the people and spread appreciation of art among the masses.

And though the National Socialist spokesmen still entreated the Muses to send them geniuses great enough to express the greatness of the Third Reich, they also proudly proclaimed that under the leadership of Adolf Hitler, "protector and greatest master of German art," the German Renaissance had begun.

Despite all these official efforts, however, the cultural and artistic life of the Third Reich appeared bare and sterile when compared with the execrated pre-Nazi past. Except for the official propaganda, the tumult and the shouting died from the German art world; art criticism was forbidden, the clash of varying opinions was stilled, and with them went the pleasurable anticipation of new masterpieces about to be presented to the world.

Private art exhibitions and private art galleries worked under tremendous handicaps and the private art trade virtually died. The whole cultural and artistic activity seemed to exhaust itself in a cult of the old classics rather than the creation of new classics; the creative vein of Germany became cramped, and the increased official patronage obviously was unable to replace the fructifying effect of the free interplay of forces during a more liberal era.

The principal reason for this was that, with all that the National Socialist regime gave to the arts, it was unable to give them the one thing, which, in the eyes of the Western World at least, was the very foundation of all art and culture, namely freedom of artistic and cultural creation. In the totalitarian State, all things must serve the ends of that State, and a regime which, in the mobilization of all national energies, considers it necessary to regiment politics and economics, capital and labor, the press, the school and even the church, could never permit freedom to the arts that form the highest synthesis of the age and provide the inspiration for the future.

For that reason, the arts, like everything else in the Third Reich, were put in uniform, and the artists were mobilized as soldiers of the National Socialist *Weltanschauung*.

In line with the dictum that the private citizen had ceased to exist and that all individual activity must be an expression of the community, the Government established a monopoly in the arts as well, and arrogated to itself the exclusive right to determine what was "good" and what was "bad," not according to artists or cultural criteria but according to political usefulness. In the sciences and in philosophy, this process was completed early through the reorganization of the universi-

ties, but in the subtler field of art the National Socialist
revolution first precipitated a hot debate on just what
National Socialist art was, and this debate continued until the summer of 1937.

Then, however, Hitler spoke, and his word automatically became the law of the land. This law was laid down
at the dedication of the House of German Art, the monumental art temple built at Hitler's command in Munich. It must have been with special satisfaction that he,
whose first hopeful paintings had been rejected by the
Vienna Academy of Art, now illustrated his artistic doctrines mainly in the language of painting, but the principles he laid down naturally apply to all the fine arts, to
architecture and sculpture, to music and to literature.
Henceforth, German artists violated this law at their
peril, for he denounced all who differ with him either as
unfortunates suffering from a disturbance of their senses
who should therefore be sterilized, or as frauds fit for the
criminal courts.

These principles, as expounded by Hitler and his authorized spokesmen, may be summarized as follows:

Art is the highest manifestation of the genius of each
race; it is therefore racially determined and timeless.
There is no art of the Hellenic Age or of the Renaissance, but only Greek art and Roman art and French
art and German art. The art of the Third Reich must
be, therefore, neither "international" nor "modern,"
which would mean transient, but German and "eternal."

It must be born of the German racial consciousness as
revealed in the National Socialist *Weltanschauung,*

which calls for a reverent and "racial," not merely individualistic or possibly profane, interpretation, not to say idealization, of nature. And it must go back to the classic function of art, namely the creation of beauty—not for its own sake, nor for the enjoyment of a few esthetes, but for the education and inspiration of the German people, to enable them to progress to that "radiantly beautiful" new type of man which is the goal of the National Socialist regime.

For that purpose, it must be both "healthy" and "natral," and comprehensible not merely to art experts but to the whole German people. As becomes a German Renaissance, it must seek its models in the masterpieces of "Aryan," meaning Hellenic, antiquity and of Germany's own past, which made sound craftsmanship the basis of all art. It must set up patterns of beauty and conduct for the German people to emulate—patterns that will exalt not merely physical beauty and strength but also the beauty and strength of the nobler emotions approved by the National Socialist regime, such as heroism, patriotism, loyalty, love and self-sacrifice, applied to topics likewise so approved, such as war, work, motherhood, family, love of the native land, peasant life, sport and, of course, the National Socialist movement itself.

No longer shall art exist for art's sake, but only as a new German confession of faith, portraying the good, the beautiful and the strong, not necessarily the true. And in that sense the arts become part of the vast propaganda machine of the National Socialist regime, which already suggests that, to promote the German birth rate, family pictures should display at least four children instead of the usual one or two.

These principles automatically exclude all "un-German," that is, Jewish, art which could not be expected to glorify the National Socialist *Weltanschauung;* there was no *Zeitgeist,* only immutable German *Geist,* which might stray but never changed. For this reason, all Jews, and those with Jewish relations, were barred from membership in the Kultur chambers and so from all artistic work.

That Heinrich Heine should have written the best German lyrics, that Max Liebermann, late president of the Berlin Art Academy and founder of the Berlin *Sezession,* should have been the only modern German painter worth mentioning in international handbooks along with Adolf Menzel, the Wilhelmian court painter; that Felix Mendelssohn should have composed some of the best German music, were considered aberrations of nature that must be prevented in the future and, as the past, must be either suppressed or corrected by National Socialist artists.

But the same principles also excluded all other forms of art which fell short of the propagandistic function of art. They excluded, first of all, the so-called "abstract art"—cubism, futurism, constructivism, neoplasticism, purism, dadaism, and surrealism—which dissects nature through the intellect instead of synthesizing it through an emotional urge. They likewise barred all "unnatural" art, including most of the impressionists and post-im-

pressionists, who subordinate design to color effects and
so violate the tenet of "sound craftsmanship." They excluded all "unhealthy," morbid, depressing or nihilistic
art, which specializes in portraying the ugly, the de-
formed, the grotesque, the degenerate, the "primitive,"
the merely sensual, the animal or material and mecha-
nistic aspect of things rather than the sublime.

Finally and most emphatically, they excluded the
consciously Communist-revolutionary or so-called "proletarian" art, which, with equal perversion of the
function of art, sought to storm the citadels of the "bourgeois Philistines" by de-deifying their world, by profan-
ing the accepted gods and mocking the sacred symbols
and customs of "capitalist" society.

All these manifold forms of art, which together com-
prise almost the whole art developments of the last few
decades, were thrown into one pot and denounced as
"Jewish cultural bolshevism," in conformity with Hitler's dictum that all enemies, no matter how varied,
must be combined into one for greater effectiveness of
the attack on them. In place of this "bolshevism" would
arise the new German art, conceived according to Hitler's own principles. This new art was admittedly still
meager. Nevertheless, the beginnings were made, most
auspiciously, it was held, in the field of architecture, the
queen of the arts, which is also Hitler's own pet art.

In 1937 the new architectural style was mainly exemplified in the many public and party buildings erected
under Hitler's personal supervision, sometimes with his
help in design. They were hailed as the monuments that

would transmit the glory of the Hitler epoch to the coming generations. The most ambitious effort toward that end was the House of German Art in Munich, the Parthenon of the Third Reich, but the Air Ministry in Berlin, the party office buildings in Munich, with the honor temples between them, the party congress buildings in Nuremberg, and the German pavilion at the Paris exposition were likewise representative examples.

It was, however, obvious that the claim of a new architectural style advanced for these buildings was over-optimistic. Even the layman could detect their models. Despite all differences in design they all represented what might be characterized as a romantic classicism in which Greek and Roman motifs were combined with the severe outlines of modernistic architecture and applied to the monumental. The style had Hitler's personal approval however, and was intended to dominate German cities.

Admittedly in that year of change, painting and sculpture had not attained the excellence of architecture, but a representative cross-section of these arts was presented in the exhibition with which Hitler dedicated the House of German Art.

The first impression of this exhibition was one of general uniformity. Barring some notable exceptions, there was a sameness to the exhibits which expressed itself in painting in a painstaking technique and a smoothness of brushwork giving the pictures an almost photographic, not to say lithographic, sleekness; the sculptures showed a trend toward the monumental which, in the absence of life-giving genius, in some cases suggested grossness rather than strength.

The impression of uniformity was further emphasized by an extensive similarity of subjects which dealt largely with "blood and soil," with war, the National Socialist party, peasant life, comradeship and similar topics. There were ten portraits and busts of Hitler himself, including one as a knight in shining armor on horseback; seventeen portraits of leading members of the regime, including a bust of Julius Streicher with a very Mussolinian chin; fourteen pictures and sculptures of storm troopers and other uniformed National Socialists, besides numerous scenes of the National Socialist struggle and reconstruction.

But Hitler was also credited with having avoided an overemphasis on the heroic, not merely for reasons of artistic policy but also his own artistic taste ran more to the idyllic and romantic than to the bloodcurdling. In sculpture, his favorite artist was said to be Josef Thorak, who executed the monumental figures before the Paris pavilion; in painting, his own field, his favorites were Adolf Ziegler, president of the Reich Chamber of Static Arts, who painted figures that excel in smooth brushwork, and Max Zaeper, who did landscapes with very green trees, reflected in very still waters, under very blue skies.

According to a quotation from Hitler, inscribed on the house of German Art, "art is an exalted mission making fanaticism a duty." Thus the Munich exhibition was to lead the way toward the purge begun by Goering and directed against those forms of art which were pilloried in the show of "degenerate art," likewise opened in Munich, to emphasize the difference between "German" art and "cultural bolshevism." In this "chamber of horrors," containing 300 examples of most of the barred art schools and subjects, the main point made in the placards attached to the exhibits was that all these objects had been purchased by German museums at public expense.

Museum and exhibition directors guilty of having purchased "degenerate" art were likely to lose their posts (one had already fled the country) and a shakeup in the personnel of the art schools was expected. All directors were to undergo schooling so that they might infallibly distinguish between "German" art and the wrong kind.

In regard to literature and the drama, even National Socialists admitted in 1937 that progress had so far consisted mainly in exterminating the undesirable rather than in substituting something better. In all these fields, Germany was compelled to live largely on the treasures of the pre-Nazi past. Despite all official promotion, despite public subsidies to theatres and operas, despite numerous State orders to authors, dramatists and composers, and despite numerous public prizes, the new geniuses, whom the old regime was charged with repressing, had so far failed to come forward, and to the outside world German literature, drama and music were represented principally by men exiled from the Third Reich.

In literature the new spirit had so far been able to express itself only in the political writings of the National Socialist leaders and in some lyrics and epic poems for chorus or radio recitation, all of which dealt with patriotic topics and stressed the tragic and pathetic note. There had been some attempts at dramatizing these same topics, but only with indifferent success, and the German stage had been forced to take refuge either in the classics or in foreign plays. Humor was the greatest rarity, which may explain in part why the greatest dramatic hit under the National Socialist regime was "Jolanthe," a rural comedy in which a pig appearing on the stage in person was the star.

For the most part, however, German authors were producing what might be called "escapist" literature, mostly by delving into the past. There had been a flood of historical novels and biographies with or without attempts to establish parallels with the present. The reason was, of course, that no author could picture the realities of the present and survive, and no author living could impart a semblance of reality to the picture presented by National Socialist propaganda.

In music a similar situation prevailed. All modernistic atonal music was barred as "un-German," together with Paul Hindemith, master experimenter in it; Richard Strauss was in retirement because of the uproar caused by his use of a libretto by Stefan Zweig, a Jew, for his opera, "The Silent Woman," which remained the last creative work of note in the Third Reich. Because of these developments, German composers used "Aryan" librettos, with National Socialist contents, and at most sought to strike a middle course between the modernistic and the classic music, with a close approach to popular folk melodies. But though nearly a dozen new operas were produced in the early years of the National Socialist regime, none proved an outstanding success.

For the most part musical activity in Germany consisted of excellent reproductions of the classics, but German isolation and absence of the former interchange with other countries, the lack of soloists and the drain on musical talent through the expulsion of all Jewish conductors, greatly reduced this activity as well. The younger German generation especially was forsaking the concert halls to follow the brass and drums of marching bands which dominated the music of the Third Reich.

IX

RELIGION

EARLY an effort was made to change the religion of the German people.

It became evident at the Christmas season in 1934 that a serious conflict between Church and State might occur in Germany. In that season an effort was made to transform the celebration of the birth of the Christ-child into a pagan observance of the Winter solstice. The Nazis wanted something closer to their idea of "blood and soil."

Under the new dispensation the Christmas tree lights became symbols of the renewal of nature through the victory of light over darkness, with a tendency to supplement or replace the tree lights with the more powerful symbol of fire bursting from solstice pyres, and even the name of the celebration was changed to "the festival of Jul."

"Holy fires we light to celebrate the turning of the sun," the *Völkischer Beobachter* said in an editorial, "fires that are symbols of the decadent and the bad;

fires that are symbols of the new ascent to the light, which means life."

One Christmas celebration in which the new rites were introduced was observed by selected representatives of the labor service army in the presence of Rudolf Hierl, its commander-in-chief, at Ruhlsdorf near Berlin. The celebration started with the lighting of a huge pyre before which the inmates of the camp lined up with burning torches.

Describing this "wonderful knightly scene," the *Völkischer Beobachter* explicitly called it a solstice celebration in line with its editorial, although apparently a more orthodox Christmas observance followed.

Similar solstice celebrations were organized by the Hitler Youth in various parts of Germany.

Most outspoken in favor of the change is Wilhelm Kube, Governor of Brandenburg, who wrote in *Der Deutsche*:

"The Christmas celebration in Germanic lands is not an invention of the Christian church but our forefathers. The day of the winter solstice was holy to our ancestors and the period around the winter solstice was filled with the fairyland magic of the Nordic soul.

"In this period gifts were exchanged without an indecent hind-thought of getting a reward from Heaven in return. The Nordic man did not think of a reward for decent deeds.

"For us, therefore, even the Christian Christmas remains a festival of Germanic love, Germanic ways and Germanic benevolence."

Four years afterward Germany was in the midst of a new *Kulturkampf*—an obvious war between Church and State. There had been many such conflicts in her history, but, for the first time since the Roman Cæsars bowed to the cross, the struggle was no longer between temporal and ecclesiastical powers but between two rival faiths—Christian and National Socialist.

On one side stood all Christian churches from the Catholic to the ultra-Protestant, united beyond denominational differences by a common peril and a common platform upholding the fundamentals of Christian religion and proclaiming liberty of conscience and confession.

On the other side stood the totalitarian State pledged to "positive Christianity and religious tolerance" which, at the same time, proclaimed a totalitarian *Weltanschauung* of its own, and used all its power to eradicate conflicting doctrines.

Unlike the bolshevist Legion of the Godless, it did not deny the religious instinct as such, but through the mouths of its appointed spokesmen it was raising its own *Weltanschauung* to the level of a substitute religion which repudiated Christian universality in favor of tribal exclusiveness, Christian charity in favor of ruthless heroism, which summed up its theology and Ten Commandments in one word—Germany—and which divided Heaven along racial lines as it did the earth.

Four years of intermittent fight and compromise had convinced both sides that between the Christian cross and the swastika cross there was no compromise. The attempt to co-ordinate the churches into the totalitarian State had failed and the churches remained the sole stronghold of opposition to National Socialist ideology.

But the four years had also shown that the religious struggle could not be won by secret conferences or with police club and concentration camp. Both sides had been forced to carry the battle to the German people, and Hitler on one side and the Pope and the Protestant Bishops on the other had issued their challenges. The clergy of all confessions thundered from the pulpit against the new paganism, the State took the youth away from the churches by monopolizing education and sought to alienate adults by propaganda and "show trials" of clerical offenders.

X

"BEHIND ME... THE WHOLE GERMAN PEOPLE"

THE German nation went to the polls on March 27, 1936 to endorse, with practical unanimity foreordained, Adolf Hitler and all his works and, incidentally, to elect a new Reichstag chosen by him to shout approval whenever such demonstration was deemed advisable.

Taken at face value—as the world was supposed to take it—the spectacle of a great people being at last welded into national unity through the struggle for resurgence from defeat, and for freedom from foreign encroachments upon their sovereignty, was not without grandeur. For though the election results required careful analysis to discern the drift of German public opinion, nevertheless the majority was bound to remain so overwhelming that Hitler was still able to repeat with a show of justification the taunting challenge he had flung out at foreign statesmen during the election campaign:

"Behind me stands the whole German people. Who stands behind you?"

126

But even more awe-inspiring was the spectacle of a nation of 68,000,000 putting its fate into the hands of one man for better or worse. This spectacle became truly alarming when viewed as what it really was: namely, the result of the skillful wielding of the weapons of propaganda backed by the persuasive power of force.

This was no new combination. It was Machiavelli who pronounced the dictum that armed prophets conquer while the unarmed perish. But the use of this combination on such a vast scale as we saw exemplified at this time in Fascist Italy, Soviet Russia and National Socialist Germany was entirely a modern phenomenon. And the greater of the two weapons is propaganda.

Propaganda had made possible the modern dictators, who no longer sat on bayonets alone but were able to cushion their seats with the genuine and contagious enthusiasm and loyalty of such large masses as dragged along, in decisive moments, the even larger mass of the discontented and indifferent, until visible opposition became negligible. Force was indispensable in crushing avowed opponents and discouraging secret antagonists, but it was propaganda which mobilized the millions who shouted themselves hoarse for the leader and finally went to the polls to cast valid "yes" ballots when it would have been just as easy to vote "no."

Judged by results, the National Socialists generally and Hitler in particular were perhaps the greatest propagandists of modern time. They had conquered the German people more completely than either Stalin or Mussolini had conquered theirs; they dared, therefore, to submit to the rule of popular vote oftener and in a more genuine election test than any other dictatorial regimes could, and be more confident of the result. To all outward appearances there was something to that "ennobled democracy" of which the National Socialists boasted, giving point to Hitler's exclamations: "I don't want to be a dictator! I want to be your leader, and you are my judges!"

To the Western mind this "ennobled democracy" may have seemed rather warped because at best the established tyranny of the majority made even that majority artificial by annihilating all parties and organizations which might overtake the government, thus confronting voters with a choice between the existing regime and possible chaos.

But as an election steamroller the National Socialist system must have aroused the envy of election campaign managers everywhere. For, as Reich election director, Goebbels had a complete monopoly of all election propaganda and had furthermore at his disposal an organization which was unsurpassed in its striking force, a variety of methods that nobody dared criticize and funds that were unlimited.

There was only one legal party and only one ticket. Names on the ticket did not matter, inasmuch as they were all determined by the party machine, anyhow, and only a few of the top ones were mentioned at all. The ticket was not so much an election ticket as an expression of faith in Hitler. The election itself was not so much a Reichstag election as a plebiscite, which Napoleon also knew how to employ, frequently with good effect.

There was no opposition. The formation or attempted formation of any other party outside the National Socialist party was forbidden by law; so was all criticism of either the regime or its representatives. Even dissent from party doctrine often led to the loss of one's job or even became the subject of a Gestapo investigation.

The entire State apparatus, with its monopoly of patronage, public relief and police powers, was put at the service of the National Socialist party's election campaign. This included not only the vast body of government officials and employees, from Cabinet Minister to rural mailman, but also all social, business and cultural organizations which were under party control. All of these issued urgent appeals—now is the time for all good men to come to the aid of their party; stand by the leader; let the Reich show the nation's foreign and domestic enemies what's what. Count Helldorf, Berlin's police president, frankly instructed his police force: "You must be propagandists of the National Socialist idea. Helpers of the Führer must see to it that every man and every woman follows the call of the Führer and goes to the polls."

It was difficult to imagine a German who would stay away after that; and nine times out of ten a voter brought to the polls was a voter for the government.

Finally, all the means of influencing public opinion—press, film, billboard; above all, radio, and even the pulpit—were converted into vehicles of National Socialist election propaganda. In the official press the periodical German press was frankly told that it was an instrument of political leadership and must devote every page, from first to last, to election propaganda, which could be only National Socialist. Yet by Hitler's dictum, by National Socialist experience, the greatest instrument of propaganda remained the human voice, provided it was employed amid appropriate surroundings, with proper oratorical skill and lack of scruples. Through oratory the National Socialist movement first became a power.

A talent for oratory was therefore a first requirement of every aspirant to National Socialist leadership. The flood of election oratory poured out upon the German people was, therefore, assuming unprecedented volume; and since the Germans never before had had orators worth mentioning, they were virtually helpless before the flood.

Radio, which in Germany was owned by the government, had extended the range of the human voice to embrace the entire nation simultaneously and had so created a new political force for good or ill which was revolutionizing political practice not only in Germany but in other countries as well.

Still, in organizing, in trimming the contents of election oratory so as to make it most effective, National Socialism surpassed perhaps every other propagandist organization in the world. It was especially remarkable that *Mein Kampf*, written when Hitler was 34, was still the standard work on organizing "legal revolution," as Lenin's works were on organizing illegal revolution. At any rate, the National Socialist propaganda machine still followed its maxims, not to its loss.

The first of these maxims was that oratory was most effective at big mass meetings held in the evening amid carefully created atmosphere of both solemnity and enthusiasm. In his book Hitler recounted how he learned this maxim by painful failures in his early attempts to stir crowds with speeches in broad daylight; how he came to realize the three conditions of successful political oratory. The big mass meeting, he explained, is necessary because in it an individual feels safe and courageous; the crowd produces its own spirit, which feeds enthusiasm and carries the individual along. In the evening, he continued, everybody's resistance is lowest and the mass succumbs all the more easily to the suggestive power of a stronger will.

Finally, said Hitler, he learned in the Catholic Church that twilight cathedrals in which incense burned amid solemn ceremonies created an atmosphere which made the words of the priests most effective; he determined to employ an equally appropriate atmosphere for the propagation of his own doctrine.

So far as possible these methods were employed during the National Socialist struggle for power; the attainment of power put at the disposal of the National Socialist regime unsurpassed facilities for enlarging upon them. At this time—1936—the regime not only had a monopoly of oratory but also control of all meeting places, all State party organizations, which enabled it to assemble mass meetings as large as desired.

It mobilized for election purposes such huge organizations as the Storm Troops, the *Schutzstaffel,* the labor service, the Air Defense League, the Women's League, the Hitler Youth and, above all, the German Labor Front, with its shop organizations embracing almost every worker and office employee. Sometimes tens of thousands of the most loyal supporters were shipped by special trains to points where they could do the most good in leading cheers and creating enthusiasm.

In staging such mass meetings no bets were overlooked. There were flags, banners, bunting, magnesium lights, bands, songs, trumpets, fanfares and torchlight parades. A regal atmosphere surrounded the main speakers, who often operated their own spotlights from their desks. Not least was the ceremony of the solemn opening, which usually consisted of the trooping of the Nazi colors into the meeting amid the silent salute of all present; and the chanting by a male chorus of an anthem of heroism, hate and heartburning devotion, which put the audience in a proper frame of mind to applaud anything from an abstruse dissertation upon National Socialist *Weltanschauung* by Alfred Rosenberg to a ribald attack on the Jews by Julius Streicher.

How large mass demonstrations could become is illustrated by the fact that some 300,000 assembled in Therese Meadows in Munich to listen to Hitler; the opening speech of the 1936 election campaign, delivered by Goebbels, was heard by even more hundreds of thousands assembled in 230 of Berlin's biggest halls, interconnected by loudspeakers.

But this concentration of technical organizational machinery, however imposing, would have remained an empty shell and, therefore, ineffective if the Nazis hadn't known how to fill it with the living breath of the effective word uttered at the right time. It was here that they display their real mastery. And here again they merely followed the precepts of Hitler's book.

These precepts may briefly be summarized as follows: In order to be effective, propaganda must be of a popular order, and to be popular it must be primitive. For, said Hitler, the mass itself is primitive. In overwhelming majority, asserted the Führer, are people so feminine that their thoughts and actions are determined not by sober reasoning but by emotions. Therefore, he held, propaganda must appeal first of all to the emotions. Its intellectual level must be gauged to the lowest intelligence among the mass it is designed to reach, from which it follows that the larger the mass to be reached the lower must be the intellectual level of propaganda.

Oratory must therefore deal primarily with such primitive emotions and concepts as love, hate, right, wrong, patriotism, treason, without forgetting the material interest. All this must form the foundation for a few central ideas which must be hammered into even the dullest brain by constant repetition.

Above everything else, propaganda must have courage, fanatical onesidedness which paints only in black and white and knows only heroes and villains. For, said Hitler, "If even a shade of justice is admitted for the other side, the foundation is laid for doubt in the justice of our own cause."

All this was nothing new to the authors of good old-fashioned melodrama, to demagogues and yellow journalists and war propagandists, from whom, in fact, Hitler learned his trade. But the application of their principles to politics on such a "totalitarian" scale as that adopted in Germany had rarely been paralleled. It was particularly remarkable in a country which had always made a religion of its Kultur. Yet Hitler knew that the mere employment of cynical principles would be insufficient for ultimate success; he tied them up with what to Germans must appear a noble cause—namely, national racial unity in a bigger Germany—and made it seem plausible that in the service of such a cause the end would justify the means.

By their nature these principles were fighting principles, and fighting was proclaimed to be the essence of Nazi life. But to assure victory it was advisable to pick carefully both the enemy and the issue. In this respect Hitler was likewise following his own precepts. Concentrate on one enemy, he advised in his book; if necessary, lump even widely differing enemies into the same category. He proceeded to do so successfully in both domestic and foreign politics. All enemies of National Socialism were in 1936 lumped under the general category "bolshevism." This category included such diversified elements as Jews, international finance, the Catholic Church and, as a potential new member, the French nation or any other nation standing in Germany's way.

They were all being fought in the name of a crusade against bolshevism. This in turn explained why National Socialist elections were timed so that they could be connected with a vital issue of foreign politics such as Germany's bolt from the League or the scrapping of Locarno through military occupation of the Rhine.

But there was yet another fighting precept laid down by Hitler. That was challenging the enemy by appropriating his colors, his symbols, his slogans. He employed this precept so successfully that he was able to merge colors, symbols and slogans of both the Nationalists and the Communists with his own and, finally, to steal the weapons of both Nationalists and Communists.

This precept was in the foreground of the election campaign, placed even above the injunction to concentrate on a synthetic enemy. According to instructions issued by Goebbels, the election battle was waged this time for something, rather than against somebody. Ordinary enemies, like the critics of the regime and the reactionary grumblers, even the Jews and the still unco-ordinated churches, were therefore sidetracked. The National Socialist orators appeared in the role of crusaders for peace, freedom, law, order, "ennobled democracy," everything that was good, true, and beautiful.

They did not so much denounce unconverted rascals; rather they emphasized the actual and apparent accomplishments of the regime. They stressed their assertion that Hitler had saved Germany from chaos and bolshevism, clad her in "shining armor" that enabled her to take equal rank among the big powers and to defy all enemies.

They painted in glowing if too glaring colors how he had provided work for the unemployed, vacations for the employed; how he had increased wages, savings and profits; how he had fed the hungry, clothed the naked from a 300,000,000-mark winter relief fund raised by the National Socialist party in the best Tammany style; how he had sent workers in their own ships to cruise the seas and visit such blessed islands as Madeira; how what had been done so far was merely a beginning, with bigger and better things to come.

In line with this "positive aspect" of the campaign, words and concepts like comradeship, honor, decency, heart, soul, faith, truth—and lately even God and the divine grace that attends rulers like Hitler—played a dominant role. The conflict between the German God and the Jewish Jehovah was buried, along with the church fight. But if the "positive aspect" of the campaign had failed to convince some of the hard-boiled enemy, Nazi orators left little doubt that if necessary other means of persuasion would have been found for "a cur who denies the Führer his plea for a 'yes' vote."

Yet the biggest argument of the National Socialist regime, ranking high above all else, was Hitler himself. In German eyes he was already beginning to assume the stature of both superman and saint—a demigod who, like Atlas, was carrying worlds on his shoulders. Not only could he boast remarkable achievements, the reverse side of which were hidden from public view, but he was also the best campaign speaker the Nazis had.

Again he was barnstorming the country as he had during his struggle for power. The fact was that this "man of the people" had proved himself the unsurpassed conqueror of men, the master player on the keys of human emotions. Goebbels may have glittered among intellectual fireworks; Goering may have thundered like Thor; Streicher may have exhibited himself; but when Hitler spoke with that dark voice of his and fanatical sincerity in everything he was saying at the moment, he imbued crowds with his own zeal. When he stood before a vast audience against a background of many banners, when with mingled pride and self-compassion, but also with amazing self-confidence, he recounted his own struggles, sufferings and accomplishments, he seemed to his listeners the personification of the whole German people and their destiny—a man in a trance, from whom radiated a strange magnetism that escaped foreign observers but which apparently gripped all Germans present, stirred them to both heroics and tears.

In short, Hitler was his own best propagandist; as long as the spell of his propaganda was coupled with the show of success, he could continue to dominate Germany.

XI

HITLER'S MACHINE

RENEWED fear of war in Europe and the opening in the first week of September, 1938, of the annual Nazi party meeting in Nuremberg threw Germany and Adolf Hitler into the center of world affairs. It was a commonplace as well as a literal fact to say that "Adolf Hitler is Germany, and Germany is Adolf Hitler." Yet the statement was obviously too simple to contain the whole truth. The government, especially the totalitarian government of 75,000,000 people, was far too complex to be a one-man proposition, and despite all regimentation there remained numerous individual interests and separate pressure groups with their own special aims and ambitions which had to be balanced against one another and "co-ordinated" into a common front if the regime was to function at all. It is pertinent, therefore, to look a little closer into the National Socialist machine to see what made it tick and find out who besides Hitler ran it.

To make it work, a theory of society and a theory of government as a guide for all was necessary. National Socialist Germany had as yet no written constitution,

for the Constitution of the Weimar Republic, under
which Hitler came to power, had been torn to shreds by
the "legal revolution" initiated afterward. But the methodical Germans were evolving a constitutional theory,
which found its ideological basis in a synthesis of Pan-
Germanism and Hegel's doctrine of State supremacy,
and its method in the military rule of Prussia.

However, the original connotations of these terms
had been revised in that Pan-Germanism had been
replaced by the idea of racial unity irrespective of
State borders, that Hegel's abstract State had been
replaced by the national community, and that Prussian
military rule was being transformed by military economy, as developed during the last war, on the one
hand, and by progressive socialism, designed to catch
the masses, on the other.

The German people, conceived as an exclusive
oath-bound racial community of "German blood," were
acclaimed by Hitler himself as the sole source of sovereignty, and their good was proclaimed to be the supreme good for all Germans.

This racial idea, raised to almost religious heights by
the "Mythos of Blood and Soil" and reinforced by the
theory of Nordic supremacy as revealed in the German
people, was, in the words of the Berlin *Angriff*, "part
of the spiritual armament of a proud people"; for which
purpose it was promulgated as an inviolable dogma to
be accepted by all Germans, if not by reason, then by
faith. It replaced "the European spirit with racial real-
ism"; it abrogated "human rights" in favor of the com-

mon interest of the national community; and it made that interest the sole test of right or wrong.

But whether, in practice, the German people were really the "supreme political factor" or merely the "unpolitical factor growing in the shadow and under the protection of political leadership," was still subject to debate among German constitutional theorists. In any case, 75,000,000 people obviously could not act as a whole, but must act through a more concentrated agency.

To Hegel and all previous German political writers this agency was the State. But Hitler grew and rose to power in a fight against the State, or, more exactly, against the German States as constituted before him, which, as products of dynastic accidents, failed to embrace the whole German racial community.

National Socialism proclaimed, therefore, that the agency which represented the German people as a whole was no longer the State, but the National Socialist party. Having conquered the German people, it tolerated no other parties beside it and according to its doctrine, all "decent" Germans were National Socialist and the best National Socialists were party members. The party thus became the sole representative of the political will of all racially conscious Germans, just as the Communist party was (or sought to be) the sole representative of the class-conscious proletariat.

At the same time, unlike the bolshevist party in Soviet Russia, the National Socialist party had been united with the State by law. It was not, however, part of the

State; rather the State was part of the party. The party was greater, and therefore above the State; it "commanded" the State, supervised its work and spurred it onward. Thus the one-party State was reduced to an instrument of the party through which it worked the people's will.

This will incarnated itself in the person of Adolf Hitler, Führer and Reich Chancellor. Deriving his just powers, first from the consent of the governed, as demonstrated in periodic plebiscites, and second, from his manifest destiny to be the instrument of Providence, he was leader of the whole German people and, as such, head of both party and State. He was, in the words of Dr. Wilhelm Stuckard, constitutional expert of the government, "the supreme political leader of the people, supreme leader and highest superior of the Administration, supreme judge of the people, supreme commander of the armed forces, and the source of all law."

In other words, he combined in his person all executive, legislative and judicial powers; and, hedged by the divinity of such absolute power, like the Tenno of Japan he was not and could not be an "organ" of the State, but was above the State; he knew no equals, only subordinates; he was master over the life of every German, and he was responsible to nobody but himself.

Under this constitutional theory Hitler ruled, therefore, under both a popular and a providential mandate, limited neither in time nor scope, and his words, not only the formal decrees and others he issued, but also his spoken words, were the law of the land.

And that he ruled, nobody who had watched the workings of the German Government doubted. He inspired or passed on all major policies and made all important decisions, often solely on the basis of his own intuition and against the advice of the competent Ministers and experts; he personally intervened in all branches of government and directed and supervised many of the most important projects of his regime, such as the automobile roads, the reconstruction of the cities, and the *Volksauto;* he was, in particular, his own Foreign Minister and his own best propagandist. Finally, he was the last arbiter between conflicting interests.

Leon Archimbaud, well-known French Nationalist, who disliked many things in present-day Germany, gave this description of Hitler's position, which was quoted with approval in the German press:

"Hitler is the unchallenged master of Great Germany. When he issues a command, it is carried out by 75,000,000 Germans. In France Hitler is represented as a mountebank and a stage comedian, just right to make big speeches and review troops. That is our mistake. The German people are considered to be resigned for the moment, but eager to throw off the heavy hand of the Führer. Another mistake. The German people regard Hitler as their Messiah. He unites, in their view, the virtues of Frederick the Great, Luther and Mohammed. *Mein Kampf* has replaced the Bible and the Koran."

In practice, Hitler ruled through three agencies whose

joint head he was and which he balanced against one another—the party, the State and the military forces. Each of these agencies was a hierarchy more or less independent of the others, sovereign in its own domain and ruled by its own laws and courts, but deriving all authority from Hitler alone. If Hitler was the man on horseback, then the State was his horse, the army his spear and the party his whip.

Before Hitler, Germany was a federal, democratic republic of some twenty States—the fourth biggest democracy in the world. In the fall of 1938 it was a unitary, centralized, authoritarian, totalitarian, racial, one-party Führer State, in which all self-government had been abolished.

It was unitary because the federal States had been abolished; in so far as they still existed as administrative units, they were, in effect, merely provinces of the Reich, ruled by Reich Governors. It was centralized because all governmental powers were concentrated in the Reich Government in Berlin. It was authoritarian because it was run on the principle of military discipline: authority from above, obedience from below. "The command of leadership must be obeyed even if wrong, because the preservation of order is more important than the prevention of wrong."

It was totalitarian because it undertook to control, supervise and direct, not only politics, but also all other phases of human life—capital and labor; producer and consumer; industry, trade, commerce and the professions; agriculture, religion and education; art, literature, the radio and the press; sport, charity, every organization and association, and, to an increasing extent, even family life.

It was racial because it admitted to full citizenship only persons of "German or cognate blood," and not only excluded all aliens but also sanctioned their spoliation in the interest of the national community.

In its outward form the State consisted merely of the governmental bureaucracy of public officials and employes, subordinated to the various technical Ministries and headed by a Cabinet of eighteen. This Cabinet was the "government" to which the German Reichstag, in its last sovereign act on March 24, 1934, abdicated its legislative powers.

It was however, no longer a Cabinet of parliamentary Ministers, making decisions and passing laws of majority vote and ultimately accountable to Parliament; it was a "Führer Council" of administrators, technical experts and political contact men who were Hitler's subordinates, bound by oath to be loyal and obedient to him personally, and responsible to him alone. The Cabinet Ministers advised, Hitler decided.

Every Minister, like every other public official, had been endowed by Hitler with all the authority and power necessary to carry out the tasks with which he was charged, although Hitler might intervene at any time and place. The Minister and his administrative bureaucracy prepared the laws, decrees, ordinances and executive orders they considered necessary within their field of work; when published these were binding on all and not subject to court review. The more general laws might be signed by Hitler and the whole Cabinet; generally they were signed only by Hitler and the competent Minister; in merely technical administrative matters, the signature of the Minister or of a subordinate executive official sufficed.

There was still a Reichstag, consisting of 803 National Socialist Deputies and eleven "guests." It was nominally elected at the periodic plebiscites; actually it was appointed by Hitler, who selected the only admitted list of candidates. Its functions had become purely decorative. It might legislate "at the discretion of the leadership," but for the most part, it merely provided the background for Hitler's more important speeches to the nation and the world. There was also a Prussian State council, and there were city councils, but they, too, merely advised and did not decide.

The party consisted of some 6,000,000 members, conceived as a priestly order of political leadership, and bound to Hitler by special ties of fealty. Many party members were officials of the State, but for their different functions, party and State maintained separate and often parallel organizations. The State bureaucracy, obligated by law to keep in mind that National Socialism represented the German State idea, was also obligated to assist the party in its work, but the party was not supposed to intervene in State affairs directly, except through the regular channel.

This channel was Rudolf Hess, Hitler's deputy for party affairs and member of the Cabinet. He had authority by law to supervise the appointment and promotion of officials, and he assisted in the preparation of laws and decrees in order to assure that National Socialist ideology permeated the State in both men and measures.

Hitler had served notice that if the State was unable to solve some problems, he would transfer them to the party for solution. Even without his express authority, in matters in which the State seemed slow to follow the party's lead, local "little Hitlers" often took matters into their own hands, and "direct action" against the Jews, the churches, and "enemies of the State" was the result. Where the party did not care to expose itself, there were always "spontaneous" demonstrations of an indignant populace, or "individual actions" of unidentified persons in what the National Socialists themselves call "bandit mufti," which could later be repudiated.

Besides directing and supervising the State, the party had also the task of organizing the people directly in all their various interests and activities. It did so through its numerous "branches" and "associated organizations," which, in their combined membership, embraced virtually the entire population.

Among the most important of these subsidiary organizations were the black-uniformed SS, some 200,000 strong, who were Hitler's special bodyguard, the ideological shock troops of the party and its political police and intelligence service, and the SA, or brown-shirted storm troops, who, though greatly reduced in numbers and importance since the "blood purge" of June 30, 1934, were still the "political soldiers" of the regime.

Also, there was the Political Organization, some 450,-000 strong, which supervised every block and household; the Hitler Youth, which embraced virtually every boy and girl in the land and through which led the only path to public jobs and careers; the National Socialist Welfare Organization, which had a virtual monopoly on all charity work in Germany; and, finally, the German Labor Front, claiming 20,000,000 members, which was the One Big Union in Germany, embracing both employers and employes, and charged with the "human leadership" of both.

The principal task of this union was to keep the workers working and happy; it did so, first, through the *Werkscharen,* or "labor shock troops," created to supervise the rest and set an example to all, and, second, through the "Strength Through Joy" organization, which regulated the workers' leisure and provided sport facilities, entertainment, vacation trips and other recreation at small cost.

The army was perhaps the most independent of the three hierarchies. For while the party "commanded" the State bureaucracy, it was still barred from the military domain. The German Army was neither a "brown" army, as the Soviet army is "red," nor had it a Fascist militia as balance beside it. Except for Hitler's bodyguard, it was the only "arms bearer" of the nation; as such, it co-operated with the party at its own discretion but remained "unpolitical."

There were no brown commissars to dictate to it; all soldiers obeyed only their immediate superior officers, and the highest officers of the three services—the army, the navy and the air force—obeyed only Hitler himself. All attempts to bring the army under party control had been defeated—once in the "blood purge" of 1934 and again on February 4, 1939. From both these attempts the army emerged with its solidarity unimpaired.

That, summarized as briefly as possible, was the political machinery with which Hitler ruled. But all political machinery consisted of men, and even under authoritarian government, the human element remained decisive. Who, then, were Hitler's principal advisers and assistants, and what of the inevitable conflicts of individuals and pressure groups, which even regimentation could not eliminate entirely?

During the crisis in February, 1938, that shook his regime Hitler set up a Privy Council to which he named Baron Constantin von Neurath, ex-Foreign Minister; Joachim von Ribbentrop, present Foreign Minister; Field Marshal Hermann Goering, "Minister President" of the Reich, Aviation Minister and Commander-in-Chief of the Air Force, who, as Commissar for the Four-Year Plan, was Germany's economic dictator; Rudolf Hess; Dr. Joseph Goebbels, Minister of Propaganda; Admiral Erich Raeder, Commander-in-Chief of the Navy; General Wilhelm Keitel, Chief of the Supreme Command of the Armed Forces, and as such Hitler's personal Chief of Staff; and Dr. Hans Heinrich Lammers, Chief of the Reich Chancellery.

This council was appointed to advise on foreign policy only, and it rarely met; yet in so far as there existed an official consultative body in Germany, that was it. Of its members Goering and Goebbels, Hitler's companions-in-arms during the long struggle for power, were perhaps closest to the Führer personally, although they rarely agreed and thereby neutralized each other. As a result of personal rivalries and conflicting views and interests, Hitler had been steadily lifted to an ever lonelier eminence.

In so far as anybody exercised discretionary, even if delegated, power in Germany besides Hitler himself, the three most important men in the regime were Goering, who is Hitler's chief executive and presumptive successor; Dr. Wilhelm Frick, Minister of the Interior, and Heinrich Himmler, chief of the German police and head of the SS. Dr. Frick, who combined in himself the fanatic zeal of the National Socialist "Old Fighter" and the methodical training of the German public official, had been put in charge of the State bureaucracy and the reconstruction of Germany into a unitary State—a task that once baffled Bismarck. Himmler, charged with the protection of the regime from "domestic enemies," was in effect the keeper of every German's liberty. He was master of the concentration camps, and his secret police force was a law unto itself.

Yet, vast as the powers of these men were, they were too high up to deal with much more than general policies. The impact of the authoritarian and totalitarian State came to average Germans through officials much farther down in the hierarchy, and these officials, within their jurisdiction, had just as arbitrary powers as those above them.

In such complicated machinery were bound to be, despite the authoritarian principle, many overlapping jurisdictions and many conflicting interests and views. There were, in fact, so many orders, laws and decrees in every field, especially in the economic one, that even the highest officials responsible for their administration admitted they no longer knew what was legally right or wrong, and business men frankly told you that they were always standing with one foot in the concentration camp.

In the final analysis, however, even the power of Hitler depended on the willingness of the German people to follow his lead. Nobody could successfully run a complicated machine like a modern industrial nation with bayonets alone. The periodic plebiscites, which, according to National Socialist theory, were not "acts of government," but merely "acclamations" of the political leadership, might not have presented a true picture of the political sentiments of the people; but however much the democratic West scoffed at their 100 per cent majorities, they were highly effective in mobilizing the masses and breaking the moral backbone of incipient opposition—in National Socialist Germany as in Soviet Russia.

In coming to power Hitler broke the strength of the Socialists and Communists. The former socialistic and communistic masses, together with the peasants, were the main support of his regime, while the middle classes which brought him to power, and—excepting a few opportunistic concerns—the industrialists and financiers who backed him, sat on the mourners' bench.

And the principal hold that Hitler had on the masses was the growing socialization of German economy. The government and its agencies collected 40 per cent of the national income in taxes and levies, but they spent more than half of what they collected, in supporting German economy, and they controlled altogether two-thirds of it. This meant that two out of every three Germans, workers and industrialists, were directly or indirectly dependent on the government and its agencies for their livelihood, and this livelihood depended in turn on their professed loyalty to the regime.

In other words, besides possessing unlimited political power, the National Socialist regime also possessed the deadly power of the almost monopolistic employer as well as buyer in the field. But few men dared bite the hand that fed them, and thus once again it was demonstrated that the nation which surrenders its purse-strings surrenders its liberty.

XII

THE "FIELD LORD" OF THE THIRD REICH

ADOLF HITLER, Chancellor of the Third Reich and Führer of the German people, served notice on the world on February 20, 1938, that Germany was again a great power which demanded her place in the sun and that if this place was denied to her she had the military and economic means to obtain it by her own will and strength.

On that day the system of the Versailles treaty tumbled into dust and Woodrow Wilson's dream of a disarmed world governed by law, reason and a league of nations dedicated to the status quo was finally torn to shreds. In their place there reappeared a world still familiar to those who remember prewar days—a fluid and dynamic world of power politics in which might creates its own right and "blood and iron" enforce the vital interests of the strong against the weak. Woodrow Wilson's dream world had been badly battered before, but it was Hitler who on that day gave it the coup de grace; for when he spoke before the Reichstag and the world with a symbolic sun surmounted by a German Eagle shining down on him he spoke as the absolute and unchallenged master of a "nation of a hundred million" who only a fortnight previously had concentrated all political, military and economic powers in his own hands.

This concentration of power, accomplished through a "second revolution" against recalcitrant army generals, was in itself the triumph of a master politician. But it was also only a means to an end, and that end was a greater and stronger Germany.

Particularly, however, the "second revolution" was a final step toward that totalitarian mobilization of the nation which General Erich Ludendorff, "Field Lord" of the German Armies during the World War and actual dictator of the Central Powers during the latter half of it, demanded in his political testament, as laid down shortly before his death in his book entitled "The Totalitarian War."

In this book the military master mind of Germany expounded the doctrine that modern war was no longer a conflict between rulers or governments, or even armies and navies, fought frequently for immoral buccaneering purposes. He saw war as an inevitable and highly moral struggle for survival between nations, which drew within its orbit every man, woman and child and, therefore, called on the last moral, physical and material resources of all of them. Such a totalitarian war, he argued, demanded totalitarian policies which in peace

must prepare the nation for war; and his specific proposal toward that end was the immediate appointment
of a new "Field Lord," who, in view of the totalitarian
responsibility he would have to assume for the conduct
of the war, should supervise the moral, military and
economic mobilization of the nation for that war.

Despite characteristic eccentricities in its exposition,
Ludendorff's fundamental thesis of the totalitarian war
was Germany's official doctrine. It was the apotheosis
of the heroic National Socialist ideology which held
that continuous struggle was not only inevitable for the
"have-nots" among the nations but was also healthy
national discipline, the cessation of which meant
national stagnation and degeneration. In this ideology
peace, therefore, became a continuation of the war with
other means, and in such a peace a high war potential,
it was thought, often permitted a dynamic nation to
attain its aim even without resort to war.

But totalitarian war and dynamic peace both demanded the totalitarian mobilization, and that in 1938
was in full swing in Germany. In many respects it was
a product of the lessons of the last war. In some respects it was being carried out in most countries, but
nowhere with such thoroughness as in Germany.

As a matter of fact, this totalitarian mobilization of
Germany began the moment Hitler came to power on
January 30, 1933. In it was encompassed the whole significance of the "national uprising," and also the secret
of its success. But until this time it had been proceed-
ing under a technically divided supervision.

Hitler himself, and his National Socialist party, attended to the moral mobilization of the German people by attempting to weld all Germans all over the world into one solidary national, or racial, community which would blindly obey one central will; some of the party radicals followed Ludendorff's mystic nationalism to the point of repudiating Christianity in favor of a new and more heroic national religion, analogous to the Shintoism of Japan.

The German general staff, that most efficient collectivist organization in the world, under the titular leadership of Field Marshal Werner von Blomberg, attended to the military mobilization and created one of the most powerful military machines in the world, which was rapidly shifting the military and political center of gravity for Central Europe from Paris to Berlin.

But the most important and most complicated mobilization of all proved to be the economic mobilization —important because on it depended the effectiveness of the army and the morale of the nation; complicated because it involved mastering capital, labor and economic law. For the lack of it, Germans felt, they lost the World War, and their rulers at this time were determined that history should not repeat itself.

The economic mobilization really began under the magic wand of Dr. Hjalmar Horace Greeley Schacht, who conjured billions out of a country bled white of all capital. But from the very beginning it also developed into a struggle between the nationalistic and capitalistic forces led by Schacht and the equally nationalistic but socialistic forces within the party who still clung to the "Marxist" ideas of their party platform. In this struggle victory went not to the combatants but to *Wehrwirtschaft*, or military economy, which turned into a Frankenstein monster that eliminated both Schacht and the Nazi radicals.

As its name implies, the principal functions of *Wehrwirtschaft* were military. It was, therefore, not so much concerned with living standards, profits and finances, but with the strategy of raw materials. Its impetus came from the virtual conscription of capital, labor and the farmer. Its method was planned economy that was planned, not to balance supply and demand in a land of plenty, but to raise production to the maximum in a land of scarcity. Its goal was the greatest possible self-sufficiency, not in consumption goods as such, but in all essential war materials, in order to enable Germany in time of peace to withstand economic pressure and in wartime to defy another "hunger blockade" or "sanctions."

After February 4, 1938, all strings of the totalitarian mobilization had become concentrated in Hitler's hand; he had therewith become his own "Field Lord" in the sense of Ludendorff's book. The full significance of this development became evident when, on February 20, Hitler revealed that this mobilization had been greatly intensified, and the nature of it was simply documented by the decree of February 4, charging the new "Supreme Command of the Armed Forces," headed by General Wilhelm Keitel, the technical if not titular successor of Blomberg, with "the unitary preparation of the Reich's defense in all fields."

The moral and propagandistic mobilization of the nation for war remained with the National Socialist party. That the new developments meant further expansion of Germany's armed forces was proudly announced by Hitler in his Reichstag speech, although he revealed no details. In the economic field they had placed German economy completely under military command, vested not only in General Keitel by the above order, but most especially in Hermann Goering, the "Field Marshal of German Business." Goering, as commissioner for the so-called four-year plan, superseded Schacht as economic dictator and, in turn, placed active army officers in the Economic Ministry to issue orders that were finally carried out by the *Wehrwirtschaftsführer*, or military economic leaders, appointed in the various industries and sworn in to Hitler in much the same way as the military.

This set-up was part of the fundamental forces which dominated Germany but the brain that, more than any other, determined the development of economic mobilization was that of a youthful and retiring soldier whom Blomberg once called "the ablest man in the German Army," but who was still little known outside of the German business world, where he was well known indeed. His name was Fritz Loeb, his rank major general and he bore the modest title of "Chief of Division No. 1" in the Economy Ministry, which was charged with the production of German raw materials and with planning.

In point of fact, however he was the principal planner of military economy and the father of the four-year plan, who through many changes was Goering's economic chief of staff. As such he was, if not the most powerful, certainly the most influential man in German economy in 1938.

Like all army officers, Loeb shunned publicity, and to the German public he was little more than a rank and a name. But he was known by his accomplishments and these spoke for themselves.

Fritz Loeb was born in Berlin in 1895 and entered the army as ensign in a pioneer battalion in 1913. During the World War he became first lieutenant and company commander. Afterward he served as first lieutenant in the Sixth Cavalry Regiment in Pasewalk, and in 1926 became captain in the Ninth Cavalry Regiment in Fürstenwalde, where he stayed for about two years. Then his real career began.

It was still the time of German disarmament under the Treaty of Versailles, but the German army command was already preparing Germany's rearmament—had been doing so, in fact, before the ink on that treaty had dried. The full story of these preparations, which also furnishes the answer to many riddles of German post-war politics, will probably not be told until the army archives reveal their secrets, but it is as fascinating as the history of Prussia outwitting Napoleon after her defeat early in the last century; and Loeb played an important part in it.

Sometime around the turn of the year 1928-29 Loeb

was transferred to the then mysterious *Truppenamt* in the *Reichswehr* Ministry, which, "it can now be told," was merely the disguise adopted for the German Staff during the time when its existence was forbidden by the Versailles treaty. The brief official record of his career available states that he was assigned to the *Truppenamt* "temporarily," but the *Reichswehr's* rank lists reveal that he was in the *Truppenamt* for several years and that he was assigned to the department for "army organization." It was his special task during that time to study economic mobilization, and it was here that he first displayed his talents. Between times he performed his compulsory field duty as company commander in the Sixth Pioneer Battalion in Minden.

Then, on January 30, 1933, came Hitler, and the veils that had shrouded German rearmament began to fall. Within three months—on May 1, 1933, to be exact —Loeb was transferred as major to the general staff, which had immediately been reconstituted, although no public mention of that fact was made for more than two years afterward. Here he helped to mobilize German industry for military purposes.

Loeb's great chance came a year later, when Goering, then in the midst of his race to build up a German air fleet before any outside power could intervene, "borrowed" Loeb for the Air Ministry to speed up the expansion of Germany's aviation industry and to commandeer supplies for it. In that capacity Loeb did what is generally admitted to be a "magnificent job," and thereby became perhaps Germany's greatest practical expert on industrial mobilization.

By the end of 1935 the mobilization of the aviation industry had been so well organized that it ran of its own momentum. But Germany's rearmament was exhausting her raw-material supplies. Thereupon Goering took Loeb out of the Air Ministry, gave him a special office and told him to study the raw-material situation and to find ways and means for coping with the shortages. In April, 1936, Goering became special commissar for all questions concerning raw materials and foreign exchange and immediately appointed Loeb as his chief of staff for these questions. But inasmuch as the practical work was still being done by Schacht and the other Ministries, with Goering as supreme arbiter, Loeb was at leisure to continue his studies. He studied for nine months and then he drew up his plan. The result was that on September 9, 1936, Hitler announced before the Nuremberg Party Congress the second four-year plan, designed "in four years to make Germany wholly independent of other countries in all those materials which German capacity, our chemistry, our machine industry and our mining industry, can produce at home." It came as a surprise to the world, which at first did not see its significance; but it also surprised Schacht, and in the end hoisted him out of the Economic Ministry.

Loeb, who had become colonel in the meantime, took personal charge of mobilizing German capacity, science and industry for the production of the needed raw materials. German raw-material production, especially in

oil and iron, had already been speeded up by the demands of rearmament, but nowhere near enough to
satisfy the army. In fact, it soon became apparent that
the demands of military economy were wholly beyond
the capacity of private enterprise, which still had to
keep an eye on costs and the balance sheet, and that
only far-reaching economic planning, controlled and
financed by the State, could cope with the situation.
That was the function of the four-year plan.

In the execution of this plan Loeb, then major general, worked in close co-operation with Major General
Georg Thomas, head of the economic section of the
Reich War Ministry, and with Major General Hermann
von Hanneken, head of the division for iron, mining and
power in the Economic Ministry, which had given rise
to the quip about the "triumvirate of generals" running
German economy. But the production end of the four-
year plan, which was its heavy end, rested on the
shoulders of Loeb.

According to insistent National Socialist protesta-
tions, the four-year plan was not designed to isolate
Germany economically nor to hamper her foreign trade.
On the contrary, Germany was constantly stressing her
desire for economic co-operation, and was engaged in an
export drive which scored a bigger success in 1937 then
that of any other major industrial country except the
United States. Goering, like Schacht and Walther Funk,
the new Economic Minister, was particularly anxious to
expand trade with America, and the interest of military
economy in foreign trade was documented by the fact

that another officer, Major Eberhard von Jagwitz, had been put in charge of foreign-trade promotion.

But even the limited aim of wartime autarchy was rapidly forcing such readjustments in German economy as to precipitate a new industrial and agricultural revolution. It was introducing new materials, new methods, new processes, new plants, a whole new way of living, in fact; and in that readjustment foreign trade likewise assumed a new position and a new function.

The principles underlying the four-year plan, as seen by Loeb himself, were often explained by him in speeches before German business men, and these principles could be paraphrased as follows:

The aim of the four-year plan was to end Germany's dependence on foreign countries for any vital necessities in war or peace. Such dependence was dangerous in war, and unworthy of a free people in peace. To end it Germany necessarily must utilize her own resources to the extent commanded by Hitler in the four-year-plan announcement.

This aim could be accomplished because Germany had the scientists, the technicians, a hard-working population which no longer wasted its energies in class warfare, and a government able to enforce all measures necessary in the interest of the State.

The scope and speed of this effort was determined solely by the number of workers available and by nothing else. Inasmuch as a labor shortage had replaced unemployment, more workers had to be found, because already feasible projects, such as the mining of sufficient copper from (poor) native ores, had been postponed for lack of labor.

The four-year plan was not hostile to exports, but was a sworn enemy of imports. Imports were curtailed wherever requirements could be met from domestic resources, and the foreign exchange thus freed was used for the importation of materials that could not be produced at home.

Hitler had set Germany greater tasks than ever before, but these tasks were designed to make Germany safe from the outside and more beautiful inside. With the co-operation of industry, which the State guaranteed against recessions, and of labor, whom the State safeguarded in its right to work, these tasks were accomplished.

The magnitude of these tasks could be gauged, however, by the fact that of the 19 basic materials necessary for the conduct of war Germany was self-sufficient by nature in only two, coal and zinc, while the United States, for instance, is self-sufficient in 17. But this situation was rapidly being remedied. Under Goering's driving power and Loeb's direction, new industries and new industrial areas were being forged out of the ground throughout Germany, especially in the well-protected interior—all designed to correct nature's niggardliness, either by increased exploitation of Germany's natural resources, even those unprofitable by purely commercial standards, or by the creation of synthetic *Ersatz*.

This revolution affected, directly or indirectly, all industries, but the main efforts were concentrated on iron, oil, rubber, textiles, food and *Ersatz* products in light metals and plastic masses.

No war can be conducted without iron, and since the loss of the Lorraine iron mines Germany had had to import no less than 84 per cent of her iron ore. The four-year plan provided for a fourfold expansion of production from the poor domestic ores, until by the end of the four years at least half of Germany's iron needs were to be supplied from domestic sources. And as proof of his confidence Goering gave his own name to the combined State and private corporation charged with this task.

As regards oil, Hitler announced in September, 1936, that in 18 months from that date Germany would no longer be under the "compulsion" of importing foreign oil. At the end of 18 months the task was still far from accomplished, but Germany already was meeting more than 50 per cent of her liquid fuel demands from domestic sources, and additional synthetic oil plants, distilling oil from coal, were to be opened soon.

The production of synthetic rubber, made from coal and lime and called Buna in Germany, was already supposed to be adequate to supply the tire needs of the army, and it was being expanded rapidly. The program called for a supply of one-third of Germany's total needs by the end of 1938.

In textiles, the production of domestic and synthetic fibers from lumber, straw and other plants, as well as from coal, lime, glass and fish, had increased from 17 per cent of demand in 1932 to around 35 per cent in

1937, and plant capacity already enabled production of 50 per cent.

In the metal industry magnesium and aluminum, both of which are found in Germany in great quantities, had become the great *Ersatz* products, and the plastic masses, numbering more than 200 different trade names, were completely changing German articles of daily use.

Only in food production had progress been meager, first because of less than middling harvests, second because of the withdrawal of arable land for military purposes. As a result, in spite of all efforts to cut down consumption through managed shortages in various foods and "directed" consumption of what was plentiful, foreign foods were still being imported in increasing quantities. And a really bad harvest could mean catastrophe.

It was Loeb's proud boast that the first year of the four-year plan had been a "100-per-cent success." Everything had been accomplished "according to plan" and he was particularly proud of the fact that the larger part of it had been financed from private rather than governmental sources.

Yet large sections of the German people continued to regard this development with profound skepticism. They were aghast at the growing public indebtedness which threatened to leave them some day holding a bag filled with government paper; they chafed under the growing restrictions and control; they doubted the economic soundness of the four-year-plan enterprises which, however financed, must still be guaranteed and "protected" by the government; and they feared that rising costs of production and a deteriorating quality of goods would increasingly handicap Germany's export chances and reduce the standard of living.

But these were objections based on a capitalistic ideology which military economy did not recognize, and Loeb and his staff had already given the answer to them. Their argument was that costs were determined by the necessities of State; German economy must be able to produce; production depended on the enterprises of the four-year plan; *ergo,* these enterprises were economic.[1]

[1] In a brief paragraph in the *New York Times* of June 30, 1940, Loeb was reported to have been killed. The German report said merely that he had died "in the air." There was no elaboration.

XIII

THE ORGANIZATION OF THE FIFTH COLUMNS

ADOLF HITLER came to power in Germany through a hectic campaign against bolshevism, democracy and the Jews, and waged the same kind of campaign on an international scale to carry Germany to power in Europe. But like most campaigns of hate, this one also turned against its authors, and for millions of Germans scattered throughout the world it turned into a boomerang that threatened their existence.

In most countries, whatever their attitude toward the objects of National Socialist attacks, it was the National Socialists themselves who were regarded with increasing suspicion. As early as 1937, almost all countries were beginning to adopt precautionary measures against them. In many, including the United States and Great Britain, police and parliamentary investigations of National Socialist activities were common; and on the European Continent the whole German element outside the Reich, whether National Socialist or not, was being subjected to increasing restrictions that were matched only by the treatment of the Jews in Germany.

So keenly was this development felt in the Reich that the spokesmen of the regime, from Hitler downward, were taking every opportunity to assure the world that National Socialism was not imperialistic and to ridicule the idea that every German servant girl abroad was a disguised Gestapo agent or a spy. At the same time Baron Constantin von Neurath, Germany's Foreign Minister, served notice on the world that the Third Reich would tolerate no discriminatory measures against National Socialists abroad, and Dr. Hans Frank, Reich Minister and juridical leader, threatened retaliation against States making National Socialism a crime.

One reason for this growing anti-Germanism was the intense nationalism sweeping all countries in Europe. Faced with the possibility of a "totalitarian war," each nation had become suspicious of every other nationality within its sphere of power, and the life of national minorities had become more precarious than ever.

Another reason was that every ideological front created a counterfront: faced with the dictum of the dictators that "the Europe of tomorrow will be fascist," those unwilling to surrender were organizing to defend themselves.

But the deepest reason, which impelled even tolerant countries to take measures against the "National Socialist peril," was the conception of the State and nation introduced by Hitler as a new element in the modern world. Previously in Germany especially, but also elsewhere—the State had been conceived in the Hegelian sense as the final unit of human organization, which, by virtue of that character, claimed sovereignty. Within that State all nationalities, races and creeds were supposed to find their home, and every ambition looking beyond that State was "imperialism," still so regarded by Fascist Italy.

Hitler's doctrine disclaimed "imperialism" based on the conquest or "Germanization" of subject races, although it did not exclude colonies and even called for the "Germanization" of alien land when needed. But it also disclaimed the State as the final organizational unit and put in its stead a new organism, namely, the nation, or better still, the "race" as determined by the homogeneity of "blood."

In doing so, it went far beyond the national urge which led to the unification of the national States of today; even beyond the doctrines of the Pan-Germans. It not only envisaged the unification of the solid bloc of Germans in Central Europe according to the dictum that "like blood belongs within a common Reich," but it included in the new organism every member of the "race" wherever he might be and to whatever State he might belong. It put all of them—legally if they were Reich citizens, morally if they were citizens of another State— under an "inborn" tribal law which obligated them to a new loyalty and a new discipline within an "indissoluble community of blood and destiny uniting the Germans all over the world," and treated every frondeur as a "traitor" or a "renegade."

All statesmen agree that, above reason or self-interest, every State that courts permanence must be animated by some integrating principle of almost religious authority, able to command super-rational loyalty and support; and that, where such a principle is lacking or has disappeared, a new one must be created or the State perishes. Racialism, raised to mystic heights, was Hitler's method of integrating the German people not only into a State but into a "super-State" community, inspired by the community of the Anglo-Saxon world but organized with German methods in order that there might arise the "Germanic Reich of Teutonic nationality" proclaimed by Hitler at Nuremberg in 1937.

"Had the German people possessed that herdlike unity which served other nations so well," said Hitler in *Mein Kampf*, "the German Reich would today be the mistress of the earth."

This racialism, which envisaged an ideological empire surpassing all State borders, was not a biological but a political and juridical construction, designed to fit the special situation of a people conceived as a national unit owing allegiance to one central authority but scattered all over the world. It thought in terms of a nation of 100,000,000, of whom only 67,000,000 lived within the borders of the Reich—a nation whose language every sixth European spoke as his mother tongue but which, even in Central Europe, was divided among fifteen different States.

To mobilize these millions outside of the Reich, from which he himself had come, Hitler had to find another principle than the statism of the pre-war period, which, despite the various "pan" movements, thought in terms of States and governments rather than of a whole people; and racialism was the answer to his prayer.

In that sense, German racialism represented the other side of German anti-Semitism, on which it was nurtured. Like most nations of today, what is known as the *Deutsche Volk* was in itself a hybrid people, composed of Germanic, Celtic, Slavic and Lithuanian elements; even the name of Prussia comes from a Lithuanian tribe. Being a political construction, this racialism was also reared only on attacks against races without political power behind them, principally the Jews; the Japanese and Chinese Governments quickly put a stop to any discrimination against their nationals. But as long as National Socialist racialism remained a useful weapon, anti-Semitism, its counter-pole, necessarily remained a fundamental doctrine of the National Socialist regime.

To reach its aims, however, racialism had to have a world-wide organization and an instrument of power. The first was the National Socialist party and its associated bodies, which provided the new ideology with a "fighting representation, just as the Marxist party organizations free a path for internationalism"; the second was the totalitarian State, which was merely "a means toward an end," the end being "the maintenance of physically and spiritually homogeneous living beings."

By aim and nature, both State and party excluded every alien-racial element, but, conversely, made every German eligible to high positions in them, irrespective

of place of birth or citizenship. Hitler himself was born
in Austria; Rudolf Hess, his party deputy, was born in
Egypt; Richard Darré, the Food Minister, in the Argen-
tine, and Ernst Wilhelm Bohle, the Foreign Office chief
of the party's foreign organization, in England. And
party, government and German Reichstag contained
numerous Germans of foreign citizenship who merited
preferment by services to the National Socialist cause,
even if in doing so they incurred the displeasure of their
native States.

It was in this all-inclusive and totalitarian sense that
all National Socialist pronouncements and demonstrations were to be viewed. "Blood knows no borders" was
the National Socialist slogan, and the same thought
could be seen between the lines of most official National
Socialist speeches. But the most complete exposition of
the racial doctrine had been penned by Josef Huener-
fauth in an article in the *NSZ Rheinfront,* an organ of
advanced National Socialist thought, in which he wrote:

"Primarily we are not citizens of States, but racial
comrades. The certificate of State citizenship is an easily
exchanged possession, but membership within one's people is something immutable, granted by God. . . . Pro-
ceeding from the racial realization, we include in the
league of national comradeship all who are of German
blood. In addition to those who live in the Reich we
count the many millions of tribal brothers whom fate has
scattered all over the world. This produces a great community of German kind, which has its members in all
States of the world, and which finds its proud refuge and

kernel in the Reich of Adolf Hitler. . . . There lives a law which unites beyond borders and distances, and that is the law of blood and brotherhood."

This meant that there should be no further naturalization of German citizens abroad, and where other citizenship had been acquired or enforced, the perpetuation of the hyphen to the child and children's children.

And the final implications of that doctrine were drawn by those publications which objected to the restriction of the term "Germany" to the German Reich, or advocated the exemption of citizens of foreign nationality in a war against a State of their own nationality as the only solution of the "dilemma between treason to the State and treason to the race."

"This standing together of Germans with Germans," said the *Völkischer Beobachter*, "may be an unwonted sight here and there in the world. But it has become a fact. It will have to be accepted."

And it had to be accepted because, as had been so often emphasized in all National Socialist speeches, the Germany of Adolf Hitler was no longer the Germany of Versailles, but rather, "thanks to her racial attitude and her military strength, a world power governed by a sovereign national regime."

By its nature, the doctrine of racial solidarity above all State borders was a powerful lever against the solidarity of all other States with German elements, whether these States were purely German, like Austria, or "nationality States," like Czecho-Slovakia, or "melting pot" States, like the United States and Brazil. But it was also

part of the Hitler doctrine that only national States
serving the purpose of racial development had a right
to existence; "States which do not serve this purpose
are misconstructions, even deformities, the fact of whose
existence affects this statement as little as the success of
a filibustering community, for instance, justifies rob-
bery."

At the same time, the National Socialists were not
only prophets of a new dogma but also political realists
who believed in politics as the "art of the possible."
Hitler, in particular, was regarded by his followers, to
use his own words, as that rare combination of "program-maker and politician which arises only once within
long periods of humanity"—a combination in which "the
greatness of the program-maker lies in the absolute abstract rightness of his idea, while the greatness of the
politician lies in his right attitude toward the existing
facts, and an efficacious use of them, in which the aim
of the program-maker must serve as his guiding star."

And Dr. Joseph Goebbels, Minister of Propaganda,
was constantly exhorting the German people to think
and act "politically"; to realize that in politics they
must at times be "wise as serpents and harmless as
doves" because history decides right or wrong not according to the methods used, but according to success.

The reality facing National Socialist racialism was the
existence of other States which exercised sovereignty
over all their citizens and residents, including those of
German "race." This reality forced the National Socialist regime, both party and government, to separate

theory from practice and to make a strict distinction between Germans of German citizenship living abroad and Germans of foreign citizenship, to which could be added as a third category the "lost tribes" of Germanism, such as the Netherlanders, Scandinavians and German-speaking Swiss.

This distinction was rarely stressed in National Socialist speech or writing, which almost invariably addressed themselves to the "nation of 100,000,000," and it was almost unknown among the Germans abroad. All kinds usually attended the Pan-German congresses and had, by special appointment of Hitler, their own home capital in Stuttgart. But for legal and diplomatic purposes the three categories were strictly separated in name and organization as follows:

The Germans of German citizenship living outside the Reich were called *Auslandsdeutsche* and were organized in a foreign *Gau,* or province, ruled by the Foreign Organization of the National Socialist party (NSFO) and headed by Ernst Wilhelm Bohle as provincial governor. The foreign *Gau* was formally anchored in the German State through the appointment of Bohle as "Chief of the Foreign Organization in the Foreign Office." As such he was placed under the personal and direct authority of the Foreign Minister. The greeting of the *Auslandsdeutsche,* who by Bohle's dictum are all National Socialists, was "Heil Hitler!"

The Germans of foreign citizenship were called *Volksdeutsche,* or "racial" Germans; the organization which "took care" of them was the *Volksbund für das Deutsch-*

tum im Ausland, meaning the People's League for Germanism Abroad, or more briefly the VDA. It was, technically, a private organization, financed by membership fees and tag-day collections, the token of which was the modest cornflower. But in contrast to the NSFO, its work was necessarily "quiet and without loud propagandistic effects" because of foreign opposition at the scene of action. The greeting of the *Volksdeutsche* is "Volk Heil!"

Co-operating with both these organizations was the German Foreign Institute in Stuttgart, headed by Dr. Stroelin, the burgomaster of the town. It was the scientific institute for Germanism abroad; it had a library of 45,000 volumes, kept 800 German newspapers and 400 magazines, and maintained correspondents in all parts of the world.

The only organization existing for the larger Germanic community, as distinct from the *Deutsche,* was the Nordic Society at Lübeck, headed by Heinrich Lohse, the local provincial Governor. It was a propagandistic organization in which the leading National Socialist orators expounded the idea of Nordic solidarity.

The foreign *Gau* had a population of between 2,000,-000 and 3,000,000, consisting of the German citizens living abroad and some 70,000 sailors. It had been created on the legal principle that "the penal laws of the Reich apply to offenses committed by a German national at home or abroad," which meant that the Third Reich extended jurisdiction over its citizens all over the world, and that they remained subject to its laws, including, of course, the racial segregation laws, wherever they lived. It was merely a slight extension of this principle to assert that "whatever the Germans had to settle among themselves," even when abroad, was merely a German "domestic" affair.

Organizationally, the foreign *Gau* consisted, first, of an elaborate headquarters in Berlin with 32 subdivisions including a press office, a *Gau* court and eight regional offices, among which that for North America was the sixth; second, of 1,097 seafaring and 548 local groups or "supporting points" all over the world. There were none, it was stated, in the United States and Soviet Russia, but in forty-five countries the individual groups were comprised in regional organizations under *Landesgruppenleiter*, "land group leaders."

The project advanced by Bohle to give these group officials recognition by providing for their invitation to official functions in foreign lands in company with German diplomatic representatives, and the additional project of sending "Kultur attachés" abroad, advanced by Hanns Johst, president of the Reich Chamber of Literature, were dropped in that form because of immediate foreign opposition; but the Swiss press pointed out that a successor to the assassinated Wilhelm Gustloff, land group leader for Switzerland, had been appointed— Baron von Bibra, German legation counselor at Bern.

According to Bohle, these groups of the NSFO were, in character and work, analogous to the clubs, associations and leagues of other nationals in foreign lands.

And it was constantly emphasized, first, that these particular groups were for German citizens only; second, that all German citizens abroad were under strict instructions to obey the law of the land and to keep out of its domestic politics; third, that far from trying to infiltrate the National Socialist "poison" into foreign nations, Germany was jealously intent on keeping National Socialism for herself.

At the same time the NSFO groups abroad were also supposed to be both combative and totalitarian. It was their task, first, "to propagandize and fight day by day for the adhesion of every honest German to our movement"; second, to displace the older German clubs and *Vereins* of "unpolitical" character and thereby provide for all Germans abroad a totalitarian cell or *"Ersatz* framework" of the Third Reich; third, to promote German prestige, interests and exports abroad and, in particular, displace Jewish commercial representatives of German firms. The sport periodical which urged Germans traveling abroad to note roads and landmarks exceeded, therefore, the official instructions.

Furthermore, being both National Socialist and totalitarian, the foreign groups of the party were by no means voluntary associations, and an assertion that they were, contained in the translation of Bohle's speech in London as furnished to the British press, was not contained in the speech itself. "We organize more thoroughly, perhaps, than others," said Hess; "we are, after all, Germans."

To organize successfully, however, there had to be,

first of all, organizers and, secondly, reward and punishment for those to be organized.

The organizers were trained in a special "Foreign Political Training School," founded by Alfred Rosenberg, the supervisor for the ideological indoctrination of the National Socialist movement. They were jurists, economists, commercial agents, scientists; of high technical efficiency and a knowledge of both French and English, who underwent another six months' training in National Socialist ideology, foreign policy, bolshevism, Germanism abroad, racialism, press, languages, society manners and sport. Graduation from this school assured them either admission to examinations for the foreign diplomatic service or employment in German business organizations abroad.

As to reward and punishment, all German citizens abroad loyal to the cause received full backing and support of their government, which also controlled the business organizations of the Reich. They could count on the support of the German press abroad, which comprised 37 newspapers and periodicals, including 14 official party papers; and they found other benefits in conformity, such as material aid and credit in business and relief in distress; free vacations and cures for their sick, and schooling for their children within Germany; also, an adequate supply of German reading and films, and cheap vacation trips with the "Strength Through Joy" agency; finally, liberty to return to the Reich.

Those, on the other hand, who refused to be "co-ordinated" could count on the boycott of all their organ-

ized fellow-citizens. If they still refused their passports
might be withdrawn, and if that failed to convert them,
they were likely to be deprived of their citizenship and
any German academic degrees they held. The long lists
of those so treated, continuously published in the official
gazette, were tokens of the power wielded by the group
leaders abroad. And if a prominent German should
change his citizenship, he could count on denunciation
as a "traitor" in the home press.

But the real value of the NSFO, beyond the mere "co-
ordination" of the two-million-odd German citizens
abroad, was perhaps best expressed by an article by
Bohle in the September 2, 1937, issue of the *Deutscher
Weckruf und Beobachter* of New York, which was considered an authority on the subject. He wrote:

"The creation of this organization, the round 600
groups of which are scattered all over the world . . . is
one of the boldest strokes of racial policy. That it succeeded is an achievement the consequences of which for
millions of German descent beyond the borders of the
Reich, and, conversely, for the development of the Reich
itself, cannot yet be estimated.

"Thanks to the steadily increased and improved
work of the Foreign Organization, the life of the German racial community in all foreign countries received
a firm nucleus which is strong enough to withstand, if
necessary, the heaviest strain, and elastic enough to
meet all peculiarities of the respective locality. All those
who are sincere about our Germanism abroad have long
since realized and gladly admit that we owe in increas-

ing measure the assurance and resurgence of our racial life in the midst of foreign nations to this nucleus and to the strong National Socialist spirit which animates the entire Foreign Organization."

Although, therefore, the NSFO compromised only citizens of the Reich, it naturally became the center of life for all those Germans of foreign citizenship who were won for German racialism. And that they should be so won was the task of the VDA.

The VDA was founded as far back as 1882, but before German racialism arose it devoted itself mainly to cultural and school work. When it tried to continue along that line after Hitler came to power, certain "tensions" arose which were later removed, so that at this time it was "in close contact with the whole life of the nation, with race, State and (National Socialist) movement," it devoted itself to the revitalization of German racial consciousness everywhere in order to prevent further assimilation.

"We want to grow up with all Germans to a nation and demand that all questions of our national existence shall be viewed in the extent and operation of our whole super-State racial body," said the last annual report of the VDA. "In admiration and deep faith, our racial comrades in foreign States look up to the Reich and its Führer. They feel the unity of blood, which is the foundation of the new German life."

To keep this blood pure, the German element abroad was urged to segregate itself from the surrounding "alien" populations as a minority, in the same way in

which the German people within the Reich had been
segregated as a majority, unless the urgent need of votes
required sacrifice; for "in future, German blood shall
serve German interests only."

Like the NSFO, the VDA also had an elaborate headquarters organization in Berlin, headed by Dr. Hans
Steinacher, an Austrian, and manned by other *Volksdeutsche*. But being a Reich organization concerned
with foreign citizens it could not work abroad through
branches or individuals. For this reason it worked with
organizations formed by the *Volksdeutsche* in the native
lands, rendering them spiritual and material aid in co-
operation with the Reich.

These organizations ranged from hunted catacomb
groups in Italian South Tyrol to the *Amerikadeutsche
Volksbund* in the United States, which had its own uniformed storm troops, girls' organizations, mass meetings
and a "fighting" press modeled on the National Socialist
press of Germany.

But there were many other kinds of organizations—
school associations, *Turnvereins,* youth organizations
and, last but not least, the church, with which the VDA
co-operated as far as the individual States would let it.
The school associations were provided with funds, books
and teachers; the business organizations were furnished
with credits and were favored with German purchases;
students, artisans and apprentices were brought to Germany for their last polish; and *Volksdeutsche* peasants
were brought to the Third Reich at its expense just to
see its power and glory.

Conversely, working in co-operation with other parts of the National Socialistic propaganda machine, the VDA was instrumental in sending out to the *Volksdeutsche* abroad speakers, books, magazines, phonograph records, personal letters appealing to ancestral loyalties and a radio program which ranged from classical music to the speeches of the National Socialist leaders.

Also, inasmuch as other States were beginning to bar Germans from the professions, the VDA now concentrated on the lower social strata of the *Volksdeutsche,* and here "German racial study" and "German home movements" had been most effective. In the United States, for instance, they led to the discovery of a half-assimilated German farmer population which is now being reclaimed for Germanism.

The aims of the VDA, it was stated, had been furthest advanced in Central Europe, especially in Czecho-Slovakia, where Konrad Henlein, who rose from the Bohemian *Turnvereins,* commanded the biggest political party in the State. But it was also pursued with vigor in lands overseas; in America it had attained proportions which already prompted German-American speakers to repudiate the melting pot idea in favor of a permanent "German-Americanism," while popular German authors predicted America's division in more or less autonomous racial units as the "United Nations of America."

PART III

Life In Germany Under Hitler

XIV

LIFE IN WARTIME

As CHRISTMAS, 1939, approached, German women, fretting because of the necessity of wearing patched hose or cotton socks, could look forward to the purchase of one extra pair of stockings that would not be debited from their ration cards. Men could buy one extra necktie without loss of ration "points."

The early hopes of "peace by Christmas" were gone and the German family magazines frankly commented that it would scarcely be a merry Christmas but rather a "bare" Christmas.

Like a flood, the war was spreading, and every rivulet was seeping through every crevice of German life until it was omnipresent and all-pervading, forcing everybody to adapt himself to its demands. And it was not the darkness of the blacked-out nights with their mounting accident toll, nor the occasional air raid alarms, nor the other hardships, however irksome, or even such fighting as went on, that was the most significant aspect of the war.

It was rather the intensified regimentation, the rapid drop in standards of living and the great leveling process that it initiated in the name of "German socialism," that were the most important. From them, apparently, the most permanent results would emanate to dominate German life long after the conflict has ceased.

According to official figures Germany had in 1938 the biggest nominal, as well as real, national income in her history—some 88,000,000,000 marks for Greater Germany—and, calculated on the same basis, which disregards the mounting national debt, the income would have been much higher in 1939. But never in recent history, except during the final years of the last war, were Germans able to buy as little with their incomes as for the Christmas of 1939, and the prospect was that that little would continue to shrink with the progress of the war.

This was true of rich and poor alike. For the regimentation of the rationing system, which was clapped down on the German people, was no respecter of classes or persons, and its standard was the standard of the average worker's family, reduced to the subsistence level and based mainly on *Ersatz* (substitute) products. In fact, except in so far as the well-to-do were able to live on the purchases of the past and possibly had some special opportunities for "gifts" from foreign connections, the laborers doing heavy manual work were better off in respect to food than the rich.

Germany was still far from the common wretchedness of "classless" Russian bolshevism, but the drift was unmistakable. And like all leveling processes, the German process was leveling down, not up.

The well-to-do still had their fine houses, apartments and estates, but they lived in them far removed from the style to which they were accustomed. Like everybody else they could obtain only the same rations of all the necessities of life, including food and clothing, as the mass of the population.

They still had their automobiles, but unless these were used for urgent business, they stood in garages for lack of gasoline, and the rich, like the poor, walked or used public conveyances. They still had their damask table linen, but for lack of soap it was stored away in closets, and rich and poor alike were beginning to eat from oilcloth or from bare tables laid out with paper napkins.

The well-to-do possibly still enjoyed some preference in the shops where they formerly had bought lavishly and expected to buy equally lavishly "after the war," but this preference was confined to service and perhaps to quality, but did not extend to quantity. They might buy a few still unrationed delicacies like paté de foie gras or oysters—at 50 cents each—to supplement the rationed meals; they might buy high-priced clothes, but no more than the mass.

There was, of course, a bootleg trade in food and clothes which was expanding rapidly at exorbitant prices, but only the daring ones would take recourse to it, because the draconic National Socialist justice punished both the bootlegger and the buyer with recorded sentences up to ten years at hard labor.

Though the well-to-do still had their servants, they were also at the mercy of these servants for any infraction of the rationing rules or "hamstring"; so much so that ladies with plenty of help were going over to attending their own bedrooms or boudoirs so as to keep from prying eyes any trifles that they had put away. The week-end guest who besides bringing his own food or ration coupons was also able to say it, not with flowers, but with a bit of genuine coffee or who discreetly "forgot" his cake of soap in the bathroom—for the most part he would be either an unusually enterprising individual or a foreigner—thus might make himself a welcome guest forever.

The normal rations that could be bought per head per week, are shown in the following table:

	Grams *
Meat	300.
Meat products, such as sausages	200.
Butter	125.
Lard	62.5
Margarine	80.
Marmalade	100.
Sugar	250.
Cheese	62.5
Coffee substitute	150.
Eggs	1.

* One thousand grams equals 2.2 pounds.

Bread and grain products were likewise rationed, apparently to avoid waste, but these rations were ample because Germany was well supplied with bread grains;

so well, in fact, that the admixture of potato flour in bread was dropped. Milk was supplied only to children up to ten years of age and to prospective mothers. Only vegetables and fruits were still unrationed, but these were getting scarce and tropical products such as oranges, tomatoes, coffee and tea became something of which to dream.

The normal food rations, while sufficient to avert actual hunger, nevertheless were admittedly so scant, according to official medical judgment, that if continued for long they were certain to produce deleterious effects on the national health. In view of the approach of Christmas the German people received a special food bonus of 125 grams of butter, 125 grams of artificial honey, one egg and some chocolate cake and candy. Housewives were able to obtain spices, flavoring extracts, candied fruits, etc., required for Christmas baking without drawing on ration cards.

As a rule the allotted rations were being fully consumed and hard manual work and long hours were rewarded with extra food rations, which were treasured as much as money wages. But customers were forced to take what they could get, and they could get fowl, fish or game only when their numbers were posted in shops with which they were registered.

Inevitably the rations system imposed tremendous additional burdens both on the German *Hausfrau* and on the shopkeepers. Such conveniences as ordering by telephone or getting purchases delivered at home virtually disappeared. Every housewife shopped personally and took her turn waiting while the butcher or grocer painstakingly collected the ration coupons and equally and painstakingly weighed off the exact quantities. With quantities so small, every customer jealously watched to see that she received no less than the proper amount, while the shopkeeper faced hunger himself if he made mistakes to his own disadvantage, since his supplies were measured by the customers' coupons he collected.

That such a system did not tend to improve tempers on either side is obvious. In fact, the shopkeepers, squeezed between rising taxes, fixed prices, decreased turnover and growing paper work, grew so grumpy that customers began to complain until an official warning restored politeness.

According to official statistics the German meat consumption amounted to 157.6 pounds per adult person last year or more than three pounds weekly. With a weekly allotment of only one pound weekly, two official meatless days fell in every seven, and unofficially there were likely to be more. And it required all the famous ingenuity of the German *Hausfrau* to manage, at that.

Larger families, however, in which the older children drew almost the same amount of food as adults, reported that they were faring comparatively well. By buying in larger quantities they were able to provide a greater variety and stretch their leavings. But the small families or the single person were up against it.

That life at its best was no longer opulent in Germany, however, is illustrated by the following weekly menu suggested by a household magazine for well-to-do homes:

Sunday

Noon: Beef soup with noodles, cabbage with meat and potatoes, apples.

Evening: Fried potatoes, beet salad, pickles, bread and cheese.

Monday

Noon: Potato soup with dried mushrooms, apple compote with currants.

Evening: Milk curds, unpeeled potatoes, radishes.

Tuesday

Noon: Game, red cabbage, potatoes, fruit salad.

Evening: Game with gruel sauce, endive salad.

Wednesday

Noon: Sago soup, comfrey with holland sauce, mashed potatoes, almond pudding, fruit juice.

Evening: Potato soup, bread with sausage, pickles.

Thursday

Noon: Cutlets, turnip, cabbage or spinach, potatoes, compote.

Evening: Bread soup with raisins, vegetarian breads.

Friday

Noon: Thick vegetable soup with fish or potato balls, red groats with vanilla sauce.

Evening: Pickled celery, tomato sauce, potatoes.

Saturday

Noon: Sauerkraut, compote.

Evening: Green rye soup, potato salad, blood sausage.

Breakfasts must be imagined here as consisting of barley or malt *Ersatz* coffee, bread and perhaps marmalade because most of the butter, margarine and lard must be used in cooking. But in view of the German climate, especially in winter, the meals obviously lacked a sufficient fat basis to have staying power, and workers often complained of being hungry shortly after one of the skimpier meals.

As a matter of fact most German people were beginning to develop a sort of psychological hunger which made food one of the principal concerns and induced one to eat whenever he could and whatever he could get, if necessary, for "storage." And one way of satisfying this psychological hunger was with cakes, which were still unrationed. Even strong men were becoming cake eaters during the war. A paradoxical result of this, plus the increased consumption of potatoes and starches, was that the Germans, especially the women, grew stouter rather than the reverse.

More pressing, however, than even the food problem was the problem of clothes. The days when Berlin had begun to rival Paris in the elegance of fashion had long since passed. In that December it was a question not of fashion but of covering nakedness, and the tailors and dressmakers were beginning to specialize not in designing new styles but in turning and remodeling old garments acquired in better days.

For the clothes rations were even skimpier than the food rations, and it was plain that unless the war ended soon or new supplies were obtained when the present clothes were worn out, the Germans faced the prospect of going in rags. In respect to women's stockings, in which most women were caught short, and which were wearing out more rapidly than usual because there was more walking to do, this stage had already been reached. Already the otherwise still well-dressed woman could be seen wearing tattered and mended stockings or incongruous cotton socks, and great was the outcry over that.

Individual clothing rations were laid down in clothes cards, which were to cover the needs of the entire year and which contained 100 points each that the owner might "spend" at his discretion. Each article of clothing "cost" a certain number of points. But the range of this discretion is demonstrated by the fact that one man's suit "cost" 60 points, one pair of socks eight points, and suit of underclothes twenty-seven to 35 points.

Women were treated somewhat more generously, because a woman's costume "cost" only 45 points, and a pair of stockings only four points, although of the latter a woman might purchase only six pairs a year. The authorities admitted that women needed more clothes than men because their garments wore out faster. But in order to prevent a feminine raid on the allowances of male members of the family, the cards for men, women, boys, girls, and babies were all colored differently and only articles listed on each might be purchased with it.

Shoes could be purchased only with a special permit issued on proof of need, and a hefty durable war shoe was announced for all.

All this, of course, meant more work and trouble for the *Hausfrau* who must save every piece of clothing; mending, patching, and repairing what was worn out, and figuring ways of making new clothes from old by combing scraps. All in all, the German women were charged with holding the domestic front while the men held the front in the fields, mines, and armament works. Constantly through the radio, press, and movies, it was hammered into the mind of the German *Hausfrau* that she must fight to win the war in the kitchen and in the home.

A special Reich board for economy in the home, the GHQ of the *Hausfrauen*, organized by the National Socialist women's organization, gave advice on what to cook and how to economize even more than necessity dictated. As an instance, one of the winter bulletins told the *Hausfrauen* that they still were wasteful in the matter of soap, because 30 per cent of all washing is avoidable by greater care in not dirtying anything. Forty per cent of all spots on clothes, said the bulletin, were due to improper brushing and 20 per cent were due to carelessness in eating and drinking, which could be avoided by better table manners. But if things must be washed, the bulletin suggested numerous soap substitutes from sea sand to wood ashes.

A considerable number of women, however, were also being employed outside the home and kitchen to replace the conscripted men, not only in munition and other factories but also as street car conductors, letter carriers and in similar jobs. And millions of women, enlisted by the Red Cross and the National Socialist welfare organizations, not only sewed and knitted, but served troop and hospital trains at railway stations, acted as physicians' assistants in hospitals, distributed ration cards, and organized air defense.

In the face of all the war's extra burdens, social life in Germany was perhaps more active than before, though its tone was appropriate to the times. Few people wanted to sit in hermetically shut off homes alone in those days and nights, mulling heavy thoughts; rather the common trouble and the common danger had stirred the herd instinct more than ever and to the psychological hunger had been added a psychological restlessness.

This sought relief in the society of fellow-sufferers. Social life, in the sense of "society," with banquets, dinners and festivals, was, of course, out of the question. Only diplomats with special import quotas or Germans with landed estates or special connections and opportunities could afford affairs of that kind. One of the leaders in entertaining in the diplomatic set was Alexander C. Kirk, bachelor American chargé d'affaires, whose opulent lunches and dinners were the talk of official and diplomatic circles.

The social life of ordinary mortals divided itself into either "picnic" socials at home or visits to public amuse-

ment places. "Picnic" socials were socials at which the
guests brought their own food drawn on their own ration cards, with the host or hostess providing the drinks.

Despite the black-out darkness, these night "picnic"
socials became the fashion and the ladies' *Kaffeekränz-
chen* were more frequent even though they were held
on coffee *Ersatz*. For everybody had the urge to talk
things over. The men talked of the political and military
situation and the women of their food and clothes problems. All grumbled over the troubles of the times.

As a result of this increased social activity the consumption of alcohol increased. Fortunately most alco-
holic beverages were not yet rationed, although hard
liquors, such as cognac, rum and French liqueurs, were
difficult to obtain. There was plenty of schnapps, however.

But beer was gradually becoming "war beer" with a
reduced body content to save barley.

In respect to public amusements, the National Socialist regime attempted at first to throttle the amusement
industry, but soon found it advisable to ease the reins,
and above all to restore dancing. The theatres, movies,
cabarets, night clubs, and dance halls were open and
fairly well filled in December, with standing room only
on Saturday nights.

The theatres were devoted mainly to *Kultur* and
therefore featured classical dramas with only a sprin-
kling of comedies. The musical comedies and cabarets,
however, were beginning again to feature the female in
the nude. The movies depended largely on German films,

which were dominated by the war note, with only an occasional American or Italian film to provide variety.

The cabarets, night clubs, dance halls and saloons were filled, partly with people who were making good money and had no opportunity to spend it, but principally with young persons facing conscription for war duty who wanted a last fling. Their fun, therefore, was likely to assume a strident and artificial note. But German sports were also as active as ever, and football games at the Olympic Stadium drew crowds up to 100,000.

Despite all the strain and stress, however, all the uncertainties and grumbling, life and its three meals daily continued somehow and with less friction than might have been expected under the circumstances. For above all the troubles there was still the hope of an early victory and peace. The slogan that the regime had given out for wartime was: "It is better to live safely than to live well."

IN COLOGNE

Even on the Western Front one could, unexpectedly enough, still "live safely." When the first shock of the outbreak of war, which paralyzed all civilian life, had passed and the agony of large-scale slaughter at the front had not yet begun, one found the ancient Hanseatic city of Cologne, not far behind the lines, settling down and making the best of what was then described as "the strangest of all wars."

Cologne, though opposite Belgium and the Nether-

lands—which then, of course, were neutral—was none
the less part of the Western Front whose Westwall, in
modified form at least, extended from the French-Lux-
embourg frontier to the North Sea. As a result, Cologne
was full of soldiers, and because of its efficient Rhine
bridge it also was a transit point for troop transports in
all directions.

Blackouts, rationing of all daily necessities and drastic
curtailment of civilian motor transport had slowed up
the business rhythm and suggested certain readjustments. Many industries, shops and offices were now
working through without a luncheon pause so that workers might be permitted to go home before dark. All
shopping was being done early in the day.

There had been no air raid on Cologne, and the city
authorities asserted that there would be none; first, because the air defense was impenetrable, second, because
it would not make sense, and thirdly because it would
mean terrible retaliation.

Because of this confidence even the sandbags which
in September had cluttered up the already narrow side-
walks for persons to stumble over in the dark, had, in
the early winter of 1939, disappeared. Although emergency air-raid shelters were provided everywhere, including one beneath the little park alongside the famous
Cologne Cathedral, this classic of Gothic architecture,
which has seen so many wars, stood wholly unprotected
as if serenely conscious of its eternal immunity.

In point of fact, superficially at least, and despite the
blackout, Cologne was perhaps one of the gayest cities

in wartime Germany. Its darkened streets resounded
nightly to the songs and banter of merrymakers whose
identity was unmistakably betrayed by the heavy thud
of army boots. Its bars, cafes and night clubs were
jammed to overflowing until the small hours of the
morning. In comparison, Berlin was glum.

The attempt to impose a one A. M. curfew in Cologne
lasted exactly twenty-four hours and the dancing prohibition fourteen days. The reason was that Cologne was
the first stop for front soldiers on furlough, and when
they returned from the front they wanted to have some
fun. What Paris was to the Americans in the World War,
Cologne was to many German soldiers.

Germans during the "breathing spell" took pride in
the fact that, in contrast to France and England where
theatres and operas were closed, German theatres and
operas, including movie theatres, remained open and
played to adequate audiences, not only in Berlin but
throughout the Reich and especially along the Western
Front, in Cologne as well as Düsseldorf and Essen and
even so close to the frontier as Aachen and Trier. Their
specialty was heavy or classical drama.

Cabarets offered the usual variety shows, with a pre-
dominance of acrobatics interspersed with some very
broad or very patriotic songs and jokes aimed at the
British. Discipline of German soldiers, however, was
such that there was little open drunkenness.

But this gayety moved rather on the edge of Cologne's
real life. On the whole, the population took the war
philosophically, or, rather, fatalistically. It had lived

through many wars before, had experienced French
sovereignty and British sovereignty, and expected to see
more wars in the future.

Whatever patriotic fervor had followed the outbreak
of the war and the victories in Poland had spent itself,
and the prospect of a long war was pushing long-range
economic problems into the foreground. As a result,
Cologne prayed for only one thing: a speedy end to the
war.

Cologne was primarily a commercial city, dependent
to a large extent on export trade, although its industries
had been growing apace. These industries were now
working at capacity for the army.

For the present Cologne was also one of the chief supply depots for the army, which therefore was one of the
best customers for the city's wholesale and retail trade.
But that was scarcely enough, and Cologne merchants
looked with concern to the future.

Wholesalers had seen many avenues of their export
trade closed, although in this respect they were, perhaps,
better off than many others. For most of their trade was
continental rather than overseas. Cologne was a per-
fumery center for more than Germany and in that capacity had many close contacts with France. These were
now cut. There remained the Netherlands and Belgium
as Cologne's principal export avenues, and there was
considerable interest in the fact that Cologne firms were
receiving inquiries from new quarters, which suggested
that old business connections might be resumed in a
roundabout way, war or no war.

For that very reason the possibility of a German invasion of the Netherlands or Belgium created as much alarm in Cologne as in those countries themselves, for it would have meant the closing of these important outlets.

This possible development raised the spectre of new unemployment in Cologne last winter. At that time, unemployment had been kept in check. The city authorities insisted that the only persons then swelling the relief rolls were the families of soldiers in the field.

Unemployment had been kept down partly because so many men had been drafted for the army, partly because the Westwall construction still continued, and partly because Cologne itself was in the midst of a large-scale city reconstruction program.

There was one "industry" that was flourishing, however, and that was marriage. Cologne's ancient City Hall had become a sort of Gretna Green for soldiers and their fiancées, for whom the German authorities had relaxed the rigid marriage laws. Happy newlyweds might be seen emerging at all times of day to pose for photographers against the picturesque background of the *Rathaus*.

And those who married in Germany at that time still had hope. For all the difficulties of life in wartime the Germans could at least believe—if they accepted the assurances of their government—that the other side was not much better off and that the daring exploits of German U-boats and airplanes and the cunning of German mines would soon turn the British blockade into a boomerang—that Britain would be starved out; not Germany.

Absolutely and relatively, Great Britain is far more dependent on the outside world than Germany. Britain must import 75 per cent of her food, 80 per cent of her bread, grain and beef, and nearly 100 per cent of her textile fiber, oil, lumber, and many other essential requirements.

In contrast, Germany could boast that she produced 82 per cent of her food, 60 per cent of her oil, and 45 per cent of her textile fiber, and that the newly conquered territories further enhanced her self-sufficiency. Moreover, recent bumper crops and heavy imports had enabled her to stock up a national grain reserve of some seven or eight million tons, sufficient for eight months' requirements above current crops. Germany's greatest admitted deficiency was in fats, of which she produced less than 50 per cent of her requirements.

The British blockade sent Germany on a restricted diet immediately, but the report that proud Albion also was forced to resort to food rationing was hailed in Germany as a great victory.

According to an official German announcement, the total losses of shipping bound for England in the first three months of the war amounted to 126 enemy vessels of 531,199 tons and 68 neutral ships of 224,569 tons, a total of 194 ships of 735,000 tons. This loss was said to be all the greater, first, because Britain went into the war with a merchant fleet already about a million tons smaller than before the last war (although the fleets of the dominions and France admittedly raised the total nearly 1,500,000 tons above 1914); second, because the loss of a more efficient modern ship equaled the loss of one and one-half ships during the last war, and third, because naval demands and slower turnover, due to convoy and other delays, entailed a turnover loss estimated at 16,000,000 tons annually, or 25 per cent of the total tonnage required for British imports which were put at 60,000,000 tons.

Nevertheless, however jubilantly the German High Command displayed these figures before German eyes, it was perfectly well aware that they were not decisive. The German counter-blockade became really dangerous during the last war only after Germany went over to unrestricted U-boat warfare and raised her total bag from a monthly average of 125,000 tons in 1915 to between 800,000 and 1,000,000 tons in 1917. The 1939 figures were far below these.

For that reason, as an alternative to unrestricted U-boat warfare Germany started doing everything possible to scare off neutral shipping from British shores. The example of the United States, which in this war had "voluntarily renounced freedom of the seas" and withdrawn American ships from the danger zone, was held up as a laudable example for all other neutrals to follow.

IN HAMBURG

Judging from accounts in the German press, in December, 1939, Germany continued to march from victory to victory.

Success of German submarines, mines and airplanes; the spectacular homeward dash of the liner Bremen and the naval fight between the pocket battleship Admiral Graf Spee and three British cruisers had been presented to the German people as irrefutable demonstrations that the waves were no longer ruled by Britannia but by Germania and that "perfidious Albion," which had again tried to starve Germany, was herself rapidly being turned into a beleaguered fortress.

However that may be a merely casual glance at Hamburg and its famous harbor revealed that what the Germans hailed as the glory of their navy was also the tragedy of their merchant marine and the entire "German front across the seas," on which still depended more than half of Germany's foreign trade.

For, however daring the German exploits might be, however great a toll they might take of belligerent and neutral shipping, the British Fleet "in being" still dictated the law of the seas, and by that law all German overseas connections were severed with the outbreak of war.

As a result Hamburg, Germany's greatest commercial center and window on the outside world, was going through its second disaster of the last 25 years, and nowhere in Germany was the war felt so keenly as there.

Hamburg's harbor, one of the greatest in the world and vastly extended in recent years, was dead. Only a tiny fraction of its humming trade that united the flags of all nations in peaceful rivalry was still moving.

Its proud liners were either tied at its own docks,

where they were quickly acquiring a disreputable outward appearance for lack of upkeep, or were scattered
in neutral ports throughout the world, where they had
sought refuge before the British Navy; and according
to all appearances, that was the larger part of the entire
German merchant fleet.

The big office buildings of its shipping companies had
becomes museums. Foreign shipping companies were
packing and going home. Many of its great commercial
houses had been reduced to skeleton staffs or were liquidating entirely, fearful that many of the markets they
painstakingly built up after the World War would be
lost forever, no matter how this war ended.

The new British blockade measures against German
exports cut the last hope of keeping up some overseas
trade through neutral countries. The neutrals were beginning to refuse to carry goods from or to Germany.
Even Italy, Hamburg noted with bitterness, if with no
surprise, was submitting to the British blockade measures; and now Germans having to travel to or from the
Far East or the Americas did not dare trust themselves
to any Atlantic vessels, but took on themselves the hardships of the 15-day railway journey across Siberia to
Japan.

As a result it was not too much to say that Hamburg
was a city of gloom. Even St. Pauli, the amusement
quarter known to all sailors in the world, though filled
with people wishing to forget their troubles, had lost its
boisterousness.

The fact that British planes, which had visited the

city several times, in the first months of the war merely
dropped tiny coffee bags to the coffee-starved inhabitants of one of Europe's greatest coffee distribution centers, was accepted with rueful smiles as adding insult
to injury.

German coffee storage houses were full; but coffee
represented foreign exchange for the Reich, and therefore it was resold abroad for essential war materials.

Although Hamburg never fully recovered from the
blow of the World War and was further handicapped by
the later economic depression, the devaluations of the
British pound and the American dollar and by the strategic economic program of the Nazi regime, designed to
produce the greatest possible self-sufficiency and shift
the remaining foreign trade as much as possible from
the "wet" to the blockade-proof "dry" border, Hamburg's ship traffic figures had still exceeded those prior
to 1914.

Although this traffic, augmented by the comings and
goings of the Nazis' Strength Through Joy fleet, no
longer provided the amount of business for Hamburg's
commercial houses that was recorded in the smaller figures prior to 1914, it gave Hamburg a busy appearance
and, together with the industrialization program undertaken by the Nazi regime, it kept Hamburg going.

After war began the overseas trade that has been
Hamburg's life blood stopped completely. The only
traffic moving in the harbor was that from the Elbe
River and the Baltic Sea. Much of the latter was being

eliminated by the German counter-blockade of the Allies that was stopping the transit of the Baltic.

If the turnover in Hamburg's port during that December was 10 per cent of that prior to the outbreak of war, it was much; and that was taken care of by river barges and tramp ships.

Import houses that were mobilized to stock Germany for war to a greater extent than official trade figures admitted, and storage houses that were charged with storing the import surplus were still faring best. The importers had been able to accumulate some financial fat on which they could live for a while, and the warehouses were collecting storage dues. But the export houses and shipping companies were dead.

The Hamburg-American Line, for one, had given notice to half its employes, among them many who had been in its service for twenty and more years, for as one of its officials remarked, "We are merely museum keepers now." The United States and Red Star Lines were shutting up shop.

And export houses, despite official pleas that the overseas trade apparatus must be kept intact, were liquidating themselves by the disappearance of their business, and an increasing number were keeping alive nothing more than their name.

Immediately on the outbreak of the war the National Socialist regime gave out the slogan to try to compensate for the loss of overseas trade by switching to European and especially Balkan trade, which had been growing rapidly in recent years. Many Hamburg firms tried, and their agents were especially busy in Rumania.

To facilitate this the German Government created a special foreign trade financing corporation, advanced credits to individual firms on the basis of their frozen assets and gave outright aid to firms in trouble so that a financial breakdown was avoided.

But the success of the attempted switch was small for three reasons: first, because Vienna and not Hamburg was the logical center for that trade; second, because both commodities and trade conditions were entirely different, and third, because transport facilities by both rail and the Danube were limited due to a lack of rolling stock and barges, which neutrals would not allow to get out of their countries, leaving the Germans completely dependent on their own.

Also, the army demands were such that a rail car embargo was imposed on all Hamburg traffic to the Balkans.

Under these circumstances it must be considered an achievement of German organizational talent that Hamburg had even been spared a major wave of unemployment up to December.

Part of this was due to the fact that Hamburg had one flourishing industry, namely, its shipbuilding yards. Except for a few tankers being built for barter purposes, all private shipbuilding had ceased, but the yards were busy day and night working for the navy.

Curiously enough, excepting the huge bulk of one of Germany's new battleships at Blohm & Voss, all the bigger shipways appeared empty, but this was generally explained by the fact that the yards were building sub-marines only, of which, according to diligent hints, Germany was producing one daily.

In any case, most of the laid-off workers had been re-employed in the shipyards or transferred to war indus-tries elsewhere and most of the laid-off office employes had been absorbed in the steadily growing bureaucracy of the State-directed war economy.

IN THE RUHR

Meanwhile the Ruhr industrial district, the "arma-ment smithy of Greater Germany," roared day and night with an iron clang amid which was being sharp-ened the German sword.

All day the forest of smokestacks and blast furnaces that gave this region its characteristic aspect belched forth fire and fumes. All day innumerable trains, both passenger trains for workers and freight trains for their products, shuttled back and forth betraying a secret car shortage elsewhere. All day hundreds of thousands of workers hammered into shape and assembled guns, carriages, trucks and other accoutrements of war, or brought forth black coal from the bowels of the earth to feed the furnaces or to ship abroad in return for food and other things that Germany needed.

But when night fell the whole busy scene also slipped into darkness as completely as German cities and the smoke pall that hung over the industrial area helped blot it from vision, while dummy plants, smokestacks and blast furnaces helped confuse the contours on moon-lit nights. It was one of the miracles of modern camou-flage that the whole industrial region could hide itself so thoroughly that German fliers, searching for its vulner-able spots, in many test flights, were unable to find them.

The success of this industrial blackout was not at-tained, however, without the cost of some readjustments which interfered a trifle with efficiency. For besides the usual covering of windows and light-sluicing doors it also necessitated banking and covering the telltale blast furnaces, casting forges and whatnot that in normal times paint the sky red at night. This meant that certain kinds of production could proceed only during the day. But this trifle, together with the most elaborate air de-fense in all Germany, had kept the Ruhr safe from air raids so far.

At the same time beneath the darkness that covered this district, like most of Germany, another sector of war-time Germany sprang to life. For at night the troop transports began to move. Roads were choked with marching troops in full field equipment and so were the railways and railway stations.

Even this kind of warfare, however, has its casualties, as was amply proved by innumerable accidents. The big, new hospital at Cologne, for instance, was filled with military accident cases, and in the customary death no-tices in the German newspapers the "fallen at the front" was being replaced by "killed in an accident while on duty."

At any rate all the Ruhr was working—and working at capacity. Virtually its entire industry was now readjusted to war-material production and only the most essential wares were manufactured for domestic consumption and export.

The coal industry worked at 120 per cent of its previous capacity to meet export requirements.

There was no apparent lack of raw materials, which for the Ruhr are mainly iron and coal. Of these, Germany produced the latter herself in more than sufficient quantities and got the first from her own mines and from Sweden over a sea route that Britain could not touch. But in other materials as well, production managers asserted that all demands based on permitted requirements were promptly being met.

Nobody, not even the German industrialists themselves, knew what Germany's raw material situation really was. That was one of the greatest secrets of German war economy, as sacred as any military secret.

Nevertheless it was generally assumed in the Ruhr that Germany had put in enough stores and was getting enough from still accessible countries to get along, despite the British blockade, until larger supplies began to flow from Russia. To get these supplies, it was fully realized here, would require substantial production and transportation readjustments in Russia, but with German help it was hoped that this would be accomplished in eighteen months.

At the same time it seemed impossible to exaggerate the expectations that German industry pinned on per-

manent collaboration with Russia—not only for the
period of the war but even more after the peace that
must come some day. It was regarded as nothing less
than a solution of Germany's economic problem and the
royal road to her future prosperity, her economic security and the liquidation of her armament and war
costs.

Despite the necessary readjustments involving the
throttling of consumption goods industries, there was
no unemployment in the Ruhr.

Even British and French civilian employes, originally interned, were being released for their jobs on the
request of their former employers, and the labor force
was further augmented by Polish war prisoners and
Communists released from concentration camps.

At the same time, for the duration of the war, the
standard eight-hour day had been extended to 10 hours,
and in certain occupations the work-day stretched even
to 12 and 14 hours.

Simultaneously production costs had been lowered by
what amounted to a substantial wage reduction, though
the government had preempted a good part of the savings for itself. Overtime bonuses, formerly paid for all
work above eight hours and for holidays and night work,
had been abolished, and paid vacations—National Socialism's pride—canceled. But workers, like soldiers,
were all "in the army now."

That all this, together with the general hardships of
war conditions, had not contributed to raise war enthusiasm was self-evident, and in realization of this fact the

National Socialist regime had already decreed some "amelio-rations." Beginning in December, overtime bonuses for work beyond 10 hours as well as for holidays and night work were to be restored, and vacations were also promised in 1940. Even more important under the circumstances than pay, food ration bonuses had been granted not only for heavy work, but also for long hours and night work to supplement the admittedly scant normal rations.

Nonetheless, as far as could be ascertained, and barring individual cases and incidents, there was nothing the matter with either German working efficiency or working morale. Private assurances of production managers tallied with official statements that the initial difficulties of readjustment had been overcome, that the bulk of workers went to it with a will and that by and large the per capita production had been "at least maintained." And Germany's enemies were warned not to pin any hopes on any disgruntlement among German workers.

XV

MORE PEOPLE, MORE LAND

BESIDES being a military war, a war of nerves, an economic war and several other kinds of a war, this war has been first and foremost a war of populations in which the Germans enlisted their greater biological potency against the West.

According to estimates of the Reich statistical office, the number of Germans born in Greater Germany in 1939, excluding births among Slavic and Jewish subject populations, totaled approximately 1,640,000 and the birth rate rose from 14.7 to the thousand in 1933 to 20.7 to the thousand in 1939.

This, the German press jubilantly exclaimed, was sufficient to maintain the German population in substance and signified that the German people had overcome the menace of gradual "national death," which, on the basis of previous figures, was supposed to have begun in the near future when the "mortgage" of delayed deaths because of the lengthened average life would inexorably be called.

But it was also pointed out that the above birth figure

was more than 300,000 higher than that of France and England combined, both of whom faced the prospect of a natural population decline that a new blood-letting could only hasten.

In the last hundred years, France's population increased from 34,000,000 to 42,000,000. The population of the British Isles increased from 18,000,000 to 47,-000,000, making the present total 89,000,000. But the German population increased from 32,000,000 to 80,-000,000, and counting the Czech and Polish subject populations, Greater Germany's total population was early in 1940 put at 105,000,000, making it the greatest in Europe, outside Russia.

This towering and steadily widening population discrepancy, the Germans argued, created its own law in Europe, and in the long run rendered futile every Allied effort to impose on Europe a "law of the weaker."

At the same time, while the Germans formerly called themselves a "people without room," that slogan had long since been abandoned in favor of a new one reading, "More people, more land." "More land" was to be attained by political and military conquests; the "more people" were being attained by methods equally remarkable.

These methods may be summarized under the three headlines:

First and foremost was the increase of the native German population through child welfare, marriage aids, social sanitation, tax and other bonuses to large families, and later, during the war, a new and urgent appeal for children, even beyond the normal law, custom and morals.

The most remarkable step in that direction, unprecedented in modern history, was taken by Heinrich Himmler as chief of the German police and leader of the Elite Guard, that represented the picked favored ones in the Third Reich. In an order issued to the Elite Guard and the police under the date of October 28, 1939, Herr Himmler decreed:

"Beyond the borders of perhaps necessary middle-class laws, customs and views, it will now be a great task, even outside the marriage bond, for German women and girls of good blood, not in frivolity but in deep moral earnestness, to become mothers of the children of soldiers going off to war, of whom fate alone knows whether they will return or fall for the Fatherland.

"On the men and women whose place remains at home by order of the State, these times likewise impose more than ever the sacred obligation to become again fathers and mothers of children."

During the last war, the order points out, many soldiers decided not to have children because of the feeling of responsibility for their wives and children. To relieve the men of the Elite Guard of these considerations and worries, the following regulations were made in 1940:

1. In the name of the leader of the Elite Guard, a personal representative of his would take over the guardianship for all legitimate and illegitimate children of good blood whose fathers were killed in war. Mothers

and widows would be assisted materially and humanly in bringing up the children until they were of age.

2. All legitimate children conceived during the war would be taken care of by the Elite Guard in case of distress.

This order was read to all Elite Guards and all police recruited from the Elite Guard. Each one of them signified his knowledge of the order by signing his name in a book.

That it was also read in the army, as asserted by some, was officially denied. It was also pointed out that the reference to "women," who were urged to become mothers even outside the marriage bond, did not refer to married women, but to unmarried, widowed or divorced women.

"Many a victory of arms," said the order, "also has been for the nation an annihilating defeat of its vital power and its blood. In that connection, the necessary death of the best men, however regrettable, has not even been the worst. Much worse is the lack of children, not begotten by the living during the war and the dead after the war. Only he can die calmly who knows that his kin and all that his ancestors and he himself wanted and strove for will find continuation in his children.

"Let us never forget that the victory of the sword and the blood of our soldiers is senseless unless it is followed by the victory of peace and the settlement of new soil."

The second measure taken to increase the German population was the recall of Germans from foreign lands

—from the Baltic States, from Russian Poland, from South Tyrol and from other parts of the world, including the United States. More than 400,000 people were to be added to the German population in that manner.

The third method was the acquisition of subject populations, so far consisting of Czechs, Poles and Jews, to a total number of some 25,000,000. According to German plans, these were to be enhanced by the populations of colonies overseas. As to their status, the Inner Front, organ of the National Socialist party, published an article that extended the application of the "racial" doctrine from Jews to all subject "races."

"After the victory," it said, "we shall have open to us the same raw material resources as other nations. Our volume of work will then not fall but will rise mightily, and we shall continue to give work to alien-blooded laborers. The demand for a clear separation of races will, therefore, become all the more urgent with the rise of the Greater German Reich.

"The foundation for the life of alien peoples in the Greater German area can be only an economic one. We will draft no alien racials for the army as they do in England and France, and never will we give them influence in political leadership.

"We must be clear that these borders can be maintained only if we guard the strict separation of blood from the very start. We do not want to become haughty because greater values live in our people than in others. We must never forget that a great Reich can be led only by a master nation, and that a master right is based at all times only upon better blood."

This declaration was made in connection with sentences of between seven and fifteen years at hard labor imposed upon German women for having had intimate relations with Polish war prisoners. It concluded:

"For us it is a matter of course that the Pole deserves no equal rights. He is a member of his people and that people is our enemy. The living laws set up for every people by nature distinguish themselves by simple clarity but also an extreme hardness. The German judge, who expressed this realization in his sentences, obeys, therefore, the law of his inner voice, which creation gave to our people as well."

XVI

MANLY MEN AND WOMANLY WOMEN

ONE of the earliest aims of the National Socialist regime was that of returning women to the home. The victory of the party in Germany had been greatly facilitated by the invention of one magic word which covered many sins. That word was *Gleichschaltung*, which literally means "switching in the same direction," and is generally translated as "co-ordination." In most cases it meant equalization, uniformity, the application of the Potsdam goose-step to politics, economics and all other realms of mind, spirit and soul. Only in one field had *Gleichschaltung* become synonymous with greater differentiation, and that was in the relative position of the sexes.

National Socialism prided itself on the fact that it was wholly a masculine affair. The National Socialist State is a "manly State." Under Nazi rule, Germany was to become a place "where men are men." It was to be made a land, not only "fit for heroes to live in," but it was also to be filled with heroes, fighters, Nietzsche's supermen,

and German workers of both "fist and brow" were to be-
stride the world in the consciousness that they were
Herrenmenschen, that is, "lordly men."

In such a State there could be no room for the equalization of the sexes. Or for the emancipation of the female. The entire social development, not only of the last
fourteen years of "German shame" but of the whole last
century, which led to the emancipated, the intellectual,
the professional woman; which took women out of the
home and placed them in offices, shops and factories and
finally put them into politics—all this was roundly condemned by the Nazi chieftains in the first year of their
reign as the unholy product of materialistic and egoistic
liberalism which flouted all human and divine laws and
therefore rightly met its doom amid the storms of a new
epoch.

A great differentiation between the sexes in all walks
of life was inherent in the Nazi *Weltanschauung.* Nazism did not concern itself with the individual. It was
interested only in the State and race. Everything, and
everybody, that contributed to the defense, the perpetuation and the growth of the State and of the race was
good; everything and everybody else was either worthless or worse, including the sick and the disabled. In an
iron age of international anarchy, Nazism turned back
to the primitive, tribal law of mankind's infancy.

For this State and race, Nazism demanded the manly
man and the womanly woman—the manly man as
fighter and provider, the womanly woman as mother,
nurse and guardian of the domestic fireside. Nazism

scorned the effeminate man as much as the boyish-look-
ing, neuter-minded, self-centered woman. It had as little
use for the "bourgeois intellectual," whose life's ambition was the development of her own sovereign personality, as for the "Marxist materialist" who lost herself
in her profession. In Nazi ideology, woman became
synonymous with mother rather than wife, and motherhood replaced sex appeal as woman's greatest attraction. Womanhood changed from a biological condition
into a moral mission.

Like fascism, Nazism followed the conviction that
numbers are decisive in the battle of nations for supremacy. It regarded the birth rate as the most important indication of a nation's vitality and fitness for survival. The slump of the German birth rate from 36 per
thousand population in 1913 to 15 in 1932, which made
it—with one exception—the lowest in Europe, haunted
the Nazi chieftains.

The 30,000,000 Poles, it was pointed out, produced
more children than the 66,000,000 Germans, so that in
twenty years it was warned that Poland would be able
to put more soldiers into the field than Germany.

"The greatest victory which a nation can win is the
victory of births." The Nazi leaders therefore took up
the fight against the empty cradle as part of their battle
for Germany's regeneration. The State needed soldiers
and it was woman's business to produce them. That the
Germans were already, as they liked to call themselves,
a "people without room" could not discourage this drive
for more people, for a heroic nation takes the room it

needs. The first Nazi aim was "the normal five-child family"; the fashionable two-child, or one-child family, was denounced as a crime against the nation. In Germany, the slacker who failed to provide the State with children was to be regarded as much a menace to the State as the slacker who dodged "national service" either in the regular army or the labor army then about to be created.

There was another consideration, based on the following theory: Women's natural career is marriage. By invading business, industry and the professions, women threw men out of jobs and became competitors of men instead of their companions. In so doing, they killed the goose that laid the golden egg. Women not only robbed themselves of their greatest happiness but also became mainly responsible for the economic crisis, which in the end left women financially worse off than before. When both men and women turned into producers, there were not enough consumers left to consume what they produced.

To prove this theory was adduced the fact that despite the 30,000,000 unemployed in the world the actual number of persons still employed was greater in proportion to the population than ever before. In the view of Dr. Fritz Reinhardt, the State Secretary of Finance, every girl who, instead of marrying and staying at home to bear children, held down a job, was a double menace of the community; she put two men out of work, one directly and another indirectly through the decreased demand for furniture, housing and household necessities; and she further damaged the State by swelling the unemployment dole, decreasing tax returns and endangering the national defense and the future of the race.

Thus patriotism, economics and self-interest of the male combined to drive the German woman back to the three K's—*Küche, Kinder, Kirche,* meaning kitchen, children, church.

The German woman never objected to identifying herself with the three K's; it was her pride that she was the *Hausfrau* par excellence. And anybody who expected to hear cries of protest and revolt against the reactionary Nazi plot was sadly disappointed. If anything, the women were more ardently for this part of the Nazi program than the men. Even that master of domineering rhetoric, Dr. Paul Joseph Goebbels, grew sheepish and apologetic when he assured the ladies at the Women's Exhibition that the Nazis had too much respect for women to admit them to politics.

The women themselves were far more robust and realistic about the matter. They did not want equality, they wanted a home. Feminine emancipation was never much more in Germany than the pet enthusiasm of a few feminine intellectuals whose accomplishments were not in proportion to their earnestness; it meant little to the masses of women except hard work at meagre wages, and it turned completely sour when the economic crisis often made the men dependent on their womenfolks. Any measure which held out the hope of changing this situation could count, therefore, on the

enthusiastic support especially of the so-called emancipated generation.

Thus the Nazis were able to recruit the most ener-
getic advocates of a woman's program among the women
themselves. Which was a happy solution all around. For
while Mussolini practiced what he preached and was
able to announce a new member of the family at frequent intervals, Adolf Hitler still shunned matrimonial
duty to his country and preferred to stay in single bless-
edness. The Nazis further had the wisdom to enlist the
women intellectuals themselves in organizing and prop-
agandizing a movement which was, after all, more con-
genial to them than tariff reform or industrial reorganization.

For the three K's were not to be left to chance. Like
everybody else in Nazi Germany, the women were to
be organized, trained and "co-ordinated," but in their
own special tasks and under their own feminine leaders.
These leaders were so willing and so efficient that the
entire woman's program was placed in the hands of
women.

In this program, there was a theory and a practice.
The theory was this: marriage as a profession was to
assume an entirely new meaning. The married woman
was to be neither the *Gnädige Frau* (gracious lady)
who presided at bridge and tea tables, nor a dowdy
drudge who merely waited on her lord and master and
sewed the buttons on his shirt. On the contrary, she was
to take her place as an equal partner beside her man,
and the center around which family life turned was not

to be the father but a steadily growing brood of children. Some of the more ebullient enthusiasts already were urging that the cities be rebuilt in order to provide each *Hausfrau* with a large living room and kitchen in which she might prepare the family food, do her sewing and mending and supervise and educate her children simultaneously, while her man within his "estate" was working both for the common good and for his family. Thus both men and women were to contribute their equal though different shares to the greater glory of the nation. The laborer of the Third Reich was to be a *Herrenmensch*—the *Hausfrau* of the Third Reich was to be not only the physical but also the spiritual mother of the race and the guardian of its Kultur.

This theory however was best presented in the words of the leaders of the German Woman's Front, which is the unitary federation of all women's organizations. The leader of the German Woman's Front was Frau Lydia Gottschewsky, who explained in phrases that for all their national altruism bore the Nazi stamp:

"The State of Weimar [the German Republic] did not win the love of the German woman, despite the political right which it conferred on her. Its center was the individual; his rights and his happiness were the only concern of the democratic state. National Socialism arose out of the soul of the people for their rescue. Despite the fears of many women to whom it seemed ungentle, National Socialism maintained far more intimate contact with the woman than the vanished epoch because it sought to return her to her real field of work, namely, to the family as the basis of the community.

"There must arise out of German ranks a new womanhood which has nothing to do with the old liberalistic principles. Happiness and freedom of the individual, which were the aim of the old woman's movement, mean nothing to us. The German Woman's Front, incorporated into the front of the nation, is not a purpose in itself; it recognizes only service to the whole and demands willingness to sacrifice. It takes life seriously and earnestly. It possesses a heightened sense of responsibility. Our motto is: 'Germany must live, even though we die!' "

Frau Paula Siber, called to the Reich Ministry of the Interior as "co-ordinator" of all women's organizations, amplified:

"Beyond the task of racial and national maintenance is the sacred task of both man and woman to raise and develop their own spiritual and human personalities, which for the woman climaxes in the motherhood of the soul as the highest ennoblement of every woman, whether married or not.

"The highest calling of the National Socialist woman is not merely to bear children but also to bring up these children with the whole devotion of her motherhood and her mother's duty. She is the guardian of all national culture, which she transmits to the child in fairy stories, legends, play and customs, which, in turn, determine the child's attitude toward the nation and the race throughout life.

"National Socialism is the battle for the redemption of the German woman from the domination of her own tiny self. National Socialism does not mean the crippling of the woman, but her highest development."

"The world of bourgeois capitalism, of rationalism, liberalism, humanism, is dying," explained Frau Karin Homann. "A neo-romantic epoch of irrationalism and mysticism returns. Intellect and reason are being dethroned in favor of emotion and instinct. This epoch demands unconditional faith, for which woman is predestined. National Socialism rejects the intellectual woman, but it is necessary to distinguish between spirit and intellectualism. The latter ends in bloodless, overwrought thinking without inner experience, the former is tantamount to creative vision and a recognition of the essence of things."

Putting the theory into practice these measures were effected as a beginning.

The State granted a "marriage aid" to young couples up to one thousand marks if the bride gave up a job she had held for at least six months, and obligated herself not to take another job as long as her husband earned at least 125 marks a month. The aid was granted in scrip good only for the purchase of furniture and household utensils, and represented a loan without interest, which must be repaid at the rate of 1 per cent per month. It was thus a State-financed installment buying plan.

But every child reduced the loan by 25 per cent and postponed further payment for twelve months. The "marriage aid" was granted only to "politically reliable" couples; Jews and other "non-Aryans" were excluded from it. Nevertheless the Reich Finance Ministry hoped to unite two hundred thousand couples a year who otherwise would not have established a common household. This "marriage aid" was to be financed by a heavy "bachelor tax" on both unmarried men and women. Some travel bureaus, anxious to get into step with the government, financed free wedding trips. To discourage women from taking up careers other than marriage, all women under thirty-five years of age, and all women whose husbands or fathers earned enough to secure their economic security, were to be barred from appointment as officials. This included the women teachers. Those who were appointed would receive less pay than men in like positions. The same principle of eliminating "double earners" was to be extended to business generally by "persuasion." But special reductions in taxes and welfare insurance assessments were granted to housewives who employed domestic help, which was recommended as a career to girls.

The existing help and welfare organizations were to be co-ordinated and extended with a special view toward protecting mother and child. Health certificates for bride and bridegroom, State aid and health supervision for expectant mothers, war on social diseases with the aid of the penal code, vacations and assistance for mothers—these were some of the measures planned.

Chief emphasis, however, was laid on the education of the younger feminine generation in order to create

the new National Socialist woman needed for the
National Socialist State. According to Frau Hedwig
Foerster, counselor for girls' education in the Prussian
Ministry of Culture, this education would place emphasis, not on the creation of an independent personality,
as in the past era of liberalism, but on service—service
to the family, the community, the State.

Less book learning but more training in the duties
of motherhood was the motto. Mere humanistic girls'
schools and colleges were to be reduced and more household and agricultural academies established. But included among the studies would be religion, philosophy,
biology, social and national subjects and racial research
in conformity with the Nazi doctrine of racial exclusiveness. As Frau Lydia Gottschewsky put it: "Leaders among us can be only women who by blood and
faith stand under the law of the German people, not
half-Jewesses and democrats."

Perhaps the great innovation in women's education,
however, was to be the feminine labor service, a coun-
terpart of the labor service army of the men. Voluntary
labor service camps in which girls might stay for twenty
weeks were established, later, this service was to be
made compulsory for all girls. But whereas the men
were to build roads, regulate rivers and reclaim land,
the girls were to be prepared physically, mentally and
morally for their own career of motherhood.

It was necessary, said Frau Foerster, that "for one
year, at least, the girls should be taken out of the liberalistic, class-conscious, morally debauched or overly

tender 'atmospheres' of the homes, in order practically to experience the unity of all German people, of whatever class they may be, by living and working together in closest community, and to carry this living experience into home or profession." City girls ought to be encamped in the country, it was held, and country girls near the cities, so that each might learn from the new environment.

One important function of a labor service camp was to be "physical invigoration." This implied not so much sport as suitable exercises and calisthenic dances to promote "proper harmony of a healthy body." Too much sport, in the view of Dr. Wilhelm Frick, Minister of the Interior, "hampered family formation as much as too much education." Included in "physical invigoration," was the study of the proper diet, and there the virtues of domestic foods, such as millet and buckwheat, were to be stressed to help German agriculture and improve Germany's balance of trade.

But diet did not include fasting for the sake of slenderness. Such practice was unanimously condemned by all German doctors as dangerous to a German mother, and by the Nazis as remnants of a liberalistic age with its concentration on the individual. There was no intention to return to the "portliness" of the beauty types of antiquity, "but a certain buxomness is to be considered beautiful."

Since Germany still contained 1,900,000 more women than men, and there were not enough husbands to go around, some provision had to be made for the unwed.

Professions fitted to the nature of such persons were to remain open, principally in sociological, education and welfare fields. But the work of the unmarried woman, too, was to assume a new significance. Not the idea of having something to do, or the development of her own personality, was to be the driving motive, but only service to the community. When "sickly ambition" disappeared with the creation of Nazi womanhood, woman's profession would turn into a calling, and only such a calling was to find favor in the Third Reich.

XVII

THE "PEOPLE'S CAR"

ONE of Hitler's schemes that the war made abortive was a method designed to satisfy the mass demand for a fuller life and to bolster up Germany's own economy. This method was symbolized by the *Volksauto*, or "people's car," which was to be sold by the millions for the basic price of 990 marks, or $396.00.

In embarking on this project the National Socialist regime threw down a challenge in achievement to both capitalism and bolshevism. It challenged capitalism because it undertook, as recompense to the people for their surrender of individual liberty, to emulate capitalism's most spectacular achievement—namely, the motorization of the masses.

As it was planned in 1938, the new *Volksauto*, or, as Hitler named it, the "Strength Through Joy" automobile, was to be produced under the patronage of the Führer himself and under the auspices and responsibility of the German Labor Front, the One Big Union of all of Germany's "creative" workers. The *Volksauto* was designed to do the same thing for Germany as Henry

Ford did for America—to convert German civilization, up to then a distinctly sedentary civilization centering around the home, into a civilization on wheels.

The road toward that goal was long and steep. Although Germany was the second biggest industrial country in the world, she was far behind all other Western powers in motorization. The number of automobiles had doubled in the first five years of Hitler's power, but in 1938 there were still only 1,500,000 passenger cars in Germany, or one automobile for every 50 persons, as compared with one automobile for every five persons in the United States.

At the same time the *Volksauto* was born of quite different considerations from those that brought the cheap car to America. The cheap American car is an industrial article produced for profit; the *Volksauto* was a device of National Socialist political economy, which depended on full employment and operated with fixed wages, fixed prices, and the greatest possible self-sufficiency, to accomplish three purposes:

First, to deflect the rising national purchasing power, resulting from full employment, away from increased demands for food, clothes and the commoner luxuries of which Germany was short, and to direct it toward an article produced exclusively of domestic materials.

Second, to take up any slack in employment when rearmament was finally completed.

Third, to increase the fixed wages, not by raising the nominal wages themselves, but by increasing their purchasing power through a reduction in prices.

To some extent this "socialistic" method of raising "real" wages and directing consumption had already been put in practice through the German Labor Front's "Strength Through Joy" organization, which provided recreation, entertainment and vacation trips for the masses at small cost, and through the $14 *Volksradio* produced privately under governmental standardization. But the *Volksauto* was the most ambitious project of that kind.

The *Volksauto*, like the motorization of Germany in general, was Hitler's own personal contribution to Germany's resurgence. As a preliminary to its manufacture he ordered reduction of automobile taxes, which stimulated automobile production and sales and was largely responsible for the doubling of the number of cars in the nation.

Furthermore, almost immediately after coming to power, he ordered the construction of a vast network of new high-speed, double-track, crossingless, long-distance motor highways, which, like the railroads, connect the most important cities of Germany by the shortest routes, and which have found universal praise from both German and foreign motorists.

Built of solid concrete, with a green strip of grass between the two tracks, they stretch like white ribbons across the landscape and form the new landmarks of the new Germany. Approximately 1,500 miles of them had already been completed by the fall of 1938, and the total program called for 6,835 miles for Germany and Austria. Compared with the latest American road and boulevard developments, the German highways are not extraordinary, but they are the best in Europe.

Beyond that, however, the *Volksauto* itself was also Hitler's own creation. He conceived the idea for it, advocated it at every automobile show in Germany beginning with that in 1933, and, according to authoritative accounts, laid down the basic principles for its construction and even drew preliminary sketches for it, emphasizing especially the need for body room in order to make it a "family conveyance."

Finally, when private industry declared itself unable to produce such a car at the stipulated price he transferred the task to the German Labor Front, in conformity with his dictum that "if private industry is unable to fulfill the national tasks imposed on it by the political leadership, it will cease to be a private industry."

In general, an automobile had been a luxury in Germany, completely beyond the means of the "little man." The spectacle of clerks, stenographers and factory laborers coming to work in their own private cars, as in the United States, was unknown in Germany. The minimum price for an automobile in that country in 1938 was 1,700 marks, payable on a virtual cash basis, and the average wage of the German worker was only 30 marks a week.

Yet there was little doubt that the financial basis for a popular-priced car existed in Germany. In 1938 about 5,000,000 out of 15,000,000 workers earned above 2,000 marks a year. A good proportion, if not most of them, could, therefore, afford a *Volksauto* at 990 marks, especially when it could be paid for under the special installment plan announced by the Labor Front. And to them must be added several more millions of independent artisans, and professional and business men.

German "socialism" had been able to take up this task only because behind the German Labor Front stood the power and prestige of the National Socialist regime, permitting it to do things which no private enterprise could undertake. This enabled the Labor Front to institute a "pay-before-you-get-it" installment plan forbidden to private enterprise except for the building loan associations; they crowded private enterprise from the small-car market through restrictions on raw material in order to reserve it for the *Volksauto;* they invoked the right of eminent domain for the factory as well as *Volksauto* garages; they saved all advertising and promotion costs because the whole National Socialist regime, including the press, was enlisted in its promotion; they also saved all dealer's profits because the "dealer" was the far-flung organization of the Labor Front itself.

Despite all this it appeared that every successive announcement raised the effective prices of the *Volksauto* just a notch above the previous announcement. The original statement had been that the price of 990 marks included insurance for two years, garage charges and the cost of periodic overhauling, so that the net price of the car would come to only about 574.20 marks, or $230.00. But by 1938, the effective price of the limousine were as follows:

Basic price at factory	990 marks
Two years insurance	200 marks
Delivery cost, average	50 marks
Total ....1,240 marks

These prices were valid only for members of the Labor Front; others were to pay in addition to the regulation price the Labor Front dues fitting their income. The delivery charges might be saved by driving the car home from the factory, to which special buses were to transport purchasers, but the insurance had become an extra charge and there was no further talk of free garage or overhauling. Nor was there any guarantee; the buyer bought on trust.

The installment plan provided that every would-be purchaser should save for the car five marks per week, or sums in multiples of five, which were paid by means of purchasing a savings stamp and pasting it upon a card, a method earlier made familiar by the governmental social insurance system. This five marks a week included the insurance premium, and when 750 marks had been paid in, the buyer got an order number entitling him to a car when the factory was able to deliver it. But the total to be paid was not 990 marks, but 1,190 marks at the minimum, which at the five-marks a week rate stretched payment over about four and three-quarter years. Cash payments were excluded for domestic purposes. The cancellation of the order forfeited the amount paid in, save in exceptional cases, and even in these 20 per cent was retained. This system was designed to prevent an installment-purchase inflation.

The *Volksauto* was actually designed by Dr. Ferdinand Porsche, a Sudeten German who exhibited an "electro-automobile" as early as the Paris Exhibition of 1900, and who later, as director of the Austro-Daimler works, supervised the motorization of the Austrian artillery at the Skoda works.

The production of the car was planned at Fallersleben, near Braunschweig, where, according to Dr. Robert Ley, head of the German Labor Front, was then being built "not only the biggest automobile factory in the world but the biggest factory in the world of any kind." This plan, moreover, was to become a "socialistic" model factory as regarded beauty of the working place, housing, social settlement work, craft education and workers' health.

Toward its construction, the Labor Front, which had in 1938 an annual income of almost 400,000,000 marks, had already advanced 50,000,000 marks, which was double the capital stock of the biggest German automobile concern. But the savings plan was thought enough to provide adequate capital for further construction. The prospective customers became the *Volksauto* financiers.

For this plant, which was planned to begin production toward the end of 1939, and was not to be completed until the end of 1946, the German Labor Front had in 1938 already placed large orders. American automobile engineers, fully versed in American production methods, had arrived to lend their aid.

The *Volksauto* was planned as a four-seater, driven by a four-cylinder, air-cooled motor in the rear, which developed 24 horsepower and gave the car a speed of 62 miles an hour on a fuel consumption of only three gallons per hundred miles. The speed, it was asserted, was due in part to exact streamlining, while the position of the air-cooled motor at the rear permitted a saving in weight by elimination of the radiator and the long transmission gears. The car weighed only 650 kilograms, or less than 1500 pounds. It could be left outdoors in any cold without fear of freezing, according to its makers.

From the standpoint of National Socialist economy, however, the chief aspect of the car was that it was to be produced entirely of domestic raw materials. The body was to be all-steel, but so light that one per cent of the German steel production was to be sufficient for it. For the rest, the new German light metals, especially the magnesium alloys, were to be widely employed. The upholstery was to be synthetic leather, and the tires were to be made of Buna, Germany's synthetic rubber.

According to the 1938 plan, production was to be concentrated on a gray-blue limousine and a cabrio-limousine with removable top. An open car was to follow later. The final capacity of the plant was to be 1,500,000 a year or more than Ford's. The problems of supplying garage facilities and driving instruction were already being tackled, and the savers as well as future drivers would be under the supervising care of Labor Front agents.

Most of the first contingents allotted to the different regions were already sold out. Besides satisfying the workers and the demands of her national economy, Germany also hoped to capture the export market with this car, and British automobile interests were highly apprehensive.

PART IV

The Blow Falls

XVIII

"THEY WANTED WAR!"

UNDER the general motto, "They wanted war: they shall have it," Chancellor Hitler and his paladins issued on December 30, 1939, a series of New Year's proclamations which, while pointing with pride to military and political achievements in the last year, nevertheless admitted that "the heaviest battle is still to come" and called on the German people to stand fast and fight until final victory was achieved.

Contrary to a whispering campaign predicting a smashing German blow at Great Britain and with it peace early in the coming year, the proclamations appeared designed to emphasize rather the seriousness of the coming struggle and the necessity for further sacrifices.

Although 1940 was called "the most decisive year in German history," the question whether the new year really would bring a decision was answered merely with a prayer that it "may do so." In this connection the name of God was invoked repeatedly.

In general, the proclamations repeated the German

thesis about the wrongs Germany suffered at Versailles, Herr Hitler's efforts to right these wrongs peaceably and "the impervious egoism, stupidity and deliberate bad-will" of the Western powers, which foiled these efforts.

Now the Western powers, supposedly dominated by "Jewish international capitalism and social reactionary classes," were accused of plotting to murder Herr Hitler himself and exterminate the German people. Therefore, the German people were told, for them the war had become a question of to be or not to be.

At the same time, while holding their own conquests invitingly before German eyes, Herr Hitler and his aides likewise announced that they were fighting a "war of liberation." This liberation was for both Germany and all Europe from "the rape and constant menace" of malignant but senile and decadent Britain and beyond that a war for a "new Europe" to be created by "young and productive nations to whom belongs the future."

What this latter war aim meant was amplified at great length in that December by innumerable inspired articles in the German press. These no longer represented the war as merely a German struggle against the Versailles treaty, but as a great "international revolution" destined to make an end both to capitalistic society and the Western idea of the national (sovereign) State in favor of the "socialistic millennium," which was to usher in socialistic planning not only within nations but also among nations.

The nations, it was explained, were to be organized

in great collaborating "communities" free from the
interference of "room alien" powers and led by the
history-shaping nations that acknowledged a moral im-
perative even if in executing it their leaders must be
"hard and ice-cold."

And since Germany was "the greatest Reich and the
greatest people in Europe," it was her mission and duty
to be the leader of this revolution.

Translated into practice, this "socialism of nations"
was nothing more nor less than the old National Socialist idea of "Grossraumwirtschaft," or a regional
economy in which a lot of smaller adjacent States were
to be economic and political satellites of a big power.

In the days of frank power politics, the idea was symbolized by the term "Mitteleuropa." In the days of economic preoccupation, it became *Grossraumwirtschaft*.
In the days of German-Russian collaboration, it assumed a socialistic guise, but empire was its real name.

All the proclamations extolled the striking power and
achievements of German arms in the war as a guarantee
of final victory. But both Herr Hitler and Field Marshal Hermann Goering also emphasized Germany's
economic armament. Marshal Goering, as economic dictator, placed special stress on it. But he also warned:

"New sacrifices are inevitable; we shall not shrink
from them, for without sacrifices there is no victory."

What this warning portended was not clear at the moment, but predictions were that the new year would
bring more taxes, which already absorbed more than 40
per cent of the national income. This created a situation

for the civilian population drastically illustrated by the fact that stores that were unable to replenish their stocks, sold out during the Christmas rush, were by New Year so empty they scarcely were able to keep displays in their show windows. For this reason they were beginning to post signs that goods in show windows were either "sold" or "not for sale."

The longest proclamation, and the one outlining the program in most detail, was issued by Herr Hitler to the National Socialist party, while Marshal Goering, as heir designate, issued another proclamation to the German people.

In addition, Herr Hitler, as supreme commander and German "field lord," issued another proclamation to the armed forces, whose three branches also were addressed separately by Colonel General Walther von Brauchitsch, army chief; Marshal Goering for the air force and Grand Admiral Erich Raeder, commander of the navy.

Baldur von Schirach, Reich youth leader, issued a proclamation to the Hitler Youth announcing that he had entered the army and appointed his deputy, Hartmann Lauterbacher, as the new commander. The Reich labor leader, Konstantin Hierl, addressed the Reich labor service, which was continued despite the war.

Simultaneously Herr Hitler announced a series of promotions in the army, navy and air force. The most striking among these was the promotion of Admiral Alfred Saalwaechter to admiral general, a recently created rank held hitherto by Admiral Raeder as Commander-in-Chief of the navy.

As during the last war, the usual New Year reception to the diplomatic corps by the head of the German State was canceled for the coming year.

Field Marshal Hermann Goering, in his proclamation to the German people, declared that the nation entered the new year confidently, "strong in hope and certain of victory."

"Most tremendous and most difficult tasks press up against us," he continued. "We shall solve them and overcome every resistance in indestructible confidence in our own strength.

"The German people stand as a block as hard as steel, conscious of their rights and their duties, united in their will, unfearing and thinking of their common allegiance to their Führer. . . .

"In the new year the old watchword that made the Reich great, strong and united holds good: Führer, command; we follow."

In his other proclamation Marshal Goering heaped lavish praise upon the air force for its exploits in the Polish campaign and in the present war.

"They [the Allies] do not want peace," he declared.

"Well, then they shall have battles. . . . The German Air Force stands at the threshold of the new year with confidence as firm as rock. . . . The air force renews in this hour its oath to the Führer and Supreme Commander, to the whole German nation united in National Socialism to stake all—when and wherever it may be—in fighting for German liberty.

"The watchword for the German Air Force for 1940 is: Victory!"

General von Brauchitsch declared the German Army's spirit and strength "give us certainty of final victory."

"In steady loyalty to the Führer," he said in his order of the day, "in clear realization of our strength, in unswerving belief of the justice of our cause and with iron will we will go together into war in the year 1940.

"True to the traditions of German soldiery, the army in 1939 stood the test before the enemy. Victorious battles in Poland and successful fighting in the West are unequivocal witnesses of the army's spirit and strength in the history of the new and greater German Reich."

The text of Admiral Raeder's order of the day to the navy was:

"The German people begin the year 1940 in a severe struggle for the Reich's existence. The German Navy has shown that it is able to challenge and hit the enemy. In accordance with its great tradition, the navy will do its duty in the year ahead of us, trusting in God, in unwavering obedience to the Führer and firmly believing in victory."

Heinrich Himmler delivered the following proclamation to the Elite Guards and police force as chief of all German police:

"In the new year of 1940, which probably will be one of the most important in German history, let us be as always the Führer's and his Reich's loyal men, prepared to stake everything. Long live the Führer!"

The following is the text of Herr Hitler's proclamation for New Year 1940:

"The new Reich finally took the right into its own hands.

"From the first day of assuming power, I sought undeviatingly to achieve the necessary revision of Germany's political position as well as her vital economic rights. All attempts to do this in co-operation with other powers were shattered on the stubborn egoism or conscious bad will of Western powers and their statesmen.

"Freeing of the German people, therefore, had to be accomplished by means of that self-help which is holy at all times of great need. Following the settlement of inner struggles, nationalistic Germany step by step threw off the fetters of slavery and in the welding of the German people into a greater German Reich crowned the longing of a thousand years.

"All these measures neither robbed nor harmed the rest of the world.

"As distinguished from Herr Chamberlain [British Prime Minister Neville Chamberlain], we are convinced that a new Europe can be established not from the aged forces of a crumbling world or by the so-called statesmen who are not even able to solve the simplest problems in their own countries, but that the construction of a new Europe belongs to those people and forces which, on the basis of their attitude and accomplishments thus far, can be described as young and productive.

"To these young nations and systems belongs the future.

"The Jewish capitalist world will not survive the twentieth century.

"Germany and Europe must be freed from the ravishment and the endless threats that have their origins in the past and present-day England.

"Weapons must this time definitely be struck from the hands of the warmongers and declarers of war.

"We fight, therefore, not only against the injustice of Versailles but to prevent the even greater injustice intended to replace it. We are fighting for the construction of a new Europe.

"Through the publication of documents giving the history leading up to the German-Polish conflict, it is proved that responsible warmongers in England not only rejected a peaceful solution of German-Polish problems but did everything possible through Poland to abuse the German Reich.

"As this failed, there remained only one possibility; that Poland should be misled by international warmongers to achieve her injustices by force. In eighteen days weapons decided. The Poland of the Versailles dictate exists no longer.

"The year 1939 was marked in German history by tremendous occurrences; firstly, by the incorporation of the age-old German territories of Bohemia and Moravia into the German Reich, securing the German *Lebens-*

raum. Germans and Czechs, as in the past hundred years, will in the future live and work together peacefully.

"Secondly, Memel was returned to the Reich; thirdly, through destruction of the Polish State, the old Reich frontiers were re-established. In these three cases, Versailles restrictions were unable to survive and were removed.

"This year's fourth contribution is the non-aggression and consultative pact with Russia.

"The attempt of plutocratic statesmen in the west to bring Germany and Russia to fight one another for the profit of a third party has been nipped in the bud. Germany's encirclement has been hindered.

"That these political developments could be successful we have exclusively to thank our National Socialistic education of the German people.

"Economically and militarily prepared, we enter this most decisive year in German history.

"One thing we all recognize is that the Jewish capitalistic world enemy who face us know only one aim, namely, to destroy the German people. Firstly, they swore to aid Poland. They could best have helped Poland only by not hurrying her into war. At the instant when Poland was felled by a blow from our army, their war aim was no longer re-establishment of Poland but the removal of myself and the destruction of National Socialism.

"When they saw the German people did not respond to any such foolishness they decided to exterminate the

German people and destroy the German Reich. In the cowardly hope of winning other helpers in their task they do not shun using so-called neutrals nor engaging murderers.

"The German people did not want this fight. Until the last minute I tried to offer England our friendship and in addition, after Poland's elimination, I was willing to make proposals that would have secured peace in Europe for a long time.

"In this I was supported by Il Duce [Premier Mussolini], who, in accordance with the sense and spirit of our friendship, made every effort to halt the development, which was accompanied by misfortune.

"But the Jewish reactionary warmongers in the capitalistic democracies have awaited this hour for years. They had prepared and were unwilling to cancel their plans for destruction of Germany.

"These warmongers want war. They shall have it.

"Already the first phase of the war has shown two things:

"Firstly, they [the Allies] did not attack the German Westwall.

"Secondly, everywhere where German soldiers have engaged the enemy the glory of German soldierdom as well as German weapons again has been justified.

"May 1940 bring a decision. Come what may, it will be our victory. Everything that will be demanded in the way of sacrifices cannot be compared with that which the entire nation has at stake and is not comparable to the fate that threatens her should the mendacious criminals of Versailles again come into power."

The following was Herr Hitler's proclamation to his armed forces:

"Soldiers! the year 1939 was for the German armed forces a year of proud test. You have used victoriously the weapons that the German people entrusted to you for this war that was forced upon us.

"In a scant eighteen days we were able to re-establish the Reich's security in the East. The Versailles injustice was removed.

"At the end of this historical year we gratefully remember those comrades who sealed with their blood their loyalty to the people and their country.

"In the coming year we ask the Almighty, who in the last year took us under His protection, to give us His blessing again and to strengthen us in the performance of our duty, for before us lies the hardest battle for existence of the German people.

"I and the German people look upon you with proud confidence.

"Soldiers, Germany must be victorious.

ADOLF HITLER."

XIX

BEHIND THE PACT

In the fateful hours when, after many preliminary soundings and tentative approaches, an offer of a Russo-German non-aggression and consultative pact was definitely made and accepted, the world changed its political face and the explosive effect of the coup showed how instinctively this fact was appreciated.

For this pact, behind which lay many plans and agreements with world-wide implications, completely changed the political, military, economic and ideological values on which statesmen and nations had based their politics heretofore.

That such a pact should have been brought about between two revolutions, deadly enemies heretofore, and between nations whose rival aims for aggrandizement touched off the last war and were still part of their respective ideological programs, was an astounding fact. Yet some development had always been within the range of possibility, and it was more than a gesture when, following announcement of the pact, a German and a Russian who had played important roles in the negotiations sank into each other's arms with the Russian exclaiming, "At last we've found each other."

It had perhaps been difficult for democratic statesmen, elected for a definite term by orderly processes, to appreciate the dynamics of revolutions and the revolutionary nature and strength of the men at their heads.

The story was told that not one British statesman had read Adolf Hitler's *Mein Kampf* except, perhaps, for a brief glance at the innocuous version first circulated in Great Britain, until some time in 1935 when Ivan M. Maisky, Russian Ambassador in London, circulated typewritten excerpts among them which they referred to as "very interesting."

But Joseph Stalin, Herr Hitler and for that matter the late Polish dictator, Marshal Josef Pilsudski, fully appreciated each other's character and the strength inherent in revolutionary moments commanding substantial popular support. And they acted accordingly.

That a German-Russian rapprochement that upset all political calculations once before following the last war had always been the sheet anchor of all real German statesmen, and the dream of all German soldiers plagued by the nightmare of war on two fronts, greatly facilitated its consummation and particularly helped the *Realpolitiker* in Herr Hitler to overcome his hatred of the first enemy he had fought and conquered at home.

The Russo-German pact, in which Italy was a tacit partner and to which the Axis hoped to attach Japan as well, created what looked like a totalitarian bloc of three or even four of the world's seven big powers which could checkmate the three big but divided democratic powers. By virtue of its might and breathless dynamics this bloc hoped to reorganize the world in favor of the "proletarian have-nots" among nations which were the losers in the last settlement at the expense of the "rich but decadent democracies."

This meant "a fourth and final partition of Poland," and beyond that the reorganization of all Central and Eastern Europe by Germany and Russia for their mutual benefit and to the exclusion of France and Britain.

Neither Berlin nor Moscow made any secret of these plans, and what veiled and involved sentences of diplomatic correspondence merely hint at was freely revealed in the private talks of political activitists. In fact, according to the German view, the whole fallacy of the British and French efforts to include Russia in their "encirclement front" consisted in their demand on Russia to defend the possession by others of territories that once belonged to her. Neither Britain nor France felt able to pay the price Russia wanted. Germany did.

Just what details of the division of Eastern Europe were discussed in Moscow, was, of course, the negotiators' secret. But if vague hints dropped in political quarters were a clue, there was a prospect of restoration of "historic borders" and fulfillment of "natural destinies" that would give Germany that Mitteleuropa that had been her dream and Russia that outlet to the sea that she lost—except for a tiny strip at Leningrad—after the World War.

That this would mean the doom of Independent Poland was not only not denied but was openly declared to be one of the German war aims. And these hints already referred to were to the effect that Germany would retake Danzig, Pomorze (the Polish Corridor), Poznan and perhaps a little more just to round off her borders, while Russia would take the Polish Ukraine and White Russia, with Lithuania getting perhaps Vilna.

This would leave what is known as Congress-Poland, with approximately the borders of the Duchy of Poland Napoleon created, which might be left as either a small buffer State or a protectorate of one or other of the two powers.

Beyond this, however, such a bloc also expected to dictate the terms of a new world settlement that would redistribute colonies, *Lebensraum,* and the world's riches generally in proportion to the "numbers, courage and work" of the various nations. These frankly imperialistic aims were the sense of Hitler's National Socialist revolution, but they had heretofore been anathema to the proletarian class revolution of bolshevism.

Such a revolution within bolshevism was precisely what the Germans assumed as a basis for their calculations. Stalin, they held, had turned Right and international bolshevism has become national bolshevism, which eliminated the menace of an international communism backed by Moscow.

The dead Marshal Tukachevsky had triumphed over George Dimitroff with the paradoxical result that the Communist parties in various other countries were left high and dry. However, according to the German view, they had been regarded in Moscow as "Trotskyists" anyhow, as revealed during the Spanish conflict, which was regarded in Berlin as a turning point in bolshevist developments. They were, therefore, expected to adopt Leon Trotsky as their leader and perhaps even to start a revolutionary campaign against "Stalinism" within Russia, which would complete the revolutionary circle.

This turn of bolshevism from internationalism to nationalism the Germans assumed to be a product of the bolshevist fiasco in Spain; and if the assumption of the turnabout was true, then the difference between National Socialism, fascism and bolshevism narrowed considerably. All three were products of mass movements, all three were directed against the domination of old powers—the church and "plutocratic capitalism"—and all three used authoritarian methods in attaining their aims. By the inescapable consequences of planned and controlled economy all three were forced into totalitarian control of all phases of life, and their ultimate common destiny seemed to be more or less developed state capitalism.

Finally, having barred the Rhine with their Westwall and having placed German divisions and guns in Italy, the Germans considered themselves militarily impregnable from the worst and a general European war impossible for lack of a battlefield. This left as the only real menace British sea-power and the dreaded blockade; and the Russian pact, which, it was thought, assured Germany of Russian food and materials, was held to have made Germany "blockade-proof."

Even as late as November, 1939, the daily press still presented this rosy picture of Russian supplies of all sorts beginning to roll to Germany in the very near future along Polish railroads (that had been quickly repaired for that purpose) or being brought by water over the Baltic Sea or the Danube, protected by German sea and river fleets. But strictly military publications and military commentators were growing skeptical.

There was no doubt of Russia's natural resources as such, but it was pointed out that to make them available to Germany they would have to be exploited and developed first, because in most cases Russian production fell short of Russia's own requirements. Only in food, iron, manganese and lumber could Germany count on any increased supplies from Russia.

But in such basic war materials as copper, lead, zinc, nickel and tin, of which Russia has vast but undeveloped resources, she was not only unable to export anything but must import large quantities for her own use. And even regarding oil, of which Russia was one of the greatest producers, German hopes were melting.

Reasons for Russia's inability to supply more to Germany were outlined in a survey by Colonel Ritter von Niedermayer before the Cologne Geographic Society. These reasons were summarized as follows:

1. Russia's own industrialization, which had increased Russian consumption of raw materials faster than production but which suffered from its centralized, dictatorial direction, suppressing personal interest and

therefore leading to quantity production according to prescribed plans at the expense of quality.

2. The vast territory through which the natural resources were scattered and the backwardness of the transportation system. According to Colonel Niedermayer, while Russian production increased 250 per cent, railway facilities increased only 48 per cent; while passenger traffic rose 600 per cent the number of locomotives increased only 48 per cent. Only 30 per cent of the Russian railways were double-tracked. The Russian railways had been virtually unrepaired since the days of the Czars, paralyzing the country economically and militarily.

3. The lack of foreign experts and technicians, without which, in Colonel Niedermayer's view, Russia would be unable to keep going.

Even regarding food and fodder Colonel Niedermayer's anticipations apparently were not too large because he said Russian agriculture was entirely collectivized and industrialized and that having been made entirely dependent on tractors, it often lacked gasoline to operate them.

XX

ATTACK

EUROPEAN peace appeared to take a new lease on life on Monday, August 28, when Chancellor Hitler received the British reply to his latest proposal for a solution of the war crisis and after a preliminary study of it with his closest collaborators found it to be "not wholly negative."

That at least was what percolated out of the Chancellery together with the definite information that Germany would send a written reply to Britain. The British reply was brought from London by Sir Nevile Henderson, who arrived in Berlin in a special plane and who was received by Herr Hitler amid the customary honors in the presence of Foreign Minister Joachim von Ribbentrop and an interpreter at 10:20 o'clock on Monday night. Later Field Marshal Hermann Goering joined the conference.

The British answer consisted of a note and a lengthy oral explanation, and it was considered a good sign in itself that the conference lasted an hour and a quarter.

Although little more than the first German impression

of the British answer was available, nevertheless the general assumption of its contents in well-informed quarters checked more or less with that circulating in London. That was, that the British Government, while emphasizing its determination to stand by its pledge to Poland even at the risk of war, nevertheless suggested negotiations with Warsaw under British assistance and under conditions that were held to permit the Germans to continue negotiations, especially since they held that in urging such negotiations Britain had also abandoned the defense of the status quo.

But it still remained to be seen whether the first favorable impression of the Germans was based on the hope of a peaceful solution of the conflict with Poland or merely on the hope of localizing that conflict, keeping France and Britain out of it and thereby escaping a general war. For many indications, including comments in the semi-official news service, *Dienst aus Deutschland*, suggested that Germany was coming to the conclusion that Poland was not Czecho-Slovakia and that there was no Polish Government in sight able or willing to agree to Herr Hitler's terms. Therefore the only method of effecting them was to impose them by force of arms.

This meant war against Poland.

From that viewpoint, therefore, the German diplomatic moves represented efforts to make this conflict a local conflict; a little war instead of a big war.

Also once the conflict was regarded as inevitable, there arose the question of war guilt, which each side tried to put on the other. In view of that all diplomatic notes, letters and other communications were being written with an eye to future white, blue or yellow books for the benefit of national morale or later history. The German press, at least, asserted that this was true of the documents from the other side.

Nevertheless, official quarters took great pains to emphasize Germany's determination to end the crisis with a "German solution."

Official and unofficial pronouncements were based on the constant reiteration of what Chancellor Hitler had said in his letter to Premier Edouard Daladier of France, and what he was understood to have told Reichstag deputies—namely, that he was determined to get what he demanded peacefully if possible, and if that was impossible he did not shrink from war. The press put the fateful alternative in the words that the Polish question must be solved "so or so," and all suggestions in the foreign press that Germany was weakening were denounced as "sabotage of European peace."

At the same time it was emphasized that, while the time was running short, the doors to a peaceful settlement had not yet closed. But in anticipation of the British reply, several other points also were being emphasized with urgent insistence.

First, the one method of procedure that Herr Hitler heretofore had excluded was just the one reported to have been proposed in the British reply, namely, direct negotiations between Germany and Poland.

Herr Hitler had considered such negotiations hopeless so long as Poland was backed by British and French guarantees. Therefore, in the words of the *Hamburger Fremdenblatt,* "Britain and France, by virtue of their promise of support given to Poland, alone held the possibility of bringing about a solution of these [Hitler's] terms and the wire that alone opened up the prospects was the wire between London, Paris and Warsaw."

Second, while Britain and France, and also President Roosevelt, put all the emphasis on peaceful methods, which, in respect to revision of the eastern borders, they failed to take advantage of while Germany was disarmed even though the machinery was provided in Article XIX of the League Covenant, Germany put the emphasis of her case on the acceptance of her basis of negotiations and the only basis acceptable to Germany, and proclaimed to the world in Herr Hitler's letter to M. Daladier, "Danzig and the Corridor must return to Germany."

These demands were explained in official quarters as based on the Lansing note of November 5, 1918, which Germany regarded as a preliminary but binding peace pact with the Allied and Associated Powers on the basis of the 14 points among which the thirteenth promised an independent Polish State embracing only territories with indisputably Polish populations, possessing free and secure access to the sea, but nothing more.

This, the Germans claimed, was the legal basis of all their revision demands. The Lansing note was characterized here as binding a word of honor as any that had been given afterwards.

Germany demanded the return of Danzig and that sec-

tion of the Polish Corridor which, on the basis of the
Reichstag elections of 1919, had German majorities
ranging between 60 and 80 per cent. This, it was suggested, would include a corridor from the Baltic to the
regions around Bromberg (Bydgoszcz) and Kelmar
(Chodziez) and presumably Thorn (Torun), but not
the larger part of the former German province of Posen.

Beyond that Herr Hitler in his letter to M. Daladier
demanded the removal of the "Macedonian conditions
on the eastern border" and refused to "renounce nearly
2,000,000 people" who were "maltreated." Just what
these terms implied even the best informed were unable
to explain, but it was suggested that they might mean
the reimposition on Poland of the minority safeguards
that she had repudiated some years ago. The possibility
was not ruled out that they might also include the return of Upper Silesia, which would have solved Germany's coal shortage.

As regards the promised free access to the sea for
Poland, the technical methods for achieving it were left
open to discussion although the method suggested was
that of a free port and extraterritorial transportation
facilities to it as in the case of Lithuania and Memel.
But it was emphasized that the mere promise of such
free access precluded territorial cession since otherwise
the phrase was meaningless.

On that basis official quarters stated that Germany
was willing to negotiate but that the basis itself was un-
alterable. And it was further stated that any attempt at
dilatory tactics by the other side would not be tolerated

and might hasten the catastrophe. No definite time was set but the time-table of German mobilization.

It started Saturday. The initial mobilization necessary for more than defense was to last four days, which meant that it would be finished August 29. Full mobilization was figured to last ten days more, which meant it would be finished September 9. Inasmuch as Germany then expected to stay on the defensive in the west whatever happened and the German army command did not consider isolated Poland a hard nut to crack, Germany would not lose much by waiting till mobilization was completed. But she was also ready to strike at any time.

Meanwhile the German press continued to campaign against Poland with increasing intensity and a profusion of atrocity charges. At the same time it was also concentrating the burden of guilt for the present crisis, not on France, not even on Poland, but on Britain, which was accused of trying to keep Germany down. This accusation, insistently hammered into the German people's mind, was beginning to take effect sufficiently to produce something like a revival of the wartime *Gott strafe England*.

But the time for action came sooner than had been anticipated.

Charging that Germany had been attacked, Chancellor Hitler at 5:11 o'clock on Friday, September 1, issued a proclamation to the army declaring that from then on force would be met with force, and called on the armed forces "to fulfill their duty to the end."

The text of the proclamation read:

"To the defense forces:

The Polish nation refused my efforts for a peaceful regulation of neighborly relations; instead it has appealed to weapons.

Germans in Poland are persecuted with a bloody terror and are driven from their homes. The series of border violations, which are unbearable to a great power, prove that the Poles no longer are willing to respect the German frontier. In order to put an end to this frantic activity no other means is left to me now than to meet force with force.

German defense forces will carry on the battle for the honor of the living rights of the re-awakened German people with firm determination.

I expect every German soldier, in view of the great tradition of eternal German soldiery, to do his duty until the end.

Remember always in all situations you are the representatives of National Socialist Greater Germany!

Long live our people and our Reich!

Berlin, September 1, 1939.

ADOLF HITLER."

The commander-in-chief of the air force issued a decree effective immediately prohibiting the passage of any airplanes over German territory excepting those of the Reich air force or the government.

The naval authorities ordered all German mercantile ships in the Baltic Sea not to run to Danzig or Polish ports.

Anti-air raid defenses were mobilized throughout the country.

Foreign correspondents at an official conference at the Reich Press Ministry at 8:30 o'clock (3:30 A.M. New York time) were told that they would receive every opportunity to facilitate the transmission of dispatches. Wireless stations were instructed to speed up communications and the Ministry installed additional batteries of telephones.

The Reichstag was summoned to meet at 10 o'clock (5 A.M. New York time) to receive a more formal declaration from Herr Hitler.

The Germans announced that foreigners remained in Polish territory at their own risk.

Flying over Polish territory as well as the maritime areas was forbidden by the German authorities and any violators were to be shot down.

When Herr Hitler made his announcement Berlin's streets were still deserted except for the conventional early traffic and there were no outward signs that the nation was finding itself in the first stages of war.

The government area was completely deserted, and the two guards doing sentry duty in front of the Chancellery remained their usual mute symbol of authority. It was only when official placards containing the orders to the populace began to appear on the billboards that early workers became aware of the situation.

An increasing number of border incidents involving shooting and mutual Polish-German casualties were reported by the German press and radio. The most serious was reported from Gleiwitz, a German city on the line where the southwestern portion of Poland meets the Reich.

At 8 P.M. according to the semi-official news agency, a group of Polish insurrectionists forced an entrance into the Gleiwitz radio station, overpowering the watchmen and beating and generally mishandling the attendants. The Gleiwitz station was relaying a Breslau station's program, which was broken off by the Poles.

They proceeded to broadcast a prepared proclamation, partly in Polish and partly in German, announcing themselves as "the Polish Volunteer Corps of Upper Silesia speaking from the Polish station in Gleiwitz." The city, they alleged, was in Polish hands.

Gleiwitz's surprised radio listeners notified the police, who halted the broadcast and exchanged fire with the insurrectionists, killing one and capturing the rest. The police were said to have discovered that the attackers had been assisted by regular Polish troops.

The Gleiwitz incident was alleged in Berlin to have been the signal "for a general attack by Polish *franctireurs* on German territory."

Two other points—Pitschen, near Kreuzburg, and Hochlinden, northeast of Ratibor, both in the same vicinity as Gleiwitz, were the scenes of violations of the German boundary, it was claimed, with fighting at both places still under way.

The attackers were all said to have been heavily armed and supported by details of the regular Polish

Army. It was reported that German border guards repulsed all the attempts.

Polish insurrectionists and soldiers were alleged to have stormed the Hochlinden Custom House, which was recaptured by Germans after a battle lasting for an hour and a half.

On Sunday, September 3, according to well-informed quarters, Moscow was already supposed to have notified Paris and London that if France and Britain joined in the present Reich-Polish conflict Russia would find herself compelled to revise her Western borders.

This was tantamount to the threat that any British and French help to Poland would merely hasten the partition of Poland between Germany and Russia. There were hints that Russia might also seek other "compensation" in regions even less convenient to Britain.

As an impressive demonstration of this new co-operation there arrived by air from Stockholm a new Russian Ambassador and a new embassy secretary, both of whom were said to be very close to Premier Vyacheslaff Molotoff, and a Russian military mission headed by a commanding general.

The new Ambassador was Alexander Shkhartzeff, who, it was pointed out, collaborated with Mr. Molotoff in the Commissariat of Foreign Affairs in Moscow. The new embassy secretary was Vladimir Perloff, up to then Mr. Molotoff's secretary and interpreter.

The military mission consisted of General Maxim Purjakoff, designated as the Military Plenipotentiary of the U.S.S.R., and his staff; Brigadier General Michael

Beljakoff, Colonel Nikolai Skornjakoff, Major Basanoff and Captain Alexander Seditch.

To show the importance of the occasion the members were met at Tempelhof Airfield by Dr. Ernst Woermann, Under-Secretary of State in the Foreign Office; Baron Alexander von Doernberg, Chief of Protocol, and other Foreign Office officials. Lieutenant General Seifert, commander of Berlin, headed the list of army officers greeting the Russians. A guard of honor presented arms.

The Russians received an ovation as their automobiles, flying the hammer-and-sickle flag of the Soviet Union, passed the Reich Chancellery. Those assembled along the street gave the Nazi salute.

Adding importance to all this was the fact that it was announced at midnight that Herr Hitler would receive the new Ambassador, together with the Military Plenipotentiary, for the submission of credentials later that day, which set a precedent for diplomatic speed.

That such a formidable military mission was sent here to work out close collaboration with the German Army was taken for granted. But German quarters still held that the consultative clauses of the German-Russian pact were sufficient to cover all the collaboration necessary and a formal military alliance might be signed only as the last trump card to impress London and Paris.

Ambassador Joseph Lipski and his whole embassy staff left Berlin that morning under safe conduct en route to Sweden, which had also taken over the representation of Polish interests. The German Embassy staff was supposed to have left Warsaw at the same time. German interests in Poland were being represented by the Netherlands. Official quarters held, however, that this merely represented a "cessation of direct diplomatic relations," not a formal break of relations, just as there was no declared state of war.

Meanwhile, since the German-Polish conflict was now being arbitrated by the roar of cannon, the reported military successes also dictated the German answer to the British and French ultimatums that the Germans get out of Poland. For that reason it was safe to say that the German reply, which was to be delivered to Sir Nevile Henderson and Robert Coulondre, the British and French Ambassadors, would bluntly and categorically reject any such suggestion, irrespective of the consequences.

At the same time it was also foreshadowed in well-informed quarters that the rest of what promised to be a lengthy note would be in a wholly conciliatory tone in accord with the fact that British and French ultimatums had no time limit, therefore they were not ultimatums in the strict legal sense.

According to forecasts the German reply would once again present the whole German political and legal thesis in respect to the German-Polish problem. In particular it was expected to repudiate emphatically all efforts, such as made by Premier Edouard Daladier of France, to characterize Germany as the aggressor. International law, it was pointed out, was perfectly familiar with the concepts of provoked and unprovoked attack.

The German thesis claimed that the German invasion of Poland was provoked by previous Polish attacks by both Polish insurgents and regular troops and the fact, as then demonstrated by its resistance, that Wester-platte, in Danzig harbor, had been fortified in violation of all Danzig treaties, was characterized here in itself as Polish aggression.

In general the German stand still was that the conflict was merely a German-Polish affair which did not touch any British or French interests. Nevertheless the reply was also expected to detail Chancellor Hitler's efforts to find a solution without war, including acceptance of the British mediation offer, which seemed to have delayed German military action exactly one week. And according to authoritative forecasts the reply was expected to end on the note that even then efforts at mediation to end the German-Polish conflict to prevent its extension into a general conflagration were still open though, naturally, on new terms. That these terms would be higher than the last was taken for granted.

These forecasts apparently had in mind Premier Mussolini's proposal for a five-power conference. But this proposal, which apparently had been holding up the German reply, was turned down by Prime Minister Chamberlain unless the Germans retire from Poland first, which was held out of the question.

However, there was talk in German quarters that having attained all her "war aims," Germany was perfectly willing to call a truce and negotiate a new settlement in the east, which later might be followed by a general world settlement. It was always emphasized in German pronouncements that while Herr Hitler was determined to attain his objectives these objectives nevertheless were limited.

How and from what quarter the new mediation effort was to come was difficult to see.

In any case the official German News Bureau declared that despite the present situation Germany was willing to explore all possibilities of such mediation even if she did not overestimate the chances of success.

If, however, the new mediation effort failed the Germans now put their best bet not on the Italian but on the Russian card.

At the same time German official organs and the press continued to propound the German thesis that the German action was wholly due to Polish stubbornness and the blank check given to Warsaw by France and Britain who, therefore, were responsible for both the present undeclared war and any extension of it.

In reply to Prime Minister Chamberlain's assertions that Britain and Poland had not been informed of the German terms, it was pointed out in semi-official statements that the sixteen points, which were to form the basis of direct German-Polish negotiations, had been read and explained to Ambassador Henderson by Foreign Minister Joachim von Ribbentrop personally at a midnight conference on Wednesday, or thirty hours before the German troops marched, and that in view of the modern means of communication, these could have been transmitted in a few hours. Despite this, the Germans argued, the Poles had not only refused to accept them, but had mobilized by the British suggestion and still asserted that these terms were wholly unacceptable.

A semi-official statement also refuted Mr. Chamberlain's assertion that M. Lipski had told Herr von Ribbentrop on Thursday that Poland was willing to negotiate on an equal basis. What M. Lipski did say, according to this statement, was that Warsaw was informed from London that Germany was willing to negotiate directly with Warsaw and that the Polish Government was then considering this proposal.

Following is a British dispatch of September 3:

"On September 2nd His Majesty's Ambassador in Berlin was instructed to inform the German Government that unless they were prepared to give His Majesty's Government in the United Kingdom satisfactory assurances that the German Government had suspended all aggressive action against Poland and were prepared promptly to withdraw their forces from Polish territory, His Majesty's Government in the United Kingdom would without hesitation fulfill their obligations to Poland.

"At morning His Majesty's Ambassador in Berlin informed the German Government that unless not later than 11 A.M., British Summer time, today, September 3rd, satisfactory assurances to the above effect had been given by the German Government and had reached His Majesty's Government in London a state of war would exist between the two countries as from that hour.

"His Majesty's Government are now awaiting the receipt of any reply that may be made by the German Government."

At 9 o'clock that same night, September 3, 1939, Chancellor Hitler left Berlin, presumably for the Eastern Front. He had previously sent a message to the Eastern Army stating that he was joining them.

He left the city in a heavily guarded special train that mounted anti-aircraft artillery. He was accompanied by his Foreign Minister, Joachim von Ribbentrop, and by Field Marshal Hermann Goering. It was supposed that their destination was Stolp, Pomerania, where the headquarters of the Eastern Army was believed to be located.

The departure of the Chancellor ended a day of proclamations from the Chancellery. There was an appeal to the German people, a proclamation to the Nazi party, a message to the soldiers of the Eastern Army and another to the troops manning the Westwall. There was also given out the text of a German memorandum answering the British ultimatum.

Perhaps the most significant feature of all these proclamations and of the memorandum was that they did not mention France, sidetracked Poland and concentrated all the fury of German wrath, as in 1914, against England—or at least the British Government. That government was accused of rejecting frequently profered German friendship and of trying to strangle the German people in order to dominate the world—a goal to which Germany was said never to have aspired. There were, however, some significant differences.

The memorandum was a diplomatic document. It

restated Germany's case in the conflict with Poland. It accused the "British Cabinet policy" of preventing every peaceful revision of the treaty of Versailles, of encouraging Poland to commit aggressive acts against German people in German territory and of having rejected Premier Mussolini's last peace conference proposal, which the German Government, it said, accepted.

Therefore, said the memorandum, "the British Government bears the responsibility for all the misery and suffering which have now come and will come over many nations."

The semi-official news service, *Dienst aus Deutschland,* charged that "England betrays Europe," and all the press was unanimous in agreement with these words of the *Völkischer Beobachter*:

"It is not old, weak Chamberlain nor the British people who are guilty of this war, but international Jewish high finance and its Masonic general staff of the ilk of Churchill, Eden, Duff Cooper and King-Hall, on whom the peoples of the West—after their awakening—will take bloody vengeance."

"We enter this battle with a pure, believing heart," concludes the *Völkischer Beobachter,* "for a final victory of a new Europe against the powers of reactionary darkness, against the tumbling world of this Jewish-liberalistic century."

The *Hamburg Fremdenblatt* saw proof of a victory for the "English war party" in the fact that the British torpedoed Signor Mussolini's conference proposal, which France also favored, and that while no time limit was set for the German answer, even when the British and French Ambassadors called for an early reply the previous evening, a provocative time limit of two hours was set for the government of a big power at the meeting this morning.

Chronologically the last crowded hours in Berlin of what remained of peace in Europe brought forth the following:

At 9 A.M. Sir Nevile Henderson called on Herr von Ribbentrop at the Foreign Office and delivered to him what the German communiqué called a "challenging" note, that unless by 11 A.M. the German Government gave a satisfactory answer to the British ultimatum of Friday demanding that German troops evacuate Polish territory Britain would consider herself at war with Germany.

Herr von Ribbentrop immediately informed Sir Nevile that Germany would reject the demand, whereupon Sir Nevile replied that he would call again at 11:30 A.M.

When 11 o'clock had passed there was no German reply.

Thereupon Sir Nevile called again at the Foreign Office at 11:30 but had to wait four minutes for Herr von Ribbentrop to come over from the adjoining Reich chancellery where he had collaborated with Herr Hitler in drafting Germany's answering note.

The last conference between the exponent of Germany's dynamic foreign policy and one of the most convinced representatives of the British "appeasement" policy was as brief as it was dramatic. It lasted only four minutes and in those four minutes the dice were cast for war.

Herr von Ribbentrop read Sir Nevile a draft of a lengthy memorandum which later was transmitted to him in writing, which in the first blunt paragraph declared:

"The German Reich Government and German people decline to receive and accept, even less to fulfill, any ultimate demands from the British Government."

Thereupon Sir Nevile said his adieus and left.

At 12:15 Robert Coulondre, the French Ambassador, called on Herr von Ribbentrop and informed him that the French Government conformed to the policy of the British Government and that France would automatically consider herself in a state of war with Germany at 5 P.M. No further diplomatic exchanges being necessary, M. Coulondre bade his farewell and departed.

Following this both the British and French Ambassadors turned over the representation of the interests of their respective countries to Alexander Kirk, the American chargé d'affairs, and prepared to leave with their embassy staffs for home via Belgium the next morning. German interests were to be taken care of in London by Switzerland and in Paris by Sweden.

THE QUESTION OF WAR GUILT

In a communiqué bristling with charges of "brazen lies and historic forgeries," the German Government

replied in December to the French Yellow Book[1] on
the causes of the war. Germany characterized that book
as "a striking confession of Anglo-French war guilt."

The German answer was built in the main around two
points: first, that France and Great Britain did nothing
to induce Poland to submit to the German will, which
showed they wanted war; second, that the French Yellow Book lied when it asserted that Poland never rejected Chancellor Hitler's 16-point program.

This is the document that Foreign Minister Joachim
von Ribbentrop himself declared to be no longer "actual" when he first read it to Sir Nevile Henderson, the
British Ambassador, at midnight on August 30. The reason was that the Polish radio and the Polish news
agency had rejected it just before the Germans marched
into Poland.

The German communiqué specifically designated as
an "official pronouncement" read:

"The Yellow Book regarding the origins of the war,
published by the French Government, after considerable
hesitation yesterday confirms the guilt of the Western
powers for the outbreak of the war. This collection of
documents is a wholly arbitrary, incomplete selection of
writings that do not deal with the events most important
in causing the outbreak of the war.

"But even in this form, it proves anew that the Western powers did nothing to keep Poland from the road
to disaster. The aggressive will of Polish chauvinism
and the violence inflicted on the German folk, known to

---

[1] Published in the United States by Reynal & Hitchcock, New York.

the world in all its details today, was deliberately tolerated by the Western powers in order to force Germany
in justified self-defense to answer force with force so
that a pretext might be furnished to the nations of
Western Europe for beginning an encirclement war.

"In this connection it is necessary first to point out
some striking contradictions and lies in the Yellow Book.
It asserts, for instance, that the Reich Foreign Minister
on a visit to Paris in December, 1938 declared that after
his return he would immediately give new consideration
to the question of an international guarantee for Czecho-
Slovakia. The exact opposite is true.

"The Reich Foreign Minister replied to the French
Foreign Minister, when the latter touched on this subject, that any attempt to raise this question would again
darken Franco-German relations, whereupon Bonnet
[Georges Bonnet, then French Foreign Minister] likewise plainly indicated that henceforth France would dis-
interest herself from Eastern questions.

"The Yellow Book likewise attempts to warm up the
old propaganda lies regarding events during the visit of
President Hacha [of Czecho-Slovakia] to Berlin in
March, 1939. Reports by the French Ambassador, who
could have no personal knowledge of these events, must,
after all that has been published on the German official
side, be characterized as a plain historic forgery.

"Only the Anglo-French desire for war can explain,
furthermore, that the French Ambassador in Berlin
could be brazen enough in a report of August 17 to represent the echo of the German press to persecution of

folk Germans in Poland as a means of propaganda designed to furnish the pretext for German intervention.

"This will to war on the part of the Western Powers inevitably regarded the last generous proposal by the Führer to Poland as a grave danger. This, too, is openly admitted in the Yellow Book. True, it maintains that France and Britain intervened in Warsaw in order that Poland would now really accept the process of direct discussion originally demanded by England and already sanctioned by Poland.

"But the true intentions of Anglo-French policy are revealed by Ambassador [Robert] Coulondre, who reports to his government that a visit by [Polish Foreign Minister Josef] Beck to Berlin would necessarily represent a 'serious drawback' because it would mean a great 'moral success' for Germany which was to be denied to the National Socialist Government.

"The German proposal to Poland [the so-called 16 points], communicated to the British Ambassador on the evening of Aug. 30 and published to the world on Aug. 31, were acknowledged by the international public as a just, fair attempt to reach a solution. Even French propaganda must, therefore, assert that Poland never rejected this proposal.

"Actually the Polish radio at 11 P.M. on Aug. 31 characterized the German proposals as unacceptable and impudent. The French Yellow Book attempts to do away with this declaration of the official Polish broadcasting station by a brazen lie. It maintains that this Polish answer does not refer to the German plan pub-

lished at 9 P.M. on Aug. 31 at all, but to a German note
to the British Government of Aug. 29.

"As everybody can read in the German White Book,
however, the Polish radio broadcast begins with this
sentence: 'Today's pronouncement of the German official communiqué has clearly shown the aims and intentions of German policy,' and then summarizes what are
known as the sixteen points.

"For the rest, the official Polish news agency P. A. T.
expressed itself similarly regarding the German plan on
the evening of Aug. 31. It writes:

" 'Political circles in Warsaw reacted very categorically to the German memorandum with its proposals
regarding regulation of German-Polish relations. These
circles assert that at the climax of the present situation
German aggression had dropped the mask. For that reason the decision of the Polish Government to raise all
its forces for defense of the State was justified especially in view of the German pronouncement.'

"Despite a brazen lie, it will be impossible therefore
to deny that on Aug. 31 Poland flatly rejected a generous German proposal. According to the Yellow Book,
the Warsaw radio rejected not the sixteen points but
proposals contained in a German note of Aug. 29, because these—according to the French view—contained
'Draconic' conditions, fulfillment of which would have
left a scarcely independent Polish rump State.

"As a matter of fact, the German note of Aug. 29
poses a fundamental principle: Solution of the Danzig
and Corridor questions and assurance for the life of Ger-

man folk groups in the rest of Poland, which then were supplemented by moderate execution proposals in an extensive plan communicated to Ambassador Henderson on Aug. 30. There was no question of a threat to Polish independence or 'Draconic' conditions in the note of Aug. 29, for it specifically stated:

" 'For the rest, the German Government in making its proposals had never the intention to attack the vital interests of Poland or endanger the existence of an independent Polish State.'

"At the last hour Germany made Poland a just proposal. Poland rejected this proposal. The governments of the Western powers wanted this rejection and therefore did nothing to prevent it. They feared an agreement, especially since that might have represented a 'moral success' for the German peace policy.

"The French people, who today must bear the consequences of this policy, shall not be convinced by lies and misrepresentations that the 'peaceful solution of the international crisis in honor and dignity for all nations,' as [Premier Edouard] Daladier demanded in his letter to the Führer on August 26, had not been permitted by Germany. In truth, however, this Yellow Book, which will be discussed in greater detail later, is, just as the British Blue Book, a striking confession of Anglo-French war guilt."

XXI

POLAND—THE FIRST VICTIM

THE following dispatches on the fate of Poland are reprinted in the form in which they were originally written:

WITH THE GERMAN ARMIES IN POLAND, September 11.—Having hurled against Poland their mighty military machine, the Germans are today crushing Poland like a soft-boiled egg.

After having broken through the shell of Polish border defenses, the Germans found inside, in comparison with their own forces, little more than a soft yolk, and they have penetrated that in many directions without really determined general resistance by the Polish Army.

That is the explanation of the apparent Polish military collapse in so short a time as it was gathered on a tour of the Polish battlefields made by this correspondent in the wake of the German Army and, sometimes, in the backwash of a day's battle while scattered Polish troops and snipers were still taking potshots at motor vehicles on the theory that they must be German. But such is the firm confidence of the Germans that a cocked pistol in front of the army driver is held to be sufficient protection for the foreign correspondents in their charge.

289

Even a casual glance at the battlefields, gnarled by trenches, barbed-wire entanglements, shell holes, blown-up roads and bridges and shelled and gutted towns, indicates that the Poles made determined resistance at the border. But even these border defenses seem weak, and beyond them there is nothing.

It is a mystery to both Germans and neutral military experts on the tour with the writer that the Poles made no provisions for second or third lines and that in retreat they did not make any attempt to throw up earthworks or dig trenches such as helped the Germans stop the Allies after the Marne retreat in 1914.

In fact, the only tactics the Poles seemed to have pursued in the retreat were to fall back on towns from which, later, they were either easily driven out by artillery fire or just as easily flanked. But presumably neither their number nor their equipment, which, judging from the remnants thrown along the road of retreat, was pitifully light as compared with the Germans', permitted them to do anything else in view of the enormous length of the border they had to defend.

Again God has been with the bigger battalions, for the beautiful, dry weather, while converting Polish roads into choking dust clouds on the passage of motor vehicles, has kept them from turning into mud as would be normal at this time of year; this has permitted the German motorized divisions to display the speed they have.

But the Germans have proceeded not only with might and speed, but with method, and this bids fair to be the first war to be decided not by infantry, "the queen of all arms," but by fast motorized divisions and, especially, by the air force.

The first effort of the Germans was concentrated on defeating the hostile air fleet, which they did not so much by air battle but by consistent bombing of airfields and destruction of the enemy's ground organization. Having accomplished this, they had obtained domination of the air, which in turn enabled them, first, to move their own vast transports ahead without danger from the air and, second, to bomb the Poles' communications to smithereens, thereby reducing their mobility to a minimum.

Today the German rule of the air is so complete that, although individual Polish planes may still be seen flying at a high altitude, the German army has actually abandoned the blackout in Poland. It is a strange sensation to come from a Germany thrown into Stygian darkness at night to a battlefront town like Lodz, as this correspondent did the night after the Germans announced its occupation, and find it illuminated although the enemy is only a few miles from the city.

With control of the air, the Germans moved forward not infantry but their tanks, armored cars and motorized artillery, which smashed any Polish resistance in the back. This is easy to understand when one has seen the methods of open warfare attempted by the Poles and an almost amateurish attempt at digging earthworks for machine-gun nests.

To German and neutral experts the Poles seem to have clung to eighteenth-century war methods, which, in view of modern firing volume and weight, are not only odd but also futile. This does not mean that the Poles have not put up a brave fight. They have, and the Germans themselves freely admit it.

As a purely military matter, the German army is the height of efficiency. It moves like clockwork, without hurry and apparently almost in a leisurely manner. Yet that army moves with inexorable exactitude. The roads into Poland are jammed but not choked with heavy vans and motor trucks carrying food and munitions, while the Poles have to depend mainly on their smashed railroads or on horse carts. Bombed bridges are soon passable for the Germans and they move forward quickly. Communication lines follow them almost automatically.

Poland may not be lost yet and may be even able to offer further resistance by withdrawing into the eastern swamp. But as long as the present disparity between the military resources and her will to fight exists she faces terrible odds.

NOWOGROD, Poland, Sept. 26.—The victorious German Army, which early this month broke through the supposedly impregnable Polish Narew fortifications within 48 hours, to-day evacuated all the territory east of the Pissa and Narew Rivers, which form the German-Russian demarcation line in the north. The Germans left it and its population, like the larger part of all Poland, to the Soviet Russian troops and the bolshevist regime.

Now this army of veterans is moving toward the west to face the French and British. All roads in East Prussia are crammed with lines of military transports many miles long. Some of these trains are apparently heading west along the land routes; others move northward to Baltic ports, from which they are being transshipped west by German ocean liners.

The evacuation was scheduled to coincide with the arrival of the Russians at the Narew at noon today, but as the Russians were late a group of foreign correspondents, including this writer, were still able to penetrate to the ruins of what once was called Nowogrod on the Russian side of the demarcation line to view the scene of one of the decisive battles of the Polish campaign. They could also learn from German officers who participated in the battle how the Polish "national line" was broken and could witness the flight and dread of the abandoned population.

Perhaps one of the most significant things learned on the

trip was that, although Berlin official quarters still speak of a merely temporary military demarcation line, the armies look at it as a matter of course only as the new border. In fact, army circles seem surprised that it is called anything else, and this perhaps has something to do with Foreign Minister Joachim von Ribbentrop's projected visit to Moscow.

Moreover, this new "border" seems to be a compromise reached after considerable negotiations. For it appears that both the Germans and Russians asked for more than they got or perhaps expected to get, and that the solution found a middle line.

Incidentally, contact between the German and Russian armies did not take place without the classic accident. Russians mistook the earth-brown uniforms of the German Labor Service, now part of the army, for Polish troops and unleashed an artillery barrage that killed nine German labor soldiers and wounded four. Three German armored cars were smashed before the misunderstanding was cleared up. Since then, the two armies have maintained a certain distance between them.

Impressive as was the quick German victory on the Narew, even more impressive is the army that achieved it. This army today passed, so to say, in review before the correspondents. For this army was a living triumph of military motorization, which in the German view at least now has demonstrated its superiority over any other form of locomotion on every kind of terrain and in any weather.

According to the German testimony, the modern motor has been able to conquer ground where no motor was supposed to go before—even on Polish roads, which in part, however, proved to be better than their reputation—and motors received direct credit for the speed of the German victory.

The entire northern army is completely motorized. Infantry no longer marches, but rides in trucks; even horses have become a rarity. Thousands of motor vehicles of all kinds—all up to date—take the place of long columns of infantry.

There are light 7-ton and heavy 24-ton tanks, light and heavy armored cars for the so-called "fast divisions," light motorized field artillery and heavy motorized 15-centimeter fortification howitzers, motorized anti-tank guns, motorized pioneer troops and motorized communication troops, regiments of motorcyclists and even bicycle troops, but only one lonely horse-drawn field battery could be discovered on the road and marching troops could be seen only in garrison towns.

The prowess of such an army has been demonstrated. Its accomplishments are worth telling in detail for the lesson they may hold for the West.

The particular army group that broke through the Narew line at Nowogrod first came west out of East Prussia to conquer the fortress of Graudenz (Grudziadz) and then turned East against the Narew on Sept. 7. The Narew was fortified for 35 kilometers by a line of "bunkers" or huge steel and concrete pill-boxes, which protected every possible crossing not protected by swamps. A dozen such bunkers were just outside Nowogrod, built only this year according to the latest French and Czech models and located in terrain ideal for defense.

The Germans advanced on the Narew on Sept. 8, and one company even crossed it in rubber boats without one shot being fired. But then the Poles opened up with machine-gun fire from the bunkers and from artillery behind them, with the result that the German advance company was cut off and the Germans stalled.

All the next day heavy fighting continued. German artillery concentrated on pounding the bunkers but without noticeable effect. Largely from the revelations of prisoners, the positions of Polish artillery were located and the guns silenced. The Germans also succeeded in pounding Nowogrod into ruins and silencing the heavy Polish machine gun fire from the town. All further attempts to cross the Narew, however, failed because rubber boats were shot to pieces from the bunkers, which also made bridge-building impossible.

Thereupon, during the night of the 10th, the Germans moved up heavy artillery right to the river's edge, concentrating their fire on individual bunkers from a distance of only 3,000 feet. Even then, as shown by an inspection today, not one shot actually penetrated through the steel and concrete into the bunkers themselves. But, according to German officers, the impact of the rain of shells was such that the Polish crews were made to feel the whole pill-boxes were turning around and it "drove the soldiers inside crazy."

Some of the bunker crews came out and surrendered; others had to be "smoked out." For that purpose a German advance company, which meanwhile had dug itself in, "ran under" the machine-gun fire; that is, ran through the fire so close to the bunkers that the machine guns could not be trained on them. Then they used flame-throwers or hand grenades to finish the crews inside or drive them out.

Desperate counterattacks by the Poles on Nowogrod came too late and collapsed under German machine-gun fire, which virtually exterminated whole regiments. On the evening of Sept. 10 the impenetrable Polish lines had been penetrated.

In the view of German officers, the Narew line would have been really impenetrable but for two things. One was the break in the morale of the Polish troops, who had no notion of modern artillery fire and could not stand up to it although they fought bravely otherwise. The second and most important, however, was insufficient Polish artillery backing. Had the Poles possessed enough artillery to keep the German guns from advancing too closely to the bunkers and keep the German planes from bombing them, the Germans feel that they might be fighting there yet.

But the Polish arms were both insufficient and strange, a mixture of French and English with old German, Austrian and Russian guns of varying calibers which were simply outclassed by the German armaments.

Meanwhile, the whole town of Nowogrod looks like a burned forest of smokestacks that somehow still stand erect. Only one house in the market place had been left miraculously without a scratch. Some few inhabitants were returning today, possibly to search the ruins of their homes for any small belongings that may have escaped the shells and flames. They are a terror-striken, bewildered lot who have saved only what they could carry on their backs, and that was not much. Hunger is written on their faces, fear lurks in their eyes. The children especially have acquired almost an animal look, furtive and savage because of the brutal experiences they do not comprehend.

As usually happens, refugees surrounded the strange civilian group of correspondents and eagerly clutched the few bits of food we had available. But the characteristic irony of the situation, in view of the impending approach of the Russians, was that the conquered begged their conquerors to remain and not abandon them to the Bolsheviki.

These were city folk. The peasants, seemingly unconcerned, again were tending their fields, although if the Bolsheviki should be established there, they probably would be ranked as kulaks.

On the other hand, judging by the expressions of the new German rulers in the conquered territory, Poles as Poles are doomed there as well.

"The Polish collapse," said Civil Commissar Kiessling of Thorn in a speech there, "these days has proved anew the inferiority of the Poles. There can be no leniency. In future we cannot work with such people. There are also decent Poles. Rather from their attitude we shall draw unequivocal conclusions. Poland was German, is German, remains German. Outwardly these things still look different in respect to the population. But what the Poles did not accomplish in twenty years we shall accomplish in three years. That is now our main task."

WITH THE GERMAN ARMY, Before Warsaw, Poland, Sept. 28.—The German campaign in Poland came to an end today when the fortress of Modlin followed Warsaw in surrendering unconditionally at 7 o'clock this morning. At the same time the bulk of the German army had returned to the western side of the German-Russian demarcation line, which army circles regard as the new Reich border.

With that surrender of the last fort defending the city, Germany has attained her war aims in the East, namely, the partition of Poland, in exactly four weeks. She is already at work organizing the newly-won territory in order to enhance its agricultural and industrial resources.

Again Chancellor Hitler has proved himself the *Mehrer*, or aggrandizer, of the Reich. To his political triumph he has added an unprecedented military triumph as well.

But German army quarters are perfectly well aware that this new aggrandizement has been obtained at a high price that is not measured by German casualties, which are comparatively small, but by the fact that, in place of weak Poland, Germany has again put powerful Russia on her eastern flank. Army circles are so aware of this new situation that they frankly declare:

"Germany must now be stronger than ever, not only to

win the conflict with France and Britain but also to prepare for the inevitable dispute with Soviet Russia that must come some day."

In fact that is the consolation the German army offers the conquered foe remaining on the German side of the demarcation line who still fear National Socialist Germany less than they do Bolshevist Russia.

The final dramatic scenes of Warsaw's and Modlin's surrender were witnessed by this writer together with a group of other foreign correspondents who arrived at the German front line on the edge of the capital yesterday afternoon to find Warsaw in flames and Modlin still being bombed and shelled to pieces.

We stood at the same spot on the Warsaw-Modlin road where General Werner von Fritsch fell and where a Polish army officer with a white flag had appeared a few hours earlier to offer the surrender of the city.

Around us stood German troops in their first line positions and there also lay the Polish dead. In front of us some 250 yards away, stood the Polish advance guards in the shelter of a gateway, guns in hands, silently and suspiciously watching every move on their enemy's front.

Where they stood began the sea of houses that was Warsaw. Dense columns of smoke rose high above the Polish capital, which the evening sun painted with a rosy glow that turned blood red. Behind us, in the background, was Modlin, where fighting still continued and which was just being shelled and bombed by a German air attack. The roar of cannon, the bursting of bombs could be heard plainly to be followed a little later by the roar of the engines of the attacking planes. Appropriately enough, Modlin was overhung by sinister-looking storm clouds into which the evening sun put enough reflected light to convert them into an autumnal background for the columns of smoke and dust rising from the bursting bombs.

When we arrived at the front line firing had ceased, but the Germans still watched enemy movements as closely as did the Poles. For only today, after the "stop firing order" had been sounded for 9:30 in the morning, some misunderstanding arose as a result of which the Poles resumed fire with rifles, grenades, mine-throwers and machine guns about 11 A.M. The Germans replied with artillery until a few more houses went up in flames.

What most interested veterans of former wars in our party, however, was the fact that despite motorization and other mechanical improvements on the war machine, modern warfare had really changed little and that its quintessence, as represented by the front line, was still mud holes.

The mud holes of this line, which happily for their occupants were dry, consisted of tiny dugouts about five yards apart manned as a rule by one or two men armed with rifles and hand grenades, while machine guns were posted at strategic points. Behind this first line were deeper trenches manned by larger but still remarkably small troop contingents with rifles, machine guns and mine-throwers. After that, for a long distance, came nothing—at least so far as the eye could detect.

In fact, the closer one gets to the front line, the emptier the landscape appears. All outward activity, the mile-long transports and the marching troops, can be seen only far behind the front, usually out of range of artillery fire. But this emptiness behind the front is merely modern camouflage, and any flare-up of serious fighting soon converts innocent-looking woods and peaceful-looking houses into fire-spitting infernos.

The present positions, which will be maintained until all preparations are completed for the German occupation of

Warsaw tomorrow, were not established until Sunday. They were so recent and had been under such heavy fire that dead Polish soldiers still lay where they had fallen amid dead horses and abandoned equipment. In the pathetic inertness of their sprawling bodies, they somehow, perhaps because of their surroundings, looked more like inanimate objects than bodies that once were living men, and in the growing darkness their faces began to resemble those of mummies. If war robs death of its majesty, nature compensates by covering up some of the gruesomeness, enabling active men to keep sane.

A weapon more modern even than firearms, propaganda, was also being used right at the front line. A large poster displayed by the Germans announced in Polish:

"Poles! Come to us. We will not hurt you. We will give you bread."

As explained by German staff officers, Warsaw was first treated as an open city and only military objectives were bombed or shelled. Then, however, General Czuma, commander of the defense, restored the old Warsaw forts, such as Modlin, the last to hold out, and established defense lines around the city. Whereupon the German army command announced it would treat Warsaw as a fortress and shell and bomb it.

But this threat failed to weaken the city's defense. The Germans then offered a truce to evacuate diplomats and the civilian population and called for the Polish representative to appear at a designated point to negotiate.

After this the Germans sent airplanes over Warsaw, throwing millions of leaflets calling on the city to surrender, promising soldiers would be sent home instead of being made war prisoners, and that in view of their brave defense, officers would be permitted to keep their swords. The appeal to the officers was considered especially important because, in the German view, the backbone of the defense consisted of officers who had left their surrendering troops outside and had rallied within Warsaw in regiments consisting for the most part of officers only. When that failed, two truces were arranged—one for evacuating foreign diplomats, who arrived in Königsberg, East Prussia, recently, and another for evacuating 62 Soviet diplomats after the Russian occupation of Eastern Poland.

Only then, according to German officers, did the real bombardment start. The forts, and especially the old citadel, were heavily bombed and shelled, as were the barracks, airport and such inferior points as had been observed. As a result, many buildings also were damaged, including, it is understood, the former royal palace. A Polish truce officer, as well as others from Warsaw, asserted that, in fact, a large part of the city is merely "heaps of ruins."

Finally, late Tuesday night a Polish officer bearing a white flag appeared at the German front line and asked for a truce to evacuate the civilian population and the wounded. This was refused and the final unconditional surrender was announced early yesterday morning.

Shortly before midnight last night another Polish officer, a major, appeared at Army Corps Headquarters where he was cordially received, to arrange for the surrender of Modlin. He carried a letter from General Rommel, commander of the Polish army around Warsaw, ordering the commander of Modlin to give up.

Accompanied by a group of German officers and announced by a trumpet signal, the Polish major was taken to the Polish front line before Modlin at 1 A.M. A white banner held up on two sticks by two German soldiers was illuminated by a powerful searchlight supplied by a portable dynamo. In conjunction with the bright moonlight, this rather romantic scene was reminiscent of former rather than present-day practices.

The German demand was surrender by 6 A.M., to be announced by a white flag over the Modlin citadel. When the flag failed to appear promptly the bombing and artillery bombardment of Modlin was resumed and could be heard plainly at our headquarters. Only then the last Polish center of resistance excepting an isolated band on the peninsula of Hela, near Danzig, gave up. The white flag floated over Modlin. The last shot in the German-Polish War had been fired at 7 o'clock this morning.

Today German heavy artillery and munitions trains already are moving westward again, carrying Polish flags and eagles as trophies and bearing on trucks and caissons short inscriptions such as:

"To hell with Poland and England" or "Warsaw-Paris express."

Details of how General von Fritsch was killed in action just before the Polish-German War came to an end were learned here at the front today.

According to this account, General von Fritsch had helped in front-line observation posts throughout the campaign and did so again last Friday in a major reconnaissance attack undertaken with infantry, artillery and bombers to test out the Polish line's strength. Suddenly from a house where no enemy previously was observed, the Poles started a heavy machine-gun fire. A bullet hit General von Fritsch in the thigh and severed an artery. A lieutenant accompanying him tried to bind up the wound but the general merely said:

"Please do not bother!"

These were his last words. Two minutes later he was dead. Despite a heavy fire, the lieutenant carried the body of his commander to the rear.

BERLIN, Nov. 12.—The first hint regarding the policy that Germany proposes to pursue in the Gouvernement General of Poland, consisting of the German share of Poland in so far as it is not annexed to the Reich directly, is contained in the official pronouncements appearing today in the first issue of the *Warschauer Zeitung,* a German language publication issued under German Government auspices for all of rump Poland.

The purpose of the new publication in rump Poland, as outlined by Dr. Joseph Goebbels, Propaganda Minister, in an introductory article, is "to be the bearer of the political will and to be the cultural mission of the German people in the Eastland."

According to the programatic declaration by the Governor General, Hans Frank, the Poles in the Gouvernement General will be permitted in their relations with each other to do what they consider useful according to their own principles of life. But, he stresses, they must always remain conscious of the fact that in view of the neighborhood of the mighty Greater German Reich they must refrain from doing anything that might impair the vital interests of the German people.

"I am aware," Governor Frank continues, "that this country contains not only political visionaries but also diligent, active workers. These will be all the more willing to subordinate themselves to just methods of work under German leadership because it will bring them fulfillment of their own inner necessities, never realized within the Polish state.

"Those certain circles, however, which hitherto, in complete misunderstanding of the real situation, led the country from catastrophe to catastrophe, will be curbed in their trade."

From these pronouncements it would appear that the program of "reconstruction" and Germanization, which undertakes to reduce the Poles to a helot class, working under the control and supervision of the German "master race," is to be extended to rump Poland.

Moreover, as revealed by the German incorporation of Lodz—now Germanized into Lodsch—the largest part of the German share of Poland is being annexed by the Reich directly. Official quarters declare that so far nothing can be said about the ultimate border between the Reich proper and the Gouvernement General of Poland, but according to hints in the press it appears that this border includes nearly twice as much Polish territory in the Reich as was taken from the Reich by the Treaty of Versailles.

Judging by these hints the Reich border may be expected to run from just south of Maehrisch-Ostrau (Moravska-Ostrayal) along the old 1914 frontier of Upper Silesia and then northward to include the coal mines of Dobrowa, then more or less along the Pilica River to include Piotrkow, then just east of Lodz to the Vistula River, from which, according to some forecasts, it is expected to follow the Vistula, Bug, Narew and Pissa Rivers to East Prussia.

This would leave as the Gouvernement General of Poland only the districts of Cracow, Kielce, Radom and Warsaw, while the district of Lublin is to become a Jewish reservation for all Jews from Germany and Poland.

There are reports in Berlin that Colonel Josef Beck, former Polish Foreign Minister, and Marshal Edward Smigly-Rydz, former commander of the Polish Army, had approached the German Government through Field Marshal Hermann Goering with the proposal that if Germany installs them as the legitimate Polish Government they would repudiate the new Polish Government in Paris and conclude a separate peace with Germany on German terms.

Official quarters neither confirm nor deny these reports.

The name Gouvernement General given rump Poland obviously is a take-off on *Guberniya,* the old Russian name for the territorial subdivisions of Czarist Russia that included the major part of Poland. That name therefore is a program in itself. Under Russia it meant exclusion of Poles from government of their own country and ruthless Russification. The words of Dr. Goebbels and Governor Frank suggest a like program under German auspices.

BERLIN, Nov. 8.—Undaunted by the mighty problems of the war, the German Government is now carrying out the reorganization of its "East Room," comprising the German share of the conquered Polish territories, with characteristic speed and thoroughness and along lines that involve the greatest reshuffle of populations in modern history.

This reorganization is still under way and the new frontiers and the form of government are still vague, but the general outlines of the new order in the east as envisaged by the German rulers are beginning to emerge plainly enough. And these outlines provide not only drastic shifts of both political and ethnographic frontiers but also racial concentrations in line with National Socialist theories and social upheaval which, as announced by the local German rulers themselves, reduce both Jews and Poles to helots of the German master race.

A large part, though still officially undefined, of the conquered territories has already been annexed to the Reich. These parts are the provinces of West Prussia, Posen and Upper Silesia, which generally follow the borders of 1914 with some light additions that may be enlarged later. The rest of the territory is now in the process of division between the Polish rump State of a still undetermined character and status, but in any case under rigid German control, and the Jewish reservation around Lublin in which all Jews from

Poland and Greater Germany presumably will be concentrated.

For the present the civil affairs of the whole territory not annexed to the Reich are entrusted to Dr. Hans Frank as "Governor General for the Occupied Territories" who formally entered Cracow yesterday. And the fact that Dr. Frank installed himself at Cracow rather than Warsaw is taken as confirmation of current reports that if German plans are carried out Warsaw, which hitherto has been the spiritual center of the Poles but which is in ruins, will not be rebuilt but replaced by Cracow as the new Polish capital to demonstrate the new orientation of German-controlled Poland and its complete divorce from Russia.

But the outlines of the new order are beginning to appear most plainly in the annexed provinces ruled by Albert Forster in West Prussia, Arthur Greiser in Posen and Josef Wagner in Upper Silesia which includes Teschen, Maehrisch-Ostrau and Dobrowa. For here, both the ethnographic and social reshuffle is being carried out most thoroughly and most ruthlessly under the motto, "Reconstruction and Germanization."

Reconstruction is already evident everywhere in the rapid repair of war damage and the immediate utilization and exploitation of all the resources of these provinces under German control for German benefit. But the really spectacular aspect of the program is the Germanization which is introducing new methods of population treatment that already have set the whole population of Eastern Europe awhirl and if adopted elsewhere may lead to startling consequences.

In the widest aspect the ethnographic reshuffle in the east involves a quadruple population shift as follows:

Scattered German colonies in Eastern Europe, but also from the Italian Tyrol, are being recalled to settle in the newly annexed German provinces. The Poles in these provinces are being pushed out into Poland proper. Jews, both in Germany and Poland, are slated for concentration in the Jewish reservation. The Ukrainians and White Russians in the German share of Poland are being exchanged for Germans in the Russian share of Poland.

And so contagious is this process, possible only under new totalitarian nationalism, that Russia is reported proposing the exchange of Lithuanians remaining in the Russian part of the Vilna territory for White Russians in the Lithuanian part, while Premier Mussolini, who surrenders Germans in the South Tyrol, is calling back scattered Italian families from Yugoslavia to help populate the dried Pontine swamps.

At any rate, the speed and extent of the migration of Germans from the Baltic States is rapidly demonstrating both the hold that the new totalitarian nationalism has obtained even on "racial comrades" of alien citizenship as well as the feasibility of population movement as such.

For the exodus of German Balts is in full swing. Estonia is virtually evacuated by all Germans. Some 12,000 out of an estimated 15,000 Germans in Estonia already have been shipped back to Germany, which means that so far four-fifths of all the Germans in that country have followed Chancellor Hitler's call. But another thousand, it is announced, will follow shortly, and the final thousands who are still liquidating their business enterprises are to "come home" by January. Thus only about 1,000 Germans have chosen to remain to cast their lot with the country of their birth.

Similarly the exodus is now under way from Latvia, where the war-camouflaged steamer Steuben departed with the first 3,000 "wandering Aryans" from Riga Saturday. Although the German-Latvian agreement is far more unfavorable for the migrants than the German-Estonian agreement, the result is expected to be proportionately the same as in Estonia.

These German Balts, who are considered the cream of the Germans in the East, the great majority of whom are city folk engaged in industry, commerce and the professions, are being settled in towns and cities of the new provinces, and they will resume as far as possible the same occupations they have pursued in their former homes, replacing Poles whose properties and enterprises they will take over.

Only 10 per cent of the Germans in Estonia and 16 per cent of the Germans in Latvia were engaged in agriculture and they naturally are being settled on the land. But their scant number is being enhanced by the Germans who are being evacuated from the Russian share of Poland, especially Volhenia and Galicia, under the German-Russian agreement just concluded, from South Tyrol and from Lithuania, with other countries probably following later.

Most of these are small peasant farmers and they will be settled on land in the new provinces to take the places of the Polish colonists who flocked in after the last war and made that territory more Polish than any other part of Poland.

In one respect, therefore, the German *Drang nach Osten* has led paradoxically to the result that the easternmost Germans are moving west to fill up a *Raum ohne Volk* which the *Volk ohne Raum* acquired in the east. But this move also enables Germany, which is without capital abroad, to mobilize another national asset—namely, her own "racial comrades" in other countries, whose personal assets she now can utilize in the service of her own foreign trade.

Nevertheless, however speedy the reshuffle may be, it is still slow in terms of day-to-day life, and this raises the question in German minds as well: What about the Poles remaining in these provinces?

The answer was supplied by Herr Greiser in his inaugural speech in Posen, in which he said:

"Their fate will be hard, but just."

As interpreted by the authoritative West German *Beo-bachter* this means:

"The Poles must work for the reconstruction and building up of this land, and that under conditions which will be prescribed and fixed by Germans according to local conditions."

And the equally authoritative *Zeit*, the official National Socialist party organ of the Sudeten district, adds:

"Only determination and hardness can achieve results here. The cultural difference between Germans and Poles must receive clear expression in the future in all walks of life. That applies also to the right of possession which in all States with a healthy rank and order (the modern pluto-democracies are the opposite) are conditioned on certain moral obligations. A strong, thoroughly German peasantry, conscious of its rights as masters, shall find a permanent home in this land."

BERLIN, Nov. 25.—"Poland is not yet lost" has been the defiant and consoling slogan of the Polish nation during the century and a half of its previous partition. Now that which even in moments of greatest national pride every Pole dreaded at least subconsciously, again has come about—namely, a new partition, which, in the words of the German leaders, is to be the "fourth," that will make good Chancellor Hitler's word that in the case of a conflict the Polish Republic would be lost indeed.

For as revealed in both the statements and actions of the German and Russian rulers, perhaps even more in the frankly proclaimed ultimate aims of the National Socialist and bolshevist regimes, not only is the Polish State to be destroyed forever and its territory broken up into tiny particles, but the Polish nation is likewise to be annihilated as a nation and whatever is left of it either denationalized or reduced to an inferior helot people without any national consciousness, without any intelligentsia and, therefore, without a chance or hope of rising again.

The mistakes of the German, Russian and Austro-Hungarian empires which left Polish hopes alive for more than a century and finally led to the resurrection of the Polish State are not to be repeated. On the contrary, in the words of the *Warschauer Zeitung,* the authoritative German Government organ for rump Poland, the way is to be paved for the fulfillment of the mission of the "German master race," which is to be the pioneer of the principle of order and peace in Eastern Europe and the leader in all Central Europe. This, in Nazi eyes, justifies smashing everybody who dares oppose Germany in that region.

Although all the details are not yet known, the territorial partition of Poland is now fairly clear. First of all there is the partition between the German and Russian spheres of interest, the border of which runs along the rivers Pissa and Narew to Ostroleka, then over to the Bug east of Malkinia, up the Bug to its first western tributary along which it jumps over to the San River and follows that to the Hungarian frontier. But the Suwalki district, from the southeasternmost point of East Prussia to the southernmost tip of Lithuania, is also allotted to Germany.

Of the Russian part a tiny strip of the former Vilna territory, which just includes the town of Vilna and a narrow corridor northward, was turned over to Lithuania, which is now a garrison state of Soviet Russia.

The new Lithuanian border runs roughly from Merkine to include Rodune, Varanavas and Tabariskes but leaves the Lithuanian town of Svencionys in Russia. The border then proceeds parallel to the Lithuanian border to Latvia. The rest was annexed by Russia.

Of the total population of Poland, Russia got about 14,-

000,000, Germany about 18,000,000, Lithuania about 500,-000. Among the German share are 1,000,000 Germans, 15,500,000 Poles and approximately 1,500,000 Jews.

The Russian part is being ruthlessly Sovietized on the plea that it is inhabited by White Russians and Ukrainians who now are returning to the Russian motherland. However, though invoking national border lines for its new imperialistic purposes, the Soviet regime does not recognize any national ambitions within its own territory. Only bolshevist doctrine is the unifying element of some 180 nationalities.

The German part has been sub-divided by what is described as a "technical" border into provinces definitely annexed by the German Reich and the "Gouvernement General of Occupied Territories." The latter stays outside the German customs and currency borders but remains under sovereignty of the German Government and German military occupation and that, in the words of Governor General Frank's initial proclamation, "completes the transition of the regulation that converts a war territory into a State territory ruled politically and directed according to the principles of order."

The exact technical border between the enlarged German Reich and Gouvernement General has not yet been announced, but according to the division of administrative authority it appears to run about as follows: From Jablunka Pass northeastward to include the districts of Teschen, Bielitz, Biala, Kattowitz and Dobrowa, to Lublinitz and then northeastward to the region of Piotrkow, continuing northward twenty miles east of Lodz to the Vistula and then along the Vistula, Bug, Narew and Pissa Rivers to the border of East Prussia.

One doubtful point seems to be Czestochowa, which some allot to the Reich and others to the Gouvernement General.

Within the Gouvernement General, moreover, is being established a Jewish reservation east of Lublin of a wholly undefined extent.

According to an announcement in the *Warschauer Zeitung*, the annexed provinces—that is, Danzig and Warthe and presumably Suwalki—will be cleared of Poles and will be settled by Germans from the Baltic States, from the Russian part of Poland and the Gouvernement General itself in order that a "clear separation may be established between the Germans and Poles."

All Poles under German sovereignty are to be concentrated in the Gouvernement General and all Jews living under the same sovereignty, including those of the Gouvernement General—about 2,000,000—are to be concentrated in the Jewish reservation to which mass transports from Bohemia, Austria and the annexed provinces are already under way. And from all appearances the fate of Poles and Jews will be more or less the same.

That fate, *Gauleiter* Arthur Greiser announced recently, will be "hard but just." The *Warschauer Zeitung* writes:

"The Gouvernement General is a land conquered in a war provoked by the presumptions of megalomania and the insane delusion of an intellectual clique accompanied by inhuman cruelties and bestialities against the German civilian population and soldiers. Under these circumstances it is self-evident that there cannot be any thought of sentimental fraternization. . . . That would be frivolous play with the security of our own nation and would permit or even promote the creation of a new intellectual agitation clique."

And the German press amplifies the point that the difference in the cultural level between Germans and Poles must be clearly expressed in the future, even in respect to the right of property.

In the pursuit of such aims, Herr Frank has issued the

following decrees and has taken the following measures so far:

Introduced compulsory labor duty for all Poles at jobs and wages under conditions designated by his government.

Decreed death penalty for acts of violence against the new government, for damage to its property, disobedience to German decrees or incitement to violence against any German "because of his Germanism," or damage to his property, and finally for failure to notify the authorities of any plot to commit such acts or failure similarly to notify them of the possession of arms.

Called in the German police and Elite Guard Death's Head Brigades and created summary courts to enforce these decrees, although the Polish police were retained for ordinary police duty.

Reduced directors' salaries in Warsaw from between 2,000 *zlotys* monthly to between 500 and 600 *zlotys* and established strict price control.

Ordered the reopening of Polish elementary and trade schools for Polish children and the creation of German schools in all towns and villages with more than ten prospective pupils.

Confiscated Polish State property and took over Polish State monopolies.

Created a German postal service for mail in German and Polish but barring Hebrew.

Made Cracow the capital of the Gouvernement General, which is receiving German street names, where all important government offices and establishments are being concentrated while Warsaw's bombarded districts are being razed and, it is expected, will not be rebuilt.

For Jews shipped to the reservation, labor duty is also introduced for men up to 70 and women up to 55 years.

Big Polish estates are being administered for the most

part by German trustees responsible to the German Government and in view of the concentration of Poles in vastly reduced territory, the fate of the Polish peasant, already suffering from land shortage, remains to be seen.

FOOTNOTE ON POLAND

In a speech in December, 1939 in conquered Lodz, then annexed to Greater Germany, Dr. Robert Ley, Reich Organization Director and head of the German Labor Front, proclaimed that Germany's real war aims were the annihilation of Great Britain and establishment of the "divine right" of the German race to rule over others.

Dr. Ley's formulation of the German war aims, perhaps the most sweeping then advanced in public, went considerably beyond any official pronouncements, either by the German Government or by Chancellor Hitler himself, who had merely demanded "living space" and a proper share in world riches.

However, it was in line with a steadily increasing propaganda campaign based on the so-called positive side of the National Socialist racial doctrine as outlined in Herr Hitler's *Mein Kampf*, namely, the thesis that the Germans constitute a master race that had a mission to rule over inferior peoples and create a new world order.

"The German race, that is our faith!" Dr. Ley exclaimed. "It has higher rights than all others. A German laborer is worth more than an English Lord. We have the divine right to rule and we shall assure ourselves of that right."

The bitterest enemy Germany had in her attempt to realize that aim, Dr. Ley declared, was Britain. But, he exclaimed:

"Just as Poland was annihilated, so also will England be annihilated! There is a difference between now and 1914. Then we had a strong army, but our domestic front was weak. And yet we missed beating England only by a hair. Today England faces a solidified nation of 84,000,000. England will have to yield. We have accepted the battle.

"We know the issue; it is to be or not to be. But we also know that Germany will live. For England is already blockaded. The country that wants to starve us is itself shut up like a mouse in a trap. We want to be hard in this war. We are going to forget the arch-evil, our good nature, and will be hard and relentless in battling for our demands."

Whether Dr. Ley's pronouncement that the German race has higher rights than all others was meant to imply the right of that race to rule over all others or only some others was not clear. But it was meant to proclaim the right of that race to rule over Poland, as constantly stressed by official German newspapers issued in conquered Polish territory and further expounded in an authoritative article in the *Boersen-Zeitung* which started off:

"It is not true that the nations of Europe are equal. It is nonsense to maintain that all nations have equal rights. In the life of nations it is not otherwise than in the life of individuals. There are differences in rank and value. Not every people has the value and the weight of a nation. Not every people is capable of forming a State and not every people has the right to its own State.

"General equal right of peoples and nations is the same liberal fallacy as the twaddle of general human rights. There is a law of nations, but no rights of nations. And not every people has a national or imperial mission."

This outburst then applied all its implications to Poland. The very creation of a Polish State was denounced as a violation of the above-mentioned rank and order among nations, which had been rectified by German arms. For the article explained that the Poles had received their State without their own merit and without its being a genuine—that is, a necessary—State, in as much as it had merely served as a tool of France and Britain, and which the Poles had been unable to keep in order anyhow because of their stunted national instinct.

At this same time, December 1939, came significant reports of friction between the military authorities in occupied Polish territory and the National Socialist civil government of the Polish Gouvernement General, which were confirmed December 19, when the official German news agency issued the following communiqué, couched in terms that were usually employed only in connection with diplomatic conferences between representatives of sovereign powers:

"Reichminister Dr. Frank, Governor General for the occupied territories in Poland, and Colonel General Blaskowitz, Commander-in-Chief in the East, met Monday to discuss pending questions. Technical experts of the Commander-in-Chief's staff participated in the conference, while Governor General Frank was accompanied by competent department chiefs of the Gouvernement General.

"Discussion of various questions connected with administration of the occupied territory and their settlement resulted in a most complete agreement of views between the military authorities and those of the Gouvernement General."

The emphasis in this communiqué, the importance of which was emphasized by front-page display in the more discerning German newspapers, was of course on the fact that such a conference was necessary and the additional fact that the "settlement" of pending questions resulted in "a most complete agreement of views."

The pending questions, it was assumed, concerned the ruthless policy pursued in rump Poland by Governor Frank and his administration, especially by the Death's Head formations of the Elite Guard, sent in there as German State police. The National Socialist authorities never made a secret of their determination to reduce the Poles to virtual serfs of the German "master race," to which the Poles replied with a steadily increasing hatred of the German conquerors.

As a result of this atmosphere acts of violence appeared to be increasing rather than decreasing. According to reports that were trickling out of rump Poland, which was barred to foreign correspondents, the hatred of the Poles turned especially against the Elite Guard men who were drilled in the doctrine of their racial superiority and who, moreover, were constantly told they must be "hard."

According to these reports, substantiated by death notices in *Schwarze Korps*, the official organ of the Elite Guard, members were found dead in ambush with their throats cut. In retaliation the Elite Guard, if unable to find the attackers, were reported to have simply put some of the inhabitants of offending towns and villages against walls and shot them. This, however, merely created new hatreds that led to new acts of violence.

The policy of Governor Frank and his Elite Guard police was so ruthless that the German army authorities were reported to have objected to it on the ground that it delayed pacification of the country. And this attitude of the army was believed here to have been the reason for the conference.

Just what the "settlement" of pending question was and what the meaning of "a most complete agreement" was remained to be seen. Though the war had given the army vastly increased powers and though the generals had been able to veto all plans for a big offensive on the West Front so far, the fact remained that in all matters of domestic policy, including its own administration, the army had been always compelled in the end to yield to the National Socialist party authorities. All generals who dared stand in their way had been eliminated.

Appendix I

"WE ARE HUMANE"

A DISPATCH of November, 1939:

Emphasizing his complete confidence in Germany's final victory, Field Marshal Hermann Goering in an informal talk in November, 1939 with foreign correspondents, including the writer, during a large reception at the Russian Embassy today scoffed at British and French hopes of getting material aid from the United States after repeal of the arms embargo. He also doubted American ability to supply such aid.

Although sidestepping the direct question whether Germany will attack before American aid can become effective, Marshal Goering declared that the German air force had abstained from direct attack on the British mainland only for humanitarian reasons. But he added that German air attacks on the British fleet had provided "good practice" and further immunity of the British coast and ports will depened on the war methods of Germany's enemies.

For the rest, the Field Marshal, who fairly exuded good humor and self-confidence despite visible signs of strain, asserted that in respect to planes at least, Germany can outbuild not only the Allies but the United States as well. At the same time the Reich can prevent American supplies from reaching the front in time to become a factor in the war, he declared.

And it is perhaps significant that both Marshal Goering and his adjutant general of fliers, Colonel Bodenschatz, repeatedly have stressed the time factor with the implication that time was short.

The Goering talk, explicitly released for publication, marked the climax of the Russian Embassy's first formal reception in Berlin for years. It was attended by all important dignitaries of the Third Reich except Chancellor Hitler, as well as the full diplomatic corps, including Americans, Turks and Finns.

In other capitals the Russian Embassies held similar receptions in honor of the anniversary of the bolshevist revolution. But in Berlin all mention of that anniversary was avoided, the invitations simply reading that "the Ambassador of the Union of Socialist Soviet Republics has the honor, after submission of his credentials to the Herr German Reich Chancellor, to invite—to a reception from four to seven."

This, together with the coincidence that it was also the first reception of the new Russian Ambassador, at which, in line with diplomatic practice, the protocol department of the German Foreign Office acted as master of ceremonies, converted the whole affair from a purely Russian revolutionary celebration to a festival of the new "practical collaboration" of the two revolutions, the bolshevist and the National Socialist. To this Marshal Goering's talk gave a fitting touch.

The question of repeal of the United States arms embargo dominated the conversation, but the Marshal professed to take it lightly indeed. To the question whether he was not afraid of the many American planes in prospect and whether the German aircraft industry was strong enough to meet United States production capacity, Marshal Goering snapped back with a wave of the hand in which he was holding a cigar:

"If we were only that strong, we would be very weak indeed." Then he added: "I am very serious about that."

And Colonel Bodenschatz confirmed him with: "Yes, very serious."

It was thereupon pointed out to them that American reports had said 8,000 planes are to be produced and delivered to the Allies within a short time. But Marshal Goering replied:

"In the first place, it is impossible to build that many planes within a short time. In the second place, they are not over here yet."

To which Colonel Bodenschatz added:

"Exactly, and if there is anybody who has experience in building planes within a short time, it is Germany."

Further insistence on that point with the challenge that Americans talked of sending over 10,000 planes was waved aside by Marshal Goering with a laugh:

"Well, that's even harder to produce than 8,000."

Nevertheless, an indication of the size of the air fleets in which he thinks was supplied by his reply to the next question, which concerned reports that 800 American planes already were at the docks ready for shipment.

"That is nice," he scoffed. "It is something, but it is not enough."

This brought the question whether Germany will attack before the United States planes are ready. Marshal Goering replied:

"Well, we will build our planes. Let them build theirs. Then we shall see who comes out best."

Asked about the general situation, he said:

"It is exceedingly favorable for us. The mere fact that I am standing today in perfectly good humor tells you more than anything else could. And if in 1933 anybody should have predicted that such a situation could arise in a war against England and France, everybody would have called him crazy."

"Yes, and we intend to win. We will win," Colonel Bodenschatz chimed in. Whereupon his chief nodded cheerfully and exclaimed:

"Of course we shall win."

Questions thereupon turned to recent air battles, in which connection Marshal Goering was asked why German fliers had attacked only British warships instead of British harbors and docks.

"Well," he said, "warships are important, too." Then, with a smile: "Besides, they are good practice."

To a further question as to whether he did not propose to carry the Blitzkrieg to British shores, he replied:

"We are humane (*menschenfreundlich*)."

The correspondents laughed, but Marshal Goering broke in:

"You should not laugh. I am serious. I really am."

"Will you remain humane?" he was asked.

"That," he said, "depends on the others. And that is no joke either."

"The French say they are shooting down a lot of German planes," he was challenged.

"Well," he replied, "we will lose a plane now and then, of course. But if they are shooting down as many as they say, they are not ours. I don't know whose they could be."

Although the Russian anniversary reception was the most elaborate diplomatic function in Berlin up to 1935, when it was discontinued, this resumption outdid all the previous ones in lavishness of display and gorgeous uniform, among which Marshal Goering's was the most gorgeous of all.

And to emphasize the full significance of his presence, the Field Marshal, who came from day-long conferences with Herr Hitler, held a prolonged and serious conference with the Russian Ambassador right in the midst of the scores of guests.

The attractive Signora Bernardi de Attolico, wife of the Italian Ambassador, also sought to talk with Marshal Goering long and earnestly, but his attention soon wandered off to the riches of the table before him where whipped cream and cake caught his special notice.

Among the other dignitaries present were Foreign Minister Joachim von Ribbentrop, who was seen talking earnestly with the Belgian Ambassador; Propaganda Minister Joseph Goebbels, Grand Admiral Erich Raeder and Dr. Otto Meissner, Presidential Secretary of State. The United States was represented by Chargé d'Affaires Alexander C. Kirk and the full Embassy staff.

LINDBERGH ON AIR WAR

A DISPATCH of July 23, 1936:

In a speech in Berlin on July 23, 1936, Colonel Charles A. Lindbergh broke his traditional reticence and far exceeded the framework of the usual exchange of international courtesies. He warned the world the airplane had become such a powerful weapon of destruction that it had revolutionized modern warfare and stripped the armor from every nation in war.

For that reason he repeatedly emphasized the responsibility resting on all who had anything to do with aviation and urged that unless strength is allied with intelligence and "a new security is found which is dynamic, not static, and which rests in intelligence, not in force," the world generally and Europe particularly faced damage for which there was no repair.

The speech was delivered at a luncheon given to him by the German Air Ministry at Fliers House. In the words of the official German news agency, the address "left the strongest impression" on all who heard it, all the more so because the luncheon was presided over by a general of fliers, Erhardt Milch, Secretary of State in the Aviation Ministry, who, together with Col. Gen. Hermann Goering, Air Minister, is one of the principal creators of the new German air fleet, now one of the world's strongest.

The text of Colonel Lindbergh's speech follows:

"It is especially a privilege for any one interested in aviation to visit modern Germany. The name of Germany weaves in and out through the history of aviation. In the designing and operation of aircraft and in the vision which is always necessary for leadership, Germany has set an example which has stimulated the rest of the world.

"I seldom see one of our modern transport planes without thinking of Junkers and admiring the ability and foresight which enabled that man to build his metal monoplanes with their low wings so many years ago. His mind was living in the present era, while most designers were arguing about the biplane's structural advantages and about wood and fabric and wire.

"One may have complete confidence in airplanes of the future without refusing his admiration for the genius this country has shown in developing airships. It must give every German a feeling of real pride to see the Hindenburg and the Graf Zeppelin and realize that his country stands supreme and without rival in the field of lighter-than-air craft.

"I sometimes feel those of us who grew up in aviation have lived much more than an average lifetime. It seems almost as though we have had the opportunity of living in the future and looking back on our lives, of judging our work through another generation's eyes.

"Certainly the whole world has never changed faster than at the present time, and during this change nothing has developed more rapidly than aviation. If the man who sailed the first dug-out canoe could live again he would hardly see more change in ships than our own generation has seen in aircraft. Except for the fact that he had not lived through the intermediate centuries of development, the modern battleship would give him no more cause to ponder than the modern bomber should give us. He could no more have seen a 16-inch gun attached to his canoe than we were able to see five or ten thousand pounds of bombs attached to our planes of twenty-five years ago.

"Scientists now talk of time in terms of astronomy, physiology and psychology. Our concepts of time are changing, and I think it is nowhere more noticeable than in aviation. Our ideas of time and distance are entirely different from those our fathers held.

"And unlike the builder of the dug-out canoe, we have lived to see our harmless wings of fabric turn into carriers of destruction even more dangerous than battleships and guns. We have lived to carry on our shoulders the responsibility for the result of our experiments, which in other fields have been passed to future generations.

"We who are in aviation carry a heavy responsibility on our shoulders, for while we have been drawing the world closer together in peace we have stripped the armor of every nation in war. It is no longer possible to shield the heart of a country with its army. Armies can no more stop an air attack than a suit of mail can stop a rifle bullet.

"Aviation has, I believe, created the most fundamental change ever made in war. It has abolished what we call the sense of warfare. It has turned defense into attack. We can no longer protect our families with an army. Our libraries, our museums—every institution which we value most is laid bare to bombardment.

"Aviation has brought a revolutionary change to a world already staggering from changes. It is our responsibility to make sure that doing so we do not destroy the very things we wish to protect.

"We have moved so fast we have imposed aeronautical time upon military tactics, and we have taken away the old defense of astronomical time, which has probably been civilization's greatest safeguard in the past.

"As I travel in Europe I am more than ever impressed with the seriousness of the situation which confronts us. When I see that within a day or two damage can be done which no time can ever replace, I begin to realize we must look for a new type of security—security which is dynamic, not static, security which rests in intelligence, not in forts.

"And in the fact that intelligence must be combined with aviation I find some cause for hope. It requires more intellect to operate an airplane than to dig a trench or shoot a rifle. The education which is necessary in aviation must also teach the value of civilized institutions.

"Our responsibility in creating a great force for destruction may be somewhat relieved by knowing we have allied this force with intelligence and education and that we have moved power further away from ignorance. I find some cause for hope in the belief that power which must be bound to knowledge is less dangerous to civilization than that which is barbaric.

"It is aviation's responsibility to justify the combination of strength and intelligence."

The audience at the luncheon included Hans Dieckhoff, political director of the Foreign Office; Duke Adolf Friedrich zu Mecklenburg, a member of the International Olympic Committee; Wolfgang von Gronau, president of the German Aero-club, as well as Ferdinand L. Mayer, United States Chargé d'Affaires; Major Truman Smith, United States military and air attaché, and his assistant.

General Milch welcomed Colonel and Mrs. Lindbergh in General Goering's name and expressed the hope that they would enjoy their stay in Germany and obtain a good impression of German aviation. He concluded with a toast to Colonel Lindbergh and American aviation.

Colonel Lindbergh thanked him for his welcome and praised German achievements in aviation, but quickly launched into his real speech, which was probably the first political address he had ever delivered and which put him in the center of the international situation. It was obvious that, as a result of his stay in Europe, Colonel Lindbergh had become impressed with the grave menace of war and was particularly concerned about what a bombing air fleet might do to European civilization.

After the luncheon a ceremonious reception was given to Colonel Lindbergh by Dr. Julius Lippert, Berlin's National Socialist Commissar, at the City Hall, where the Colonel inscribed his name in Berlin's Golden Book. Later he inspected Tempelhof Field, Berlin's airport, and made an extensive sight-seeing flight over the city in the four-engined Field Marshal von Hindenburg, Germany's largest plane, with himself at the controls. The Berlin populace loudly cheered him wherever they recognized him. Tomorrow he will visit the Richthofen pursuit squadron at Doeberitz Airfield, near Berlin. There he will see the latest accomplishments of the new German air fleet's crack unit.

INDEX